DATE DUE

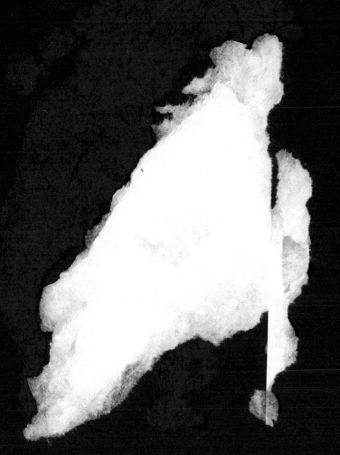

ARCHITECTURE AND COMMUNITY
BUILDING IN THE ISLAMIC WORLD TODAY

ARCHITECTURE AND COMMUNITY

BUILDING IN THE ISLAMIC WORLD TODAY

THE AGA KHAN AWARD FOR ARCHITECTURE

PUBLISHED BY APERTURE

ARCHITECTURE AND COMMUNITY BUILDING IN THE ISLAMIC WORLD TODAY

Published for the Aga Khan Award for Architecture by Aperture, a division of Silver Mountain Foundation, Inc., Millerton, New York 12546. Distributed in the United States by Viking Penguin, Inc.; in Italy by Idea Books, Milan; in the United Kingdom and in Europe by Phaidon Press Limited, Oxford, and in Canada by Penguin Books Canada Limited, Markham, Ontario.

Design by Peter Bradford and Kristen Dietrich. Production supervision by Stevan A. Baron. Composition by David E. Seham Associates, Inc., Metuchen, New Jersey. Color and duotone separations, printing, and binding by Arnoldo Mondadori Editore, Verona, Italy. Photographs by Christopher Little, Kamran Adle, Mustafa Pehlivanoglu, Najeh Abu Nab, Mokhless al-Hariri, and Nicole Toutoungi. Gouaches by Hassan Fathy.

The Aga Khan Award for Architecture was established to encourage architecture appropriate to the needs and aspirations of the Islamic world today. It recognises completed projects whose aesthetic and technological achievements and social responsiveness make them important models. Address: 32 Chemin des Crêts, 1218 Grand Saconnex, Geneva.

 The Award Logo. The name of Allah in Kufic script, reflecting itself, forms the basis of the logo design.

CONTRIBUTORS

Professor Renata Holod, University of Pennsylvania; specialist in Islamic architecture, editor. Darl Rastorfer, architect; associate editor. Professor Muhsin S. Mahdi, Harvard University; specialist in Islamic philosophy. Professor Oleg Grabar, Harvard University; specialist in Islamic architecture. Professor Doğan Kuban, Istanbul Technical University; specialist in the history of Islamic architecture and preservation. Professor Mohammed Arkoun, Sorbonne; specialist in Arabic. Dr. Mahbub al-Haq, economist; Minister for Development and Manpower, Pakistan. Charles Correa, architect, Bombay; consulting architect for New Bombay and Hyderabad. Dr. Mona Serageldin, planner; specialist in programming and land development processes. Professor François Vigier, Harvard University; specialist in urban planning. Yasmen Lari, architect, Karachi; President Institute of Architects, Pakistan. Suhail Lari, lawyer, Karachi. Dr. Ismail Serageldin, planner; World Bank, chief of urban projects division. Nader Ardalan, architect; Tehran/Boston.

ACKNOWLEDGEMENTS

Architecture and Community has been produced to present contemporary architectural projects that were honored in the first cycle (1977–1980) of the Aga Khan Award for Architecture and to manifest their symbolic, social, and cultural contexts. The essays on architectural and planning theory and practice were first presented at the Award seminars of the first cycle, and an introductory essay has been specially prepared for this volume. The Awards were presented in October 1980 at the Shalimar Gardens in Lahore, Pakistan, at the gracious invitation of President Zia ul-Haq.

Many people deserve credit for their contributions. Members of the Steering Committee for the first cycle were His Highness the Aga Khan, chairman, Nader Ardalan, Sir Hugh Casson, Charles Correa, Hassan Fathy, Professor Oleg Grabar, Professor Doğan Kuban, and Professor William Porter. The Award office was administered by Professor Renata Holod (1977–1979) and Hassan-Uddin Khan (1980). Those serving on the Master Jury were Professor Titus Burckhardt, Sherban Cantacuzino, Giancarlo De Carlo, Dr. Mahbub ul-Haq, Mazharul Islam, Professor Aptullah Kuran, Dr. Mona Serageldin, Soedjatmoko, and Kenzo Tange.

The basic information supporting the visual presentation of awarded projects came first from the architects and clients of each project. Technical reviewers then gathered additional information at each site. These reviewers included Dr. Samir Abdulac, Farokh Afshar, Dr. Mokhless al-Hariri, Dr. Nasrine Faghih, Piers Rodgers, Dr. Fredj Stambouli, Dr. Brian Taylor, and Dr. Atilla Yücel. Additional research was conducted to develop further the base of technical data and to understand each project in its proper context. Such assistance was provided by Anthony O. James, Linda Safran, Saleh Memecan, and Abdullah al-Kuwatli. Once collected, documents and research were developed for publication by Deborah Allen, Mohamed El-Malti, Deborah Gorman, Anthony O. James, and Robert MacLeod.

Mention must be made of the visual material itself. Bahman Negahban and Mehmet Selman prepared most of the architectural drawings. The line drawings in the chapter devoted to Hassan Fathy were assembled by Reinhard Goethert and provided by the Rotch Visual Collections at the Massachusetts Institute of Technology, the Aga Khan Program for Islamic Architecture at Harvard University, and the Massachusetts Institute of Technology.

The greater part of the photographs presented were made by Christopher Little except for pages 116–117, Nicole Toutoungi; 119–125, Mustafa Pehlivanoglu; 151–161, 173–181, Mokhless al-Hariri; 158, Rolf Gutbrod and Frei Otto (construction photograph); 169, Najeh Abu Nab; 180–181, VBB (construction photographs); 183–197, Kamran Adle.

A special acknowledgement is owed to the designer, Peter Bradford. Discussions with him concerning the demands of presenting the wide range of visual and written material proved invaluable in formulating the editorial approach taken.

Finally, Darl Rastorfer served ably and energetically as associate editor. —Renata Holod

CONTENTS

FOR DEVELOPING A
LABOUR-INTENSIVE BUILDING
SYSTEM INTO A COMPLETE
ARCHITECTURAL LANGUAGE,
REVITALISING MASONRY
CONSTRUCTION, AND
PROVIDING A MODEL FOR
A NUMBER OF PROJECTS
IN SENEGAL.

77 MEDICAL CENTRE
MOPTI, MALI

FOR A SYMPATHETIC RESPONSE TO BOTH THE CULTURE AND THE SENSITIVE SURROUNDINGS, MAKING EFFECTIVE USE OF AVAILABLE MATERIALS AND TECHNIQUES OF CONSTRUCTION.

89 COURTYARD HOUSES
AGADIR, MOROCCO

FOR THE RESPONSE IN PLAN FORM TO CLIMATE AND DEMANDS OF PRIVACY.

97 SIDI BOU SAID
TUNIS, TUNISIA

FOR THE EFFORTS BY A COMMUNITY TOWARDS THE CONSERVATION OF THEIR VILLAGE, RETAINING THROUGH LEGISLATION OVER A PERIOD OF TIME NOT ONLY THE PICTUR-ESQUE QUALITY OF A VILLAGE, BUT ITS VERY ESSENCE.

109 HALAWA HOUSE
AGAMY, EGYPT

FOR THE IMAGINATIVE HANDLING OF A TRADITIONAL VOCABULARY IN THE DESIGN AND CONSTRUCTION OF A HOUSE WHICH FULLY SATISFIES CONTEMPORARY NEEDS.

119 RUSTEM PASHA CARAVANSERAI
EDIRNE, TURKEY

FOR THE COMMENDABLE RESTORATION OF AN IMPORTANT MONUMENT WHICH POINTS TO AN IMPORTANT DIRECTION IF THERE IS TO BE A POSITIVE POLICY IN ARCHITECTURAL CONSERVATION.

127 ERTEGÜN HOUSE
BODRUM, TURKEY

FOR THE IMAGINATIVE CONSERVATION OF TWO SEASIDE HOUSES, WHILE DEMONSTRATING THAT NEW STRUCTURES CAN BE SYMPATHETICALLY ADDED TO THE OLD WITHOUT RESORTING TO DIRECT IMITATION.

139 TURKISH HISTORICAL SOCIETY
ANKARA, TURKEY

FOR COMBINING MODERN BUILDING TECHNOLOGY WITH TRADITIONAL IDEAS AND PRINCIPLES, PROVIDING AN EXAMPLE OF WHAT CAN BE LEARNED FROM TRADITION AND A POINTER TO A MORE APPROPRIATE ARCHITECTURAL LANGUAGE.

151 INTER-CONTINENTAL HOTEL
AND CONFERENCE CENTRE
MECCA, SAUDI ARABIA

FOR AN EFFORT TO COMBINE MODERN TECHNOLOGY AND FUNCTIONAL FORMS IN THE CONTEXT OF ISLAMIC CULTURE, ATTEMPTING TO FIND A NEW KIND OF ARCHITECTURE WHICH AVOIDS EXISTING CONVENTIONS.

163 **NATIONAL MUSEUM
DOHA, QATAR**

FOR RESTORING AND CREATING A NATIONAL MUSEUM OUT OF A GROUP OF BUILDINGS WHICH IS INTIMATELY LINKED WITH QATAR'S HISTORY AND TRADITIONS; THE PRESERVATION, ENHANCEMENT, AND ADAPTATION TO A NEW PUBLIC USE IS A NOTEWORTHY ACHIEVEMENT.

173 **WATER TOWERS
KUWAIT CITY, KUWAIT**

FOR A BOLD ATTEMPT TO INTEGRATE MODERN TECHNOLOGY, AESTHETIC VALUES, FUNCTIONAL NEEDS, AND SOCIAL FACILITIES IN A PUBLIC UTILITY.

183 **RESTORATION OF
THE ALI QAPU, CHEHEL SUTUN
AND HASHT BEHESHT
ISFAHAN, IRAN**

FOR THE METICULOUS RESTORATION OF SOME OF THE GREAT SAFAVID MONUMENTS OF ISFAHAN, AND FOR THE CONTRIBUTION WHICH THIS RESTORATION HAS MADE TO THE KNOWLEDGE OF ISLAMIC PLANNING, ARCHITECTURE, AND CONSTRUCTION.

199 **MUGHAL SHERATON HOTEL
AGRA, INDIA**

FOR AN EXPRESSION OF THE CULTURE AND RICH ARCHITECTURAL TRADITION OF THE REGION, USING A CONTEMPORARY VOCABULARY OF FORMS DERIVED FROM FUNCTIONAL NEEDS, AND MAKING USE OF THE AVAILABLE MATERIALS AND TECHNOLOGY, ABUNDANT LABOUR FORCE, AND TRADITIONAL CRAFT.

PREFACE
HIS HIGHNESS THE AGA KHAN

The first series of Awards in Architecture within the vast community of Muslims has been given. It is well to ponder at this time what they mean, what questions they raise, what implications they may have for the future, as well as for our deeper collective concern for the continuous integrity of Islamic architecture and, through architecture, for the whole of Islamic culture. I trust and hope that over the years scholars, architects, planners, officials at all levels, and users will discuss among themselves the significance of the choices made by the Jury and the Selection Committee among some one hundred eighty submitted buildings and architectural ensembles. Many even contradictory conclusions could and should be drawn from the Jury's decisions, and I would like to share with you some impressions, some thoughts, some queries, perhaps a few worries about the results of these choices.

First, let me recall that it was in Pakistan that the idea of this Award was made public some four years ago. It is in part for this reason that the first recipients of the Award were gathered in Lahore to be recognised for their achievements. Pakistan, located roughly in the geographical centre of Islam, possesses some of the wonders of classical Islamic architecture, such as the Shalimar Gardens, some of the most genuine vernacular traditions, and some of the most important contemporary architectural efforts within the Muslim world. It is only fitting that this microcosm of Islamic traditions should have served as a host for the contemporary achievements of the whole Muslim world, which ranges from the arid shores of the Atlantic Ocean to the tropical splendour of Indonesian islands. There, better perhaps than anywhere else, the richness and glory of both the past and the creations of today can be seen in the context of a vibrant and exciting concern for the environment. For it is indeed for this concern that an award has been established, and we must recognise that we are not permeating a country, a city, or a building, but the whole Muslim world, all its nations and peoples, as it enters into its fifteenth century of existence.

Second, we may well ask whether the awarded projects truly correspond to the great traditions of Islamic architecture. There are no mosques among them, no madrasas, no palaces, no gardens, no mausoleums, hardly any of the monuments that are visited by millions of tourists, cherished by those who live near them, and utilised by historians to define the Muslims' past. The paradox, however, is more apparent than real. For, great though the celebrated monuments of the past are as works of art, they were only part of the built environment of the past. They were the creations of great and wealthy patrons, often made no doubt for the use and pleasure of the masses, but rarely lacking in personal or dynastic vanity. All too frequently the settings developed by the masses themselves have been lost or changed beyond recognition. In the contemporary works, the Awards have recognised that other part, perhaps now much more important than in the past, the part of the common man creating for himself and his neighbours a setting for life and for health, preserving and utilising what nature has created, developing ways to maintain his identity rather than accepting the elephantine massiveness of so much of today's world.

This recognition of a human scale, of local decisions (even if they required outside expertise), of local needs and concerns is, I believe, a profoundly Muslim requirement. It is the expression of that societal requirement, that consideration of thousands of separate communities within the whole *umma*, that is so uniquely a central part of the Muslim message. We have recognised an architecture for men, women, and children, and not yet an architecture for history books and tourists. Through architecture we are recognising the quality of life within the Muslim world today. And, by recognising a medical centre or housing project developed by a whole community, we are preserving for all time the memory of this quality of life.

There is a deeper and more intriguing side to this recognition that forms my third observation. These Awards may indeed illustrate or sharpen an issue that has been sidetracked over the past four hundred years as scholars and patrons become fascinated with the personalities of architects as artistic and formal creators. The issue is: What architecture are we recognising? Is it the planning and design of master architects? Is it the architecture of the craftsmen, artisans, and specialists of all sorts who put a building together? Is it the architecture of the users? Is it the architecture of certain lands, with their peculiar physical characteristics? Is it the architecture of a faith that transcends national, geographic, social, or technological limits?

It is easy enough to answer "yes" to all of these questions and to identify the merits of any one project according to each one of these criteria. In part, the decisions of the Master Jury have done that. But in a deeper sense, the important point is precisely that none of these criteria has taken precedence over any of the others.

The implication is that we are recognising as unique a creative and generative process in which the imagination of one architect and the expectation of Muslim patrons and users interact constantly. Within this continuum no single moment or decision can be isolated like the element of a chemical compound, because it is creative life itself, it is the elusive process of human existence, not merely a monument, that is the winner.

A fourth observation is that the Jury used the word "search" for nearly all of the projects it recognised. What does this mean? It could mean, no doubt, that no building, no ensemble, no reconstruction or reuse has quite been able to meet some abstract criteria for architectural excellence. This is not surprising. The Alhambra probably would have been received with very mixed reviews by architectural critics at the time it was built, and many a source from ancient times is critical of architectural projects that enthrall contemporary historians. For while historians can quite often, centuries later, understand architectural quality in its purest form, contemporaries often see its social and economic costs and weigh them against the other needs of society. Clearly, architectural excellence is not enough. Therein lies the positive side of the notion of "search." We are only beginning to grasp the social, intellectual, aesthetic, cultural, and historical needs and emotions of the Muslim world. To impose from the very outset of the Award process formal or even social criteria of excellence would be not only an exercise in vanity and folly, but a profound moral wrong. We only know the issues and the problems. We know that social changes of momentous proportions are taking place everywhere. We know that expectations have arisen for both a good life and a good Muslim life. We know that we are far too ignorant of our past and far too careless in preserving it. We know that Muslim lands are subjected to pressure and temptations from cultures that are not Muslim, even though nearly all Muslim lands are independent of foreign rule.

But the solutions, the answers to these problems are still unclear. They must be sought, and this is why the Award process itself is designed to be one of the means for this collective search. A partial failure can be as important as a unique success. It is in this spirit of common search for solutions to thousands of problems that these Awards will play their part. It is a spirit which is well proclaimed in the Muslim message, for the intention of man (the *niya*) is a fundamental part of his action.

Finally, we may turn from the Muslim world to the whole world. Many of the issues that led to the creation of the Awards are not unique to the Muslim world. They are issues found in all new lands, as on our shrinking planet all new countries, or all developing countries, grope for a visible self-

identification of their own and for the satisfaction of new, worldwide expectations about the quality of their lives. But why think only of new or underdeveloped countries? Social problems plague lands with the highest per capita income, and self-identification is a concern of countries with the longest history of independence and expansion. It may just be that, as the Award highlights the search of the Muslim world for an architecture centred on man and proclaiming the potential of life, an example is given to the whole world of how this can be done. In part it is simply that the Muslim message is a universal one, not restricted to a few areas or a few ethnic groups. But, in a deeper sense, what we are trying to achieve, this environment we are looking for, is not only ours. It is also something we want to share with the whole world, not as an exercise in pride or vanity, but because of our belief that the means at our disposal may allow us to sharpen issues, to discover solutions for all mankind to use and understand.

Such are a few observations based on the Awards themselves, on recognised achievements from Morocco to Indonesia, from Turkey to Senegal, from humble houses to grand hotels, by architects and by masons, by anonymous bureaucracies or by specific individuals and collectives, by Muslims and by non-Muslims, yet always for Muslims.

But this is not the end of our effort. What challenges lie ahead? The first one is perfectly exemplified by the setting in which the Awards were given, the magnificent Shalimar Gardens. From the very beginning we felt that the Awards should be given in places of overwhelming historical and aesthetic interest. This is to remind us all of the great traditions to which we are the heirs. But what in fact *is* the relationship of our roots to what we are today? Surely we do not expect of contemporary architects copies or imitations of the past; we know only too well how disastrous such copying has been. There are two things, I feel, we may appropriately seek from the past. One is what I would call our moral right to decide on the environment that will be ours. However useful and essential outside experts may be, however international contemporary architecture has become, our past, our roots, give us the right to say that the choices we make are *our* choices and that the opportunities we have today will do for the next decades what early Muslims did in Spain, Syria, or Iraq, what the Ottoman Turks, Timurids, or Mughals did some five to six hundred years ago in Anatolia, Iran, or India: that is, understood sufficiently well what was available and appropriate in non-Muslim lands to create something profoundly Muslim. And this leads me to my second point about the monuments of our past. We must learn to understand them well, not simply to preserve them as museums of past glories, but to feel in every part of them—a stone masonry, a brick dome, a window, an ornament, or a garden arrangement—that unique spirit, that unique way that made these monuments Islamic. Only then will we be able to impart the same spirit to the technical means and to the forms of today.

A second challenge is of a very different order. As time goes on, more and more of the major environmental and architectural programmes within the Muslim world will utilise the high technology developed for the most part outside the Muslim world. As airports, office buildings, hospitals, schools, industrial complexes, whole new cities grow in numbers and in quality, they will quite naturally satisfy much less easily the originality of our traditions. The models of the past, even if available, will be technically or economically unsuited to new needs. These new creations will run the risk of becoming homogenised, internationalised monuments with an occasional arch or dome. But need it be so? While preserving and nurturing the immense variety of our vernacular architecture, how will we be able to channel the necessity of high technology without becoming its slaves? There are areas, perhaps, such as those of solar energy, of water conservation, of thermal control, or of prefabrication, where we should become leaders rather than followers, where our needs can revolutionise the rest of the world.

And, finally, let me mention one last challenge: the challenge of education. Not only do we know too little about ourselves, but we have not as yet been able to form in sufficient numbers our own experts and practitioners with the full competence to solve the environmental problems of tomorrow. Too many of our best minds are trained outside their own countries. Why is this so? Is it a question of teaching staff? Is it a peculiar trust in outside expertise? Clearly we must develop ways to make our own schools of architecture and of planning places to which others will want to come, and this will require yet another kind of intellectual and practical effort. For, even if we create an architecture worthy of praise, we will have partly failed unless we form for ourselves the men and women who will realise that architecture.

I do not claim that these are the only challenges left to us. Others exist, no doubt. But, as we celebrate the first Awards and open the way for the forthcoming ones, all these challenges can help us in defining the attitudes we must develop in thinking of the future and of the areas of discovery open to

us. It is a task we must accomplish together, fully acknowledging our diversities, but knowing, as well, that there is a Straight Path, which is that of our Faith.

Let me close, therefore, by reminding you of Attar's great poem, the Conference of the Birds, *Mantiqat at-Tayr.*

The birds, you will recall, went in search of the Simurgh, the ideal and perfect king. After many tribulations, thirty of them did reach the end of the journey and came to the gate of the Supreme Majesty. The Chamberlain tested them and then opened the door, and they sat on the *masnad,* the seat of Majesty and Glory. And, as an inner glow came into them, they realised that it was *they* together who were the Simurgh, and that the Simurgh was the thirty birds.

Is this not what these Awards mean? From the travails and labours of thousands, humble masons or expensive experts, there have emerged those works made by us and for us which we can present as being, all together, as an aggregate, as a group, the statement of our hopes and of our expectations as much as of our achievements. This is indeed the way in which Pakistan's beloved poet, Muhammad Iqbal, put it in two quotations that say best what the Awards can mean. Speaking of Islam in his vision for tomorrow, he wrote that it was

> A world eternal, with renewing flames and
> renewing leaves, fruits, and principles.
> With an immovable inside and an outside of
> Changing, continuous revolutions.

And then, in another poem, he said:
> The journey of love is a very long
> journey.
> But sometimes with a sign you can cross
> that vast desert.
> Search and search again without losing
> hope.
> You may find sometime a treasure
> on your way.

On behalf of the Master Jury and of the Award Committee, it is to this search for our new environment that I wish to invite the immense community of Muslims, and the whole world as well.

INTRODUCTION
RENATA HOLOD

This book tells the story of the first fruits of a unique initiative in the annals of contemporary architecture: to bring to light projects which, through their strategy for use, design, and execution, embody the spirit of Islam. It is a story that involves many individuals from a variety of professional and regional communities, architects from Bangladesh and Japan, architectural critics from England and Syria, historians from Turkey and Algeria, development experts from the Sudan and the United States, engineers from Sweden and Germany, community leaders from Indonesia and Tunisia, ministers from Qatar and Kuwait, restoration experts from Italy and Iran. It is a story that evokes the remarkable aesthetic and cultural achievements of Islamic civilisation. At the same time it calls for the reawakening of concern for the efficacious, the appropriate, and the beautiful in the architecture of the Islamic world today.

The story begins in 1976 when His Highness the Aga Khan called for a better awareness of the aesthetic, cultural, and social aspects of architecture on the part of architect and client alike. To encourage such concerns, an award in architecture was established which would recognise those completed projects that were successful in responding to the needs of their users and that could serve as powerful models for others to emulate in their own quest for a better architecture.

To elaborate and to refine the parameters and the governance of the Aga Khan Award for Architecture, a wide range of individuals was brought together in an ever-growing network—from the members of an international Steering Committee, to professional associations and architectural schools from Morocco to Indonesia, to the development and planning community, and to individual architects, historians, and social scientists. There developed in all of them a community of concern which helped to identify the achievements and the problems in architecture and building within the Islamic world today. A sense of excitement grew around this new venture which gave focus to already existing energies and information. Individuals who had, until then, separately and alone, striven to understand and describe transformations in their own built environment and to call for changes, suddenly found a community of like thinkers. Architects whose works were known only in limited linguistic or national circles were provided with a much larger potential audience. Clients and decision makers were exposed to other, often more desirable or more efficient, solutions. The immediate vehicle for com-

munication consisted of five seminars where opinions and attitudes were exchanged and challenged. The themes of the seminars—transformations in architecture in the Islamic world, conservation, housing, architectural symbolism, and the making of public buildings—all dealt with architectural change. Together the seminars provided specific practical information on building activities and on directions of thought, and a provisional conceptual framework for the elaboration of the selection processes of the Award itself. Preliminary though they may be, the thoughts and opinions expressed in the seminars should be considered as much part of the first cycle of the Award as the projects finally selected by the Master Jury.

Another important initial decision was to devise a network of confidential nominators who alone could suggest projects for consideration. By identifying individuals who were active in architecture within a specific country, the Award organisation aspired to be inclusive rather than exclusive in the gathering of projects and to stimulate thought about and evaluation of the nature of the contemporary built environment. Projects were nominated if, in the nominator's opinion, they embodied the concerns of the Award: to nurture a heightened awareness of Islamic civilisation and values and to encourage architecture appropriate to the contemporary era.

The network of confidential nominators yielded a wide range of projects completed between 1950 and 1977. Each project was extensively documented with materials provided by the architect and client. The nearly two hundred projects were screened by the Steering Committee and some thirty of them were then verified on site by a technical review team. All the completed dossiers were presented to the Master Jury. The detailed results of their selection and evaluation are available elsewhere in this volume.

The fifteen projects chosen by this Jury as worthy of recognition reflect the diversity of needs and resources within the Islamic world. But even more notably, the Jury defined the entire group as a search for a new architecture appropriate to the present and future Islamic world. The Agricultural Training Centre at Nianing, Senegal, with its simple vaulted forms, was seen as the result of a search for appropriate building systems, in which a new labour-intensive method of construction developed into an architectural language and into a successful model for other buildings in Senegal. The contemporary use of a traditional building language in a search for a new architectural idiom was identfied in the medical centre at Mopti, Mali. Built next to the striking Great Mosque, it chooses locally available materials and methods of construction, and thereby blends superbly with its surroundings. The courtyard form, so well known from traditional urban housing, has been explored in a group of middle-income houses in Agadir, while the most complete fit of traditional design and construction with contemporary needs was apparent in the small Halawa resort house in Egypt. On very different scales, the necessity to recognise a particular historical context and to devise a responsive vocabulary for it was recognised in three projects. The Ertegün house on the Aegean shore at Bodrum, Turkey, anchors the landscape and in a blend of old and new forms and materials becomes a model for sensitive rehabilitation of derelict structures. The Mughal Sheraton Hotel at Agra, India, recognises the close presence of the Taj Mahal through its low spreading plan and particularly its gardens. The Turkish Historical Society in Ankara fits into a lot surrounded by earlier international-style buildings and combines modern idiom in design and building technology with the internal arrangements of older teaching institutions.

The most thoroughly elaborated and successfully completed programme of restoration of ancient monuments was recognised in the Iranian-Italian one for the buildings of Safavid Isfahan; it ensured not only the accurate restoration of these monuments and the prompt publication of its scientific results but also the training of Iranian cadres who could replace foreign consultants. A different initiative in the field of restoration and rehabilitation was the moving force behind the restoration of a caravanserai built by the Ottoman architect Sinan in Edirne, as the traditional Department of Pious Foundations developed the programme of transforming the caravanserai into a modern inn. The past is preserved as a context for the Qatar National Museum, where the reception hall of the old palace became the nucleus for a multi-disciplinary educational institution. The quest to preserve and keep in use the fabric of an entire village is amply demonstrated in the community of Sidi Bou Said, where municipal legislation over a period of years is ensuring a unified and well-maintained environment.

The search for innovation was recognised in the dramatic shapes of the tensile structures of the Inter-Continental Hotel and Conference Centre at Mecca, Saudi Arabia, while the water-tower system in Kuwait with its three great landmark towers and colonies of auxiliary ones standing in parklike settings was considered a new, technologically and aesthetically worthwhile departure from the usual characteristics of a public utility.

All of these searches address critical aspects of architecture such as the development of formal language and building skills, yet the search which was considered primary by the Master Jury was the one which had the potential to provide the poor with access to housing. The innovative Kampung Improvement Programme of Jakarta, where infrastructure and services were provided without disturbing squatter settlements, stands out as a model. A solution to the needs for sheltering of rural populations was highlighted in the Master Jury's choice of the *pesantren* school system in Java and specifically of the *pesantren* at Pabelan, where building skills are taught to its students and to the surrounding population.

While the results of this process of thought and selection can in no way be considered as the definitive statement on the nature and the direction of contemporary Islamic architecture, the selected projects imply a variety of strategies in the making of a physical environment and are, perhaps, instructive not only as individual cases but as a group. To be sure, there is a host of building types and strategies which are not represented among them, such as complex institutional buildings, public parks and landscape schemes, airports, and others. These will appear, it is hoped, in the future cycles of the Award. Yet one can already consider these fifteen as a kind of barometer of architectural thinking and activity in the countries of the Islamic world.

This introductory essay is an attempt at identifying some of the lessons which can be drawn from this elaborate procedure of reflection and selection. What ties these projects together? What meaning do they have for the Islamic architecture of today or of the future or for architectural practice in general? To answer these questions in full is not yet possible, and I shall limit myself to a few observations to initiate further thought and discussion. I shall first identify some of the characteristics, often very obvious ones, which are shared by the Muslim world of today, then discuss some of the issues which arise as one looks at the projects as a group, and finally propose a broader conceptual framework for an evaluation of architecture in the Islamic world today.

The Islamic world cuts an almost horizontal swath through Africa and Asia, from the shores of the Atlantic to the major archipelagos of the Pacific. Within its widest boundaries are distinct ecological and cultural units, more than forty individual nations, and a host of languages. That this congery of nations and peoples can in any way be considered a unity is because of several factors. The key factor is the stamp that conversion to Islam and inclusion within its rhythms of life and patterns of communication have put on the history and culture of different peoples. At different moments of history various groups entered an arena where the forces of Islam as a religion and as a civilisation played the leading role in the shaping of their real and metaphysical world. The traces of the original medieval Arabo-Persian Muslim culture appear differently in any one area and are perceived differently by the many groups which call themselves Muslim, as the nature of these traces depends on the time of conversion, on distance from traditional Muslim centres, and on internal social and economic stratification; fifteenth-century Java was quite different from nineteenth-century Senegal, and the traditional culture or piety of a Damascene merchant is not that of a Pakistani farmer. Yet the same ritual of daily life, the Arabic language as the exclusive language of Divine Revelation, and the yearly pilgrimage, the Hajj, as a meeting place of far-flung believers created a centripetal pull. This unity should not, however, be mistaken for consistent sameness, as is so frequently done. The Muslim world is quite legitimately divided into separate nations, cultural spheres, and discrete cultures. What may have had an historic validity for the tenth or the seventeenth century does not necessarily coincide with the political realities of today. To treat the Islamic world as continuously monolithic has all too often been a convenience for external observers of its separate parts. We are dealing in fact with very different societies *bound together* by their participation in the Islamic experience but individually affected by many other factors as well.

What, then, are the commonalities which can be found within the discrete societies and nations of the Islamic commonwealth? What are the traits that they share and what are the problems that they confront? And, what are the issues which face them all in the maintenance and the development of an environment, of an architecture?

Perhaps the most obvious feature which all the nations of the Islamic world exhibit today is the massive migration to cities. With this urbanisation or, in other terms, the tide of rural population drowning the old urban (and urbane) centres, has come a restructuring of nearly every individual society. Changes in the patterns of life and of social networks have in most instances been coupled with an explosive rise in population. Most of the people in Muslim countries are very young, below the age of fifteen, and they vastly outnumber those who are to provide services for them. Thus, a relatively small number of adults has the challenging, nearly insurmountable, task of providing for the needs and aspirations of a vast new generation. The implications of growth and changes in population for the physical fabric of any society—for the infrastructure of its cities, for planning and architectural practices, for the forms and functions of public institutions, for access to housing—almost overwhelm the imagination. The pressures of change, gathering speed with every year, have placed a frightening drain on the often slender resources of any country and enormous conceptual and practical burdens on the often inadequate number of its professionals, architects, planners, economists, and decision makers. This small cohort, often trained and equipped with ideas and tools developed elsewhere, must conceive the new society, generate working hypotheses, and seek efficient, flexible ways to implement decisions flowing out of these hypotheses, and must also weigh the value of its own old solutions or of solutions conceived elsewhere for societies with stabilised urban-rural ratios, very slow demographic growth, and larger or different resources.

Pressed as they are by the burdens of today and the demands of the near future, most adults in nearly all Islamic countries have been shaped by a harsh and destructive past. Though varying in specific details, two major and at times coincident phenomena have left their mark on their collective consciousness and memory. The first has been colonialism, the second modernisation. The colonial experience took many forms: at times direct political rule as in Algeria or Indonesia, at other times less overt, as in the French protectorate over Morocco or the British administration of Egypt, or even quite indirect as in the cultural and economic domination experienced by politically sovereign countries such as Turkey. Whatever the experience, all Muslim peoples have had to redefine their own identity and to shape a national political and economic cohesion. Some formulations reflect the ideals, images, and rhetoric of wars of independence; others have been shaped by less violent terms. All nations have had to create a political unity and a cultural identity in response to the traumatic and debilitating effects of colonialism. Energies were turned toward the establishment of the contemporary machinery of state, at times perpetuating administrative and economic structures which had been developed for the explicit purposes of the colonising power, at others evolving new ones. The more distant, precolonial past was rarely used as a source of inspiration because there had been no natural evolution from its attitudes and forms to new ones. Rather, the intrusion of the alien body of Western and European colonial products, techniques, and attitudes was instrumental in devaluing this past. Moreover, the expulsion or withdrawal of the colonising powers left an almost unbridgeable gap between past and present. Isolated and marginalised, the precolonial past could not easily be incorporated into the making of a present. Acceptance of the products of technologies generated elsewhere has meant that modernisation came in as a finished piece, rarely filtered through collective experience within a nation and thus ill adapted to its particular needs.

This point is particularly striking in architecture, in building for shelter and for image. The rich reservoirs of experience, tradition, and public image inherent in precolonial architecture were not activated in the search for a new architectural identity. This was particularly true because at least the external forms of the older architectural traditions had at times been subverted for the official buildings of the colonial administrations themselves. The new clients, decision makers, and architects turned instead to the most current images available for expressing the aspirations of their new nations. These images, techniques, and ethos were found within the international style generated by the Modern Movement. The political control by the very centres which these nations had fought hard to reject was thereby transformed into a cultural and technological dependency. Moreover, even in nations that never experienced colonial status directly, the desire for modernisation, spurred on in some cases by possession of highly valued natural resources, now caused the appearance of a similar dependency.

The colonial experience and modernisation are shared, to a large extent, by all areas and nations of the so-called Third World. It is, however, the coincidence of these factors with a third major commonality which gives us the right to consider the Islamic world of today as a unit. That commonality is, broadly speaking, Islam; more specifically, the participation of all in Islam as a religion and as a culture. As a religion, it has a long and carefully nurtured past and a present, living form with many variants and with many differences in intensity. Yet the fact that it has been a common experience has made it one of the major ideological sources for the shaping of a modern identity. It is a living present which carries modes of behaviour and memories only partly affected by specific national or regional variances. At the same time, each contemporary nation has come to deal with the past differently, selecting those aspects of the immediate or far-distant past which help, or at least do not hinder, the formulation of a provisional ideology for today and tomorrow. Formally proclaimed connexions coexist with the informal, traditional attitudes and habits not only of the population at large but also of the leading elites. This complex relationship to Islam and to the past has had a major impact on the policies and social patterns of individual societies, an impact which has been studied by contemporary thinkers, social scientists, and historians. Its impact on the nature and form of environments built since the onset of modernisation and/or independence in each nation still awaits full investigation.

And finally, almost all Muslim countries share a rich architectural past, different in its regional aspects, but physically present throughout. The major achievements of this architectural past, its mosques and its houses, its colleges of law and its trading centres, its shrines and its gardens, its great palace plazas and intimate city squares, its courtyards and its domes, remain amid the maelstrom of change. The cultural, social, religious, and aesthetic value of a particular building to society must be questioned before often scarce resources are allocated to its restoration. Will its old functions continue, and if not, what other activities could be housed there? What lessons this heritage possesses for the new practitioners and how they can be extracted, are questions which fascinate many contemporary architects, both within the Muslim world and beyond.

Not only individual buildings remain but often entire neighbourhoods, complete parts of old urban environments with premodern functions and services. For the most part, they are no longer the loci of power. The new city, of colonial or more recent making, has drained off their traditional inhabitants. These old environments, are now the deteriorating reception centres for the new migrants to the city, providing inexpensive shelter and proximity to employment. These environments still have valuable lessons for the architect and planner creating new environments, but the prognosis for their survival is uncertain. Yet, the physical presence of a vast and varied architectural heritage, which has not, for the most part, been integrated into the international language and culture of architecture, remains a challenge to all architects building in the countries of the Islamic world. The heritage is there to accept, to reject, or to engage in a dialogue by understanding its concepts and its idiom and by building upon it.

Thus, given many regional and historical differences and taking into consideration commonalities of historical experience and present problems, the nations of the Islamic world are at once members of the third, developing world and also uniquely bound to one another by a common cultural and visual heritage and a living, religious, centripetal reality. The creation of a new Muslim architecture is set within a web of many strings. There are the great universal issues of reaction to colonialism; there are specifically Muslim issues of a strong tradition and highly charged ideals to be adapted to contemporary needs. And there is a striking variety of people working at building in the Muslim world: local clients, architects and planners, native or imported workers, international consultants, administrators of all sorts, and millions of users, rich or poor, educated or not, all of whom seek within this architecture and this environment the means to be contemporary and to be themselves.

Within this context, how can new architectures or a new architecture emerge? What are the major factors which could be called formative or even normative? What is their direct bearing on the nature and extent of building activity and through it on the formation of a new architectural language and a new architectural ethos today? Every one of the build-

ings and statements gathered in this volume has its own constraints and its own rationale. Yet, considered as a group, they suggest a number of recurring patterns which may help in understanding the nature of the emergent architecture of Islam.

The first such set of patterns is the development of a body of thought about the nature of a built environment that is culturally and economically responsive to the present and future societies of the Islamic world. It can be called the genesis of culturally valid architectural theory generated out of its own sources. It is essentially a process of reflection on the initial premises, cultural, social, and especially visual and architectural, that led to a building programme and to a method of realising it. The practicing architect, working in the Islamic world today under the pressures of immediate implementation, can only rarely reflect upon such issues. Yet they may well be the essential components in the formation of a new Islamic architecture. In the absence of one or more widely disseminated coherent statements or, in short, in the absence of manifestos of aesthetic intent, this book contains a selection of thoughts and remarks, chosen from our seminars, which may serve as provisional parameters for the development of a new architectural discourse.

The bases for such an aesthetic theory are explored by Muhsin Mahdi. Just as the sources of much of contemporary Western aesthetics were the traditions of Western philosophy, so he has turned to the great classic Islamic philosophers, al-Ghazali and al-Farabi, to find structures of thought and concepts which could serve the needs of architecture today. Relationships to past forms and environments are discussed by Oleg Grabar and by Doğan Kuban. Grabar investigates the question of an historically ascertainable symbolism of forms and the manner in which the meaning of forms could change, with obvious implications for the present day. The future of the past in the Islamic world is weighed by Kuban who sees in this past a path of cultural continuity and not a mere museum of old forms. The wider issues of the relationship of Islamic religious and philosophical stances to contemporary needs of urbanising societies have been elucidated by Mohammed Arkoun in a quest to explore the groundwork for new initiatives in nation building. Mahbub ul-Haq focusses on the responsibilty of any nation's leaders and by extension of the leaders of the Islamic world to their populations and advocates the consideration of their basic, infrastructural needs, before satisfying any impulse for image making or for large architectural gestures.

While these five statements deal with the underpinnings of the making of an architecture or, in other words, with its theoretical and conceptual bases, another series of statements deals with the more particular problems of practitioners themselves. These statements discuss a range of practical and attitudinal issues which contribute to the effective practice of architecture in the Islamic world today, and more generally in the Third World. Thus, Charles Correa voices the concerns of the professional whose desire to produce meticulously crafted and finely designed individual buildings is being continually overshadowed by the pressure on the professional to provide solutions for a healthful built environment for the poor majority. The study by Mona Serageldin and François Vigier on changing roles and procedures in the design of public buildings calls for a more careful integration of the eventual users of buildings into the programming and design process, a departure from most current government practices. Such a change would involve a different training for local architects, teaching them to be sensitive to life style and to elicit from users their needs. It would also involve a phasing out of the participation of large Western firms as consultants and would rely on the development of local professional expertise for even the most specialised projects. The comments by Yasmeen Lari and Suhail Lari are a witness to the easy reliance on ready-made Western models for tourist complexes, while revealing a completely different set of needs for recreational complexes for which a formal architectural language has not been developed or is not readily available to the practitioner. The radical change in the nature and size of educational complexes and its implications for programming and design are noted by Ismail Serageldin. Finally, Nader Ardalan confronts the problem the contemporary architect has in building perhaps the single most significant building in a Muslim community, the mosque, and offers a kit of possible design attitudes.

While the thoughts expressed during the seminars of the first Award cycle have flagged the key elements required for the creation of new architectural theory and practice, the fifteen awarded projects are in various ways exemplars of the application of at least some of the same elements within completed projects. They permit the identification of a second set of patterns which may be called applied thinking. This set involves the development of tools and programmatic strategies that ensure a close fit between the perceived needs and the designed project that identify the skills necessary to carry such a project to its successful incorporation into a particular built environment and that embody the important potential for replicability.

The agricultural school in Senegal is the end product of an evolution of a building technology without the use of expensive imported building materials. The applied research which resulted in the construction of the school began several years earlier within the international community of professionals concerned with the development of constructional solutions to the needs of poorer countries. The location of their pilot project in Senegal is a fortunate concurrence of perceived need and readily available solutions. The thinking processes which resulted in the restoration of Safavid Isfahan are more difficult to document. They certainly involved the distinct desires of the Iranian nation to preserve its architecture and to enhance a unique urban environment as well as the gradual transference not only of technical but also of programming skills from the international restoration community to the city of Isfahan. A strategy for the restoration and conservation begun on international ground was progressively tailored to local needs and requirements. Driven by the overwhelming need to create an ordered urban environment from squatter settlements, the government of Jakarta rejected all previous strategies to provide housing and formulated its own. It made a decision to use all available resources as economically as possible. The efforts of the squatters to create their own housing were recognised as a major contribution to the housing investment, and public funds were used to enhance the new built environments through the skillful introduction of a viable water, sewage, and road infrastructure. What these three examples show is that successful strategies need not be limited to one set of circumstances. Their very success projects them into the international culture of architecture and development available for application wherever similar circumstances obtain.

Yet, another kind of applied thinking may not enter into the international community as easily. It is the design thinking which seeks the roots of a cultural identity and utilises, in various ways, the conventions of past architecture to fashion new architectural languages. Thus, behind the seemingly isolated exercises of a particular designer's aesthetic, as in the cases of the Halawa and Ertegün houses, there lies an historic process of experimentation of local, vernacular architecture.

The third set of patterns which becomes discernible in the analysis of the first cycle of the Award concerns the range of complexity and appropriateness of contemporary building practices available within the Islamic world. While the latest developments in construction technology have not appeared in this cycle, what is represented are most of the building systems current in the world, from the tensile structures of the Mecca conference centre, to the reinforced concrete and cinderblock of the Agadir courtyard houses, to the bamboo and wood of the Pondok Pesantren Pabelan in Central Java. Efforts to develop building technologies, stressing labour-intensive rather than capital-intensive techniques, predominate. The Senegal experiment introducing vaulting structures, the Mali medical centre using the cinva-ram press for making bearing walls, or even the revival of a brick industry to build the Mughal Hotel, are all examples of the same approach. The message which emerges is that modernity or contemporaneity can be achieved in more than one fashion.

A particularly important aspect of building practices is the performance standards not only of imported high technology materials but, even more notably, of traditionally used or improved local materials. In large part it is a question of craftsmanship in building, of the skills available, and of the care taken to construct and finish details so that the result is aesthetically a credit to its environment, whatever the economics of the construction system. The Turkish Historical Society, built in a contemporary style with locally available materials, is not only an example of the use of high technology but also of superb detailing and overall craftsmanship which can be credited to the designers and especially to the skilled construction workers. It is one thing to impose a building technology, even to have trained architects to use it. But there is little hope for developing a regionally based architectural style if the skills to manipulate this building technology (and eventually to produce it locally) do not exist. The naturalisation of an imported building technique is an essential step whose beginnings can be observed in the Nianing pilot project where the training of masons was part of the construction programme. Although the theory and the mechanics of the building system were elaborated and designed by an international forum, the implanting of the new vaulting system on Senegalese soil required the involvement of and interaction with the labour force. Only under these conditions is there any hope of assuming that a project can have a multiplier effect on the building practice of a country or region.

Building skills are, then, the cornerstone of any architecture. There can be no valid new architectural expression without the existence of an adequate, and preferably superb, reservoir of construction know-how. This is why several projects were noted for their attention and contribution to its development. The rural school in Pabelan, Java, has as an integral component of its educational programme training in building skills utilising a mix of traditional and newer building materials. The recognition of Hassan Fathy by the Chairman's Award has been in part for his understanding and elucidation of the problem of the transfer of skills (in his case, of traditional building skills of the Nubians enhanced by the design of an architect) and for urging on-the-job training for masons. His ideas are realised in their own way in the Senegal school and were the inspiration for the UNESCO team which developed its building system.

This particular example illustrates yet another aspect of building practices, the existence of a world-wide culture of architecture and builders. Even as they contribute to the creation of a regional or local idiom, projects built within the countries of the Islamic world demonstrate more widely based trends and can serve as examples and models in an international arena. Until recently, the West and the highly industrialised countries were automatically considered the main contributors to the world of architectural and building idioms and innovations. To some extent, they still are. The Kuwait towers and the Mecca conference centre were commissioned and envisioned to answer particular local needs, but they were planned and executed not so much with locally existing building means as with tools and techniques currently available on the world market. The importance of these monuments—and monuments they are—derives from the fact that it is the countries of the Islamic world that have sponsored or are about to sponsor more and more major projects, often of unprecedented magnitude. Much of the energies of the world construction and architectural community will be directed to reshaping of that environment, from new ports and ...s to new cities, housing tracts, and shelters for new ...ctions. Just as early experiments with steel construction have become permanently identified with locations in England, so the latest experiments in fibre construction or other, as yet unimplemented, materials may in the future become identified with locations in the Islamic world. The intriguing question of today is how much of these bright new experiments and their implications will become the cultural possessions of the building and architectural worlds of the locations in which they are found.

The fourth set of patterns to be noted is the variety of roles clients have played in the realisation of projects. There are instances of the familiar role of the employer and eventual user, as in the case of the Turkish Historical Society or the

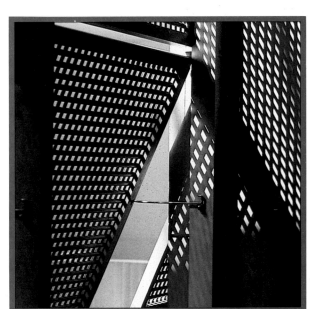

Halawa house. In large projects in particular, other bodies or individuals intervene in the client-designer relationship. In the Mopti Medical Centre, for instance, it is not clear that the formally recognised client had any real input in the programming of the design of the project. Rather, in a pattern which occurs frequently elsewhere in the Third World, to the client and designer is added the sponsor, usually some international institution which activates the search for a designer and probably sets the programme. Whether such donations of entire buildings can have an impact on the nature of architecture in a given country is a recurring, if moot, question. There are, on the other hand, several examples where the client has become the programmer, if not the designer, for a project. Particularly interesting in this aspect is the case of the *pesantren*, where building skills are taught and the school personnel have become the planners, designers and builders of its environment. What also emerges is the crucial role which governments, through their departments and bureaucracies, play in the building of new environments. While private clients do exist, there seems to be an absence of private commercial enterprise; government departments as clients overwhelm the private sector. It is thus particularly crucial for government circles to be receptive to innovations in architectural and planning thinking. Perhaps this cannot be expected as a rule; it is, however, the most important base for new practices to be launched, because even the smallest successful design has an immediate impact and a considerable potential replicability. Governments act as agents of architectural change, no matter what their professed ideology may be. Government agencies are clients of projects as varied in their symbolic intent and practical application as the Mecca hotel and conference centre, the restoration of Isfahan, the Kuwait water towers, the Qatar Museum, and the Kampung Improvement Programme. In considering the agents or factors of importance for the formation of new architecture this role of the state must be recognised and understood.

And then, what is the role of the architect in dealing with all these issues? The new and increasingly less rural population will have its aspirations shaped not only by traditional norms but by the evolving city itself. It is a population which seeks and will continue to seek access to safe, sanitary, and satisfying housing and to shelters for public functions—social, religious, commerical, and cultural. That the former cannot be provided by the commonly used building delivery systems alone has been amply demonstrated. Other means to provide access to housing, through nonarchitectural interventions such as developing public works systems or financing, may be more effective and the Kampung Improvement Programme has shown the success of such approaches.

What forms shelter for public functions is to take depends on the aspirations of every society and on its image of a desirable architecture. Though many public functions are still located in older forms (the case of the mosque is perhaps the most obvious one), this is less and less frequently so. Newly created or newly introduced functions and institutions—hospitals, airports, scientific institutions, commerical buildings—require specific new building types. Since they appear to be the most numerous new buildings everywhere they will have a direct impact on their surroundings; in fact, they become the shapers of the new urban experience and their characteristics and their forms must be properly evaluated. Their naturalisation into local idioms is a challenge to the architectural profession. How will these forms be chosen? An interesting example is that of the Turkish Historical Society, where an institution created after the secularisation of Turkey finds its home in a building that, although built in contemporary idiom with contemporary technology, evokes in plan and layout the medieval Islamic legal college, the madrasa. Does it perhaps indicate the direction of the search for new architecture? Except perhaps in countries like Turkey with a relatively high number of architects per inhabitant, architects may be called to redefine their objectives and therefore the character of their training. Instead of working in the accepted manner for smaller and smaller sectors within their entire nation they may begin to redefine their profession to expand its arena and its manner of activity, taking more managerial, planning, and finally political roles. Or, as Hassan Fathy has advocated, they may turn into specialists, "barefoot architects," working within communities to build better environments. In fact, their changing societies will reshape the architects themselves.

One last pattern deserves mention. Altogether the occurrence of expressive form which evokes or which quotes deliberately and directly from past sources is rather striking. There are the Halawa house, the Mopti Medical Centre, and the Nianing agricultural school. Even the highly technological Mecca hotel and conference centre attempts to call forth images of the bedouin tent on one hand and of traditional urban forms of the region on the other. That there should be a discernible trend toward expressive form is not surprising given the insistent search by architect and client for a particularisation of architectural idiom. What is noteworthy, however, is that the apparent sources for these forms lie almost completely outside the great metropolitan traditions of monumental Islamic architecture. There seems little evidence of learning from the Sultan Hassan Madrasa of Cairo or the Taj Mahal. Monumental architecture seems too individualised and too complex for easy evocation or quotation. The set of skills for making it available as a working language, and not only as an historical exemplar, is not yet in place. By contrast, the lessons of layout, elevation, and shape, and of the constraints of rural traditions, such as those of the M'zab or of Nubia, have been internalised and made current.

Yet there are other reasons for these choices was well. One may lie in the fact that many of the elements of the metropolitan traditions had been trivialised or devalued by their appearance in colonial architecture, as has been mentioned before. More genuine expressions of identity were to be sought and found in the countryside and in vernacular architecture. The fact that the latter forms were quite austere and could be adapted readily to the general tastes of the contemporary international idiom gave fertile ground for their study or elaboration, whether in pre-World War II Turkey, postwar Egypt, or contemporary Mali. To what extent these traditions will provide continuing inspiration for even large-scale projects and to what extent they will be taken as the true loci of identity are questions to be asked in future Award cycles. And finally, will their most important lesson, that of superb climatic adaptability, be learned on a large scale, as it was learned so successfully by the metropolitan Islamic architects of the past?

In reviewing the material presented in this book one becomes aware of several tensions which remain unresolved while the building of new environments, new settlements, and new public institutions continues apace. There are the tensions between the averred search for a local idiom or a new Islamic architecture and the nature and training of the professionals being called upon to realise or implement that search in concrete projects. To what extent can any talented designer respond to an intent which appears to be culturally grounded? Or must all building derive from primarily localised efforts? There are the unresolved tensions in the role of the client. To what extent will the client contribute to the growth of a new local idiom and to what extent will the images of the highly industrialised international idiom remain more desirable to him? Finally there are the tensions between the makers and the users of a building. Can the makers, clients, and designers accurately predict the users' reactions? Or will needs and expectations be in conflict?

But, ultimately, the significance of these projects and of the process of planning, construction, and reflection which accompanied their selection lies in something more than tensions and problems. The development of this new architecture is anchored in the awareness of a continuous communication between the universe of design and architectural thinking and the universe of building skills and construction know-how, between the potential of the construction industry and the images of a desired architecture, between the formal or informal past and the needs of today. Where the continuum has been disrupted or has never existed, the development of an architecture which is coherent with the nature and aspirations of any society is very difficult to achieve. But, if the fifteen awarded projects can in any way be used as a forecast, one can predict that the future architecture and building of the Islamic world will be able to incorporate tensions within the scope and energy of its building activities and find appropriate resolutions of its problems, as long as there remains a close relationship between architecture and the community it serves.

ISLAMIC PHILOSOPHY AND THE FINE ARTS
MUHSIN S. MAHDI

Ethnically and racially based views on Islamic art and architecture should be guarded against and not allowed to re-enter through the back door via ambiguous words such as "culture" and "religion," terms that mean all things to all people, especially when lumped together. Take an expression like "Islamic culture": one difficulty is that it tends to be seen in terms of so-called primitive cultures, as it is sometimes seen in anthropology, or of some particular, real or presumed "religious culture" such as Christianity. The attempt to look at Islam through Christian eyes and to search for symbols that parallel those of Christianity is a dubious enterprise, regardless of protestations that one is looking for specifically Islamic symbols or symbols that distinguish Islamic culture from other cultures. Christianity absorbed and transformed, and in this way preserved, pagan or gnostic symbols; Islam rebelled against these symbols and tried to remove them from the consciousness and experience of the Muslim community. We should also remember that symbols, and the symbolic functions of art and architecture as we understand them today, are predominantly nineteenth-century romantic European notions. Their relevance to the self-understanding of artistic creation and expression in other times and places cannot be taken for granted (the critical side of A. H. el-Zein's "Beyond Ideology and Theology" is rather instructive in this respect).[1]

Even if we accept the notion of "culture" or "Islamic culture" as a useful point of departure, the relationship between crafts in general, what we call "fine arts" in particular, and other "aspects" of such a culture remains highly problematic. We are dealing with the possible relationship between the fine arts in Islam and Islamic philosophy as it is available in written sources. Here I think it is prudent not to be too ambitious or too hasty, and Oleg Grabar's suggestion that written sources are important because they provide a parallel to visual phenomena is a sound starting point. One statement suggesting that such a parallel existed between the fine arts and phy is a passage from the *Alchemy of Ha*:

> The beauty of a thing lies in the appea[rance]
> tion which is realisable and in accord wi[th]
> [For example] beautiful writing combines e[ach]
> characteristic of writing, such as harmony of
> correct relations to each other, right sequence, an[d]
> arrangement.[2]

Let me, therefore, begin here and point out what else the patrons as well as the practitioners of these arts might have

learned from philosophy, either directly or indirectly, through popularised versions of philosophy spread among educated circles by mystics like al-Ghazali.

The Task of Islamic Philosophy. If I were asked by a student of Islamic art and architecture what in Islamic philosophy can enlighten us on the questions of a thing's perfection, its harmony, the correct relationships among its parts, and their implications for man and man-made works of art, my answer would be quite simple. This is what Islamic philosophy is all about: it is the search for order and harmony in the natural world, the intelligible world, the human soul, and the city. It is an account of such order and harmony where it exists, and an account of how to restore order and harmony in man and in the city. It looks at works of art as being in the service of this objective.

If a student were then to ask whether he could expect to find in the literature of Islamic philosophy an account of Islamic architectural symbols and their meanings, the answer would again be simple: written sources tell us that the overarching concern of Islamic philosophy is to find out what is true always and everywhere, and to discover the principles that govern temporal and local variations and change insofar as these are rhythmic or cyclical or the products of the interaction of permanent factors. Islamic philosophy is not a religious or cultural or national philosophy in the sense that it is the product of, or bound up or concerned primarily with, the ideas and ideals of a particular human community, not even one as large and significant as the Islamic religious community. Yet it is equally true that Islamic philosophy is very much concerned with understanding the particular character of the Islamic community, and architectural forms and decorations are temporally and locally bound to specific nations, cities.

know and take into account those needs and purposes.

How then, one may ask, can the student understand the relationship between Islamic philosophy (or the thought of the major Muslim philosophers) and Islamic architecture (or the work of the major Muslim architects)? Is the relationship "proved" to a significant degree by the fact the the architects in question were all Muslims? I should not think so; one can be an architect without being a philosopher or a good Muslim. One must therefore look for more concrete links. If they existed, it was probably because some architects were educated and intelligent men who read or heard about some of the writings of the philosophers. But the question still remains: what could they have learned from these writings?

Aspects of Divine and Human Creation.   Before looking for answers, it is useful to recall some of the characteristic ways in which Islamic philosophy deals with the arts. Although it does occasionally set down the general rules that govern the production of works of art, it does not generally engage in an analysis of these rules as they apply to the production of particular works, except by way of giving examples; nor do we find a detailed analysis of aesthetic experience or of the problems arising from the contemplation of a work of art. The particular rules that govern the production of a particular work of art, as well as the analysis of the experience of particular works, are normally dealt with by the art critic. The philosopher may also be a poet or a musician, a literary critic or a critic of music. But these activities remain distinct from what we may call his "philosophy of art," which is concerned with such questions as the relationship between art and knowledge (whether knowledge of the Creator or of the created world); the role of the powers and passions of the soul in the production and experience of art; and the civic functions of art.

The architect is a maker. If he is any good, we say he is a creative man, a creator. If he is a Muslim he knows already that the Supreme Creator is God, and one assumes that he would be interested in reflecting on His work and even in imitating His creation. There is, of course, quite a bit about God's creation in the Koran and the Hadith, but it is not difficult to distinguish between the way these sources speak about God's creation and the way philosophy investigates and presents it. Philosophy looks at it as a whole, and looks at its parts and the order of its parts as an object of human knowledge. There is an affinity between the way the philosopher looks at the work and the way the artisan conceives of his work, inasmuch as they both consider a whole, its parts, and the relationships among those parts. Both are engaged in a human enterprise: one looks at the natural whole with the aim of knowing it, the other conceives a whole with the aim of producing it. Both need to consider this whole-to-part relationship to the extent that human capacity permits. But more specific issues still have to be considered.

How is the Supreme Creator conceived? Does one give priority to His knowledge or to His will? In philosophy this question turns on whether He is conceived as the supreme intellect or as the mysterious One beyond the supreme intellect, beyond all knowledge and being. Muslim philosophers were divided on this fundamental issue, and their differences were not necessarily related to the part of the Muslim community to which they belonged. In Ismaili philosophy, for instance, the early Iranian philosophers such as Abu Ya'qub al-Sijistani thought of God as beyond being and not being, and

as the originator of the supreme intellect through His command, while the later Fatimid philosopher Hamid al-Din al-Kirmani thought of God as the first or supreme intellect, and in this he was followed by the Ismaili thinkers in Yemen. The question may seem to deal with a subject that is too remote to have any relevance to human things. In fact it is not, for it determines the end of human thought and human action. Is the end of man (who is created in God's image) the perfection of his intellect that terminates in the intellectual intuition of the whole, or is it to contact that mysterious One through deeds? The answer to this question may determine the way one looks at artistic creation in its most sublime form—whether it is considered an imaginative representation of how things are and how man ought to act, both of which can also be articulated by intellectual understanding and intuition, or an imaginative revelation that transcends all created reality and anything that intellectual understanding and intuition can achieve on their own.

This issue has something to do with the next one, which is the nature and structure of the created world, intelligible as well as sensible, the heavenly bodies as well as the bodies here below. Do stars have intellects and souls? Are they ranked in an order ascending to that which is closest to God? Such questions are more philosophic than religious, even though a philosophic interpretation may be related to or have its origin in a Koranic or Hadith text. We all know of the numerous verses about light and darkness in the Koran, especially that famous "light verse" (XXIV,35), that lend themselves to philosophic interpretations: light as the physical manifestation of intellectual or supraintellectual light, and the different parts of creation as an orderly mixture of light and darkness, an analogy of being and not being, that terminates in God as pure or unmixed light. These philosophic interpretations were current in Sufi circles and among the Sufi orders to which many of the great architects belonged.

Then there is the analogy that is drawn between the structure of the world, the structure of the soul, and the structure of the city. The structure of the soul and the activities of its various parts or powers and their relationship and hierarchy are of interest to any artist whose art consists of creating a work that pleases or conveys a message or arouses a certain feeling in the human beings who look at it or work or worship it. Sense perception, imagination, intellect, passion, and practical understanding are all parts of the soul that the architect addresses to some extent through what he creates. The power of imagination, its functions in waking and dreaming, the way it mediates between understanding and sense perception, its role as a receptacle of intellectual perception or revelation, and its creative role in representing this perception or revelation in sensible forms are all questions crucial to any discussion of symbols in architecture and any understanding of how a work of art operates.

There is also a question of the passions and desires of the human soul: pleasure and pain, comfort, security, the desire for wealth, domination, honor, and so forth. How does a work of art provide for these, order them, exploit them, or control them? Do they have a natural order which the work of art is called upon to preserve or restore? Or is the work of art meant to satisfy human feelings, desires, and passions regardless of whether they are healthy or sick, good or evil, moderate or immoderate? What is meant by the aesthetic education of man? And what is the relationship between the experience of beauty and the experience of goodness? Can a human being who lacks the experience of beauty, order, and harmony through works of art be educated in goodness, and perceive the beauty of good actions and the beauty of God's creation?

The arts provide both living space for the families and citizens of a city and symbols for a city or nation's power or purpose. These are the subjects of economics, ethics, and politics, or of the practical sciences. It is in this context that philosophy centres its attention on the "symbolic" character of these arts, and emphasises their character as sensory apprehensions that aim at pleasure as an end in itself and as accidentally useful in practical things. Otherwise they would be merely practical; that is, they would serve what is necessary in practical life or in human excellence in practical life, be it victory in war, wealth, pleasure, or virtue.

The Treatment of Language Arts in Islamic Philosophy. The arts that Islamic philosophy treats at some length are the arts of language: poetry and rhetoric. We have become sensitive to the fact that language and the arts of language are of capital importance for the study of all other human arts, and we speak of the "vocabulary," "grammar," "rhetoric," and "poetics" of this or that art, including the art of architecture. Such things as signs and symbols are thus discussed in Islamic philosophy with reference to certain forms of speech and sometimes music, i.e., generally to things heard rather than things seen. This is a paradoxical situation, since things seen have a higher rank in philosophy than things heard. The former are the objects of perceiving, speculating, or theorizing. Yet they are discussed with reference to natural rather than to man-made, to artful or artificial things. Philosophic literature considers poetry and rhetoric as part of or in the perspective of "logic"—that is, thought. In this respect, it articulates something that is present in nonphilosophic literary criticism (e.g., the "science of meanings," *'ilm al-ma 'ani*), but which is discussed there in a less coherent manner and within a narrower perspective.

In philosophy the emphasis is on the formal structure of speech and its thought content, its purpose, its impact, what it generates in the listener, and how it does this. So the question is whether poetry and rhetoric have a thought content, and if so, what kind of content it might be; whether they aim at pleasure for its own sake; whether they are meant to generate certain notions or convictions or images; and whether these are ends in themselves or are meant to educate the audience morally—that is, to form their moral character and enable them or make it easy for them to learn something or to do (or not do) something. If they do this—and the philosophic literature assumes that, for good or ill, they do—then the next question is what do they make men think or imagine; what do they persuade them of; what do they arouse them to do; what do they discourage them from doing? The arts can be all these things: they can be useful, playful, fun, pleasant, restful, morally instructive, or thought-provoking (in both directions—good or bad, true or false). All these aspects have to be considered. Such disciplines as the "sociology of litera-

ture" are modern efforts to recapture these dimensions of art.

Again, the arts (to a greater degree than the sciences) are relative to certain peoples, times, and places. They are popular or public in character. They express the human character, traditions, conventions, laws, and religious and cultural views that prevail in a certain region at a certain time. The best of them express the highest views or ideals of their audience, and lift that audience to the highest level of which it is capable, whether in terms of pleasure, moral character, or deeds. This is one aspect of the discussion of these arts in Islamic philosophy. But there is also the supranatural, supraregional, supratemporal perspective of Islamic philosophy that provides for the possibility of comparing images, conventions, moral attitudes, and deeds of various nations, and for understanding their horizons and limitations.

A "Pragmatic" Aesthetic Critical Theory. The arts (to a greater degree than the sciences) are relative to certain peoples, times, and places. They are popular or public in character. They express the human character, traditions, conventions, laws, and the religious and cultural views that prevail in a certain region at a certain time. The best of them express the highest views or ideals of their audience, and lift that audience to the highest level of which it is capable, whether in terms of pleasure, moral character, or deeds. This is one aspect of the discussion of these arts in Islamic philosophy. But there is also the supranational, supraregional, supratemporal perspective of Islamic philosophy that provides for the possibility of comparing images, conventions, moral attitudes, and deeds of various nations, and for understanding their horizons and limitations.

Thus Islamic philosophy provides an aesthetic critical theory that is best characterised as "pragmatic."[3] It deals with poetry and rhetoric (and occasionally arts such as painting and sculpture) as they exist outside the context of philosophy and as they are meant to be used by a new breed of teachers. It centres its attention on the crucial role of sensory perception and sense apprehension, and the pleasure felt by man in sensible knowledge for its own sake, for its utility, and for the way it beckons beyond itself to higher kinds of knowledge. It distinguishes between the prephilosophic experience of the arts (the experience that, among other things, led to the rise of philosophy) and the postphilosophic use of the arts by philosophers, lawgivers, and philosophically minded rulers in their efforts to educate the citizens, form their character, and teach them appropriate opinions. The philosophic contribution, then, consists of both the theory itself and the description of the new context within which these arts are to be employed, as well as how, and for what purpose.

By and large, the philosophic tradition is interested not in the technical details of the art of composing poems and rhetorical speeches, but in the overall character of these arts and in their use. In contrast, nonphilosophic critical theory in Arabic is largely devoted to such technical details. One of the models from which the two traditions work is the prophet-lawgiver. Thus the question of the use of the "art" of poetry and rhetoric (not poetry and rhetoric in the customary sense) by the founder of a religion is common to both traditions. The question is whether what is termed the "miraculous" character of the Koran consists in its unique excellence in the use of technical details (on which Arabic literary criticism tends to concentrate) or rather in its overall moral intention, educative purpose and achievement, and ability to determine the theoretical and practical opinions of the Muslim community and its way of life (on which the philosophic tradition concentrates).

This question leads back to the question of imaginative representation or revelation: of what, how, by what faculty? Does it represent the external world of nature and the individual emotions and practical objections of the poet and the rhetorician? Does it extend to common opinions, generally known or accepted notions, and the "ideals" of a particular community? Such things were, of course, known to be what rhetoricians and poets did, and Arabic literary criticism discussed the success or failure of the rhetorician and the poet on those bases. Or, does imaginative representation or revelation involve Platonic "ideas"? Following Aristotle, these are consistently refuted in the philosophic tradition (the case is different in mysticism). They are replaced by "intelligibles" in the mind, hence by things that become known or about which one can attain certainty in the theoretical sciences that deal with natural and voluntary things. This led to the philosophic distinction between the imaging in poetry and the persuasion in rhetoric that deal with theoretical things and those that deal with practical things. The former were criticised on the basis of relative proximity to the theoretical sciences (to the extent that these achieve certainty at any particular time), and on the basis of the skill of the poet and the rhetorician in convincing and moving the audience as close as possible to the truth of things. The latter were criticised in terms of what virtue and vice were thought to be, as well as on the basis of the skill of the poet and the rhetorician in promoting the practical education of the audience.

Function and Experience.   We have been trying to isolate the various functions of public buildings and spaces in the Islamic world with particular attention to public buildings and spaces that have a religious use: mosques, madrasas, and Sufi *zawiyas.* We have paid special attention to their religious-symbolic function. Much of our discussion has centred on whether certain kinds of design (decorations, inscriptions, and so on) are symbolic, and if so, whether any of them is indispensable to a building with a religious function. By posing the question in this way we are bound to reach an impasse, if not a negative answer; we are reminded that, historically, any public building that solved an immediate practical problem was considered satisfactory by men and women who were the very models of Islamic piety—in fact, by the Prophet himself, and by his companions.

My remarks are meant to suggest that we look at a work of art as something that performs a multiplicity of functions. What function a particular public religious building performs and the means it employs for doing so can be found only by considering that particular building. It seems to me that we have been trying to speculate in a general sort of way about what functions, if any, a public religious building performs above and beyond its solutions to immediate practical problems. By immediate practical problems, I assume we mean

practical utility, or what is necessary if certain practical functions are to be served, as distinguished from what appears to be useless or arbitrary. What looks useless or arbitrary in a work of art may be just that, in which case it performs the function of merely confusing and disorienting the beholder or listener; but what appears useless or arbitrary may in fact aim at a higher utility and necessity and, depending on the onlooker's or listener's taste and judgement, it may succeed in performing a higher function. For example, a public religious building may try to convey a sense of God's peace, glory, majesty, transcendence, or unity—in short, any one or a combination of God's beautiful names—and it may do this through sheer simplicity, some shape or void, colour, size, decoration, or inscription, or a combination of these. Those aspects of a public religious building that go beyond solving an immediate practical problem in a narrow sense have to be looked at individually and together as symbolic in the larger sense of this term. One has to ask what the building is trying to convey and whether it succeeds or fails.

Finally, what if one or more of these aspects that characterise the artistic traditions (in the plural) of Muslim communities is not unique to Islamic architecture, but is in fact present in one or another of the artistic traditions of some other religion? This question does not bother me at all; on the contrary, I wish that all these aspects would be present in all the artistic traditions of other religions. This seminar has pointed to the roots of spiritual beliefs and artistic traditions in Islamic countries. If the majority of contemporary examples we have seen indicate anything, it is that some architects are trying to attach dead branches to these roots with rubber bands. Our task is to find out whether others have succeeded in grafting living branches to these roots, and whether the result is a living tree that can grow and under which contemporary Muslims can take shade. We cannot perform this task if we continue to assume that architecture in the Islamic world must reproduce certain forms or symbols that we students of Islamic history or culture have identified as "Islamic," in order to help us distinguish "Islamic culture" from Western or other Oriental cultures. Whatever the use of this approach may be, it is not a substitute for a philosophy of art that considers the kind of issues I have raised, or for an art criticism that deals with the rules of artistic production and with the individual and collective experience of a work of art.

As a last remark, I would like to point out a certain difficulty for which I see no easy resolution. When I try to "experience" a great monument of Christian architecture, such as the cathedral of Chartres, I am able to read about the history of its construction, the cultural history of the period, the techniques employed in its building, the meaning of the representations in its sculpture and stained glass windows, and the stylistic features of the works of art that survive in it from different periods. I am also able to spend time looking at the monument, studying and enjoying its form and each of the works of art it contains, and attending the functions performed in it. However successful I may be, my experience is quite different from that of a convinced Catholic who has been raised in the church and has participated in the mysteries of that faith from childhood, and who experiences the same monument as a living house of God. This would seem to indicate that there are certain limits to the effort some of us make to ascertain how religious public buildings function in the Islamic world and the way Muslims experience these buildings. Furthermore, at least some great religious public buildings are themselves "works of faith," and this fact again indicates that there may be limits to an effort at understanding their spirit if we do not participate in the faith of the builders. There may be differences of opinion among us on how severe those limits are, and on the extent to which they can be overcome. But surely serious architects and their consultants, however creative or learned, need to confront these questions and constraints when called upon to design and build public buildings in the Islamic world that are meant to have religious functions.

SYMBOLS AND SIGNS IN ISLAMIC ARCHITECTURE
OLEG GRABAR

Interpretation is still obviously the central and most difficult problem. In principle, we can always bring up the question of the validity of a hermeneutics. Through cross-references, clear assertions (texts, rites, representative monuments) and half-veiled allusions, we can demonstrate precisely what such and such symbol "means." But we can also state the problem in another manner: do those who utilize symbols realize all their theoretical implications? For instance, when studying the symbolism of the "Cosmic Tree," we say that this tree is located in the "Centre of the World." Are all individuals belonging to societies that know of such Cosmic Trees equally conscious of the integral symbolism of the "Centre"? But the validity of the symbol as a form of knowledge does not depend on the degree of understanding of such and such an individual. Texts and representative monuments prove extensively that, at least to certain individuals of an archaic society, the symbolism of the "Centre" was transparent in its totality; the rest of society was satisfied with the act of "participating" in symbolism. Moreover, it is hard to state precisely the limits of such participation; it varies according to an indeterminate number of factors. All we can say is that the actualization of a symbol is not mechanical; it is related to the tensions and alternations of social life and ultimately with cosmic rhythms. —M. Eliade

Much of what follows consists in rambling views, opinions, and interpretations developed over the years by an outsider trying to understand a world which is not his own. They tend, therefore, to seek general and abstract meanings in what had been a concrete and personal experience. This is not wrong by itself, but its danger is that unique cultural experiences can much too easily be transformed into meaningless and obvious generalities. The opposite dangers are either that a unique experience becomes so specific as to be unavailable for sharing and even explaining or that an artificial search for presumably universal values falsifies the truth of any individual's culture or experience. I hope I have avoided these pitfalls, but my main concern is that what follows be construed as a statement of the truth or of a doctrine. They are merely partial and questioning signals toward the formulation of a way to understand symbolism in a specific culture. At the end an afterword puts together some implications of my remarks which have worried me as I read and reread them. It seems more and more evident to me that discussions of symbols and signs are far more complicated than, in our managerial aloofness, we imagined them to be.

The Problem. There are two reasons, one general, the other specific, for raising the question of symbols and signs. The general reason is that the act of symbolisation and cultural or personal attachment to whatever we call symbols are recognised modes of behaving, feeling, thinking, associating, and understanding. There may be now and there may have been in the past more than one "Islamic" symbolic or semiotic system, but whether one or a multitude, they form a discrete group which must by definition be, at least in part, different from comparable groups at other times or in other places. The question derives from nearly two years of deliberations and discussions in the context of the Aga Khan Award seminars about what, if anything, within contemporary architecture in Muslim countries can legitimately be considered Islamic. Furthermore, can this something be defined with sufficient clarity to be used as a criterion for evaluation?

When we dealt in the second seminar with restoration and rehabilitation, the problem did not arise, for the criterion of having been part of Muslim history was sufficient to justify the consideration of any old remains. The concerns were or could have been technical (is a given monument or ensemble accurately restored?), social (what should be preserved and why within the context of contemporary culture?), informational (how should one present and exchange knowledge about monuments?), economic (how does rehabilitation relate to tourism or to urban mobility?), aesthetic (what is a good restoration?), or ideological (what is the purpose of preserving and whom does it profit?), but the value of the activity within the context of enhancing Muslim self-awareness was not questioned. It could have been, for the argument can be made that monuments, like people and cultures, may best be left to die, that antiquarianism in architecture is a peculiarity of a very limited Western elite and that preservation is a form of congealing a meaningless past, at best useful for flag waving. But the discussion did not go that far.

Housing, the topic of the third seminar, was a much more complicated matter. It seemed clear to me that there were two extreme positions. One maintained that there is a definable Islamic typology of housing, whether its definition should derive from historical forms created in order to make an Islamic way of life possible or from a prescriptive system of religious and social requirements determined by the Koran, the Traditions, and Law. The other extreme maintained that housing is independent of the prescriptions of the faith, either because contemporary problems require solutions independent of religious and cultural allegiances or because Islam itself is prescriptive in behaviour, not in form. These extremes allow for a very extensive range of intermediate possibilities, but what was important about the debate itself was that the pertinence of Islam for housing—the system of belief and ways of life—*could* be questioned, while no one questioned the right of Muslims to a setting for whatever forms their lives may take. It was interesting that the texts quoted consisted either of very general statements (usually from the Hadith) about good behaviour and cleanliness or legal sources in which complex local practices and traditions were given a broad sheathing of theoretical jurisprudence. Statements attributed to the seventh and eighth centuries (for which we have few available forms) and contemporary urban requirements are difficult to correlate, unless one tries to delve much more deeply into the evolution of Islamic law over the centuries. But even if unanswered in any way approaching coherence, the correct question was asked: what is the pertinence of Islam to architecture, now or in the past?

While this issue was aired in very broad terms at the first seminar and has reappeared from time to time, this fourth seminar seems to be the proper moment to try to be more specific and more concrete. But, even here, it is impossible to consider in one swoop the impact of Islam on architecture from Spain to the Philippines over fourteen centuries—hence the choice of a series of questions dealing with only one aspect of the impact. One could have chosen something as concrete as inheritance law and the development of building space in cities, but the information would not be easily available and the subject is hardly exciting. In proposing to deal with signs and symbols, the assumed social and psychological need to symbolise provides a different framework within which to consider Islamic architecture.

The questions can be formulated in the following way: Is there an Islamic system of visually perceptible symbols and signs? How universal is such a system and what are its variants? What are the sources of the system, the revealed and theologically or pietistically developed statement of the faith, or the evolution of visual forms over fourteen hundred years? In what fashion and how successfully were signs and symbols transformed into building forms? How valid is the experience and memory of the past for the present and the future?

Old Approaches.   The need for an approach comes from existing literature. To my knowledge, only two studies deal overtly and formally with symbolism and signs in Islamic culture and claim, at least in theory, some kind of completeness.

One is Rudi Paret's *Symbolik des Islam* (Stuttgart, 1958). Modestly restricted to "observation on the meaning of symbols (*Symbolik*) within the sphere of the Muslim world" (p. 9) and limited to religious matter, it tends to be descriptive rather than interpretative. Paret does, however, make an important distinction between primary and secondary symbols, the former being direct and immediate transformations of whatever is being symbolised (a complete set or system), the latter being more fragmentary or diverse, at times a synecdoche (part used for the whole) and at other times in multiple layers (as when a mystic headgear made of two pieces symbolises *all* binary opposites such as paradise-hell, life-death). It is only when dealing with mysticism that Paret, under the impact of Hellmut Ritter (to whom I shall return below), moves beyond the descriptive to the visual symbolism of the Arabic alphabet. He does not, however, talk about visual architectural implications.

The second study is Jacques Waardenburg's "Islam Studied as a Symbol and Signification System" in *Humaniora Islamica*, Vol. II (1974). A theoretical essay on method, it asks appropriate questions (note in particular an interesting query about Islam as an ideology rather than as a religion) but loses itself by being so methodologically abstract that it fails in providing answers and even in indicating how these answers could in fact be found. Not even a nod is extended in the direction of visual forms.

Much more work has been done with the uniquely rich subfield of Islamic, and especially Persian, mysticism. The grand master of the field is Hellmut Ritter, whose *Das Meer der Seels* (Leiden, 1955) is one of the most elaborate and difficult systems of interpreting mystical thought. His successor, hardly less complicated, is Henri Corbin, some of whose works exist in English. An excellent introduction to all mystical matters is Annemarie Schimmel's *Mystical Dimensions of Islam* (Chapel Hill, 1975). An interesting and occasionally provocative discussion of related issues around a single theme and with a broader base than Iranian Sufism or Ibn al-'Arabi can be found in M. Arkoun and others, *L'Etrange et le Merveilleux dans l'Islam Medieval* (Paris, 1978), the proceedings of a lively colloquium. The most interesting aspect of these studies for our purposes is that they extend beyond traditional theological or esoteric interpretations into science and technology (S. H. Nasr, *Islamic Science*, London, 1976) and architecture (N. Ardalan and L. Bakhtiar, *The Sense of Unity*, Chicago, 1973). They owe little to broad symbolic theories except to an implied (Jungian, I guess) assumption that certain kinds of formal transformations (i.e., not only the visible form but its finite or infinite modifications according to one or more logical or paralogical methods) are innate within the psyche and often affected by certain physical or cultural circumstances (e.g., the land of Iran with its ecological properties, Muslims brought up in Sufi traditions).

In most of these studies, just as in several works by T. Burckhardt (*Sacred Art in East and West*, London, 1967, and *Art of Islam*, London, 1976), which are not as deeply affected by Iranian culture, I see three inherent difficulties:

1. Nowhere is there an explicit statement of the relationship between data (measurable and quantifiable in time and space) and interpretation; in other words, as opposed to the works of philologists and even philosophers such as Ritter or Corbin, there is an absence of scientific precision. Therefore, many of the conclusions seem premature.

2. The specifically Islamic character of forms is rarely clear or specific enough, except for calligraphy, which is mentioned as unique but never described; in other words the Islamic component is either absent from what are basic human needs conditioned by local limitations (no stone in Iran, colder weather in Anatolia than in Egypt, and so on) or else it is simply a sheathing, a removable skin which is an expression of *taste,* not a symbol of the faith or the culture; this last point may be further strengthened by the undeniable fact that buildings (as opposed to objects in metal or paintings) were constantly repaired and refurbished to fit a prevalent taste and by the more debatable theory of earlier decades that visual expression was a sin in Muslim eyes.

3. The contemporary context is almost always missing; we may not yet have discovered a Suger or a Procopius in traditional Islamic culture, but we do have documents of contemporary witnesses which would prevent the unavoidable impression of modern constructs, perhaps valid to modern man, applied to traditional forms.

If we turn to media other than architecture, the matching of literary evidence with works of art or the investigation of symbolic themes and ideas has been more thorough and more specific. The most conspicuous examples are various studies by Schuyler Cammann on rugs (in *The Textile Museum Journal* 3, 1972, and in P. J. Chelkowski, ed., *Studies . . . in Honour of R. Ettinghausen,* New York, 1974) and much of R. Ettinghausen's work over the last thirty years (best examples in *Ars Orientalis* 2, 1957, and in J. Schacht and C. E. Bosworth, *The Legacy of Islam,* Oxford, 1974, pp. 274–291). Over the years several other scholars have made specific contributions to this general theme (Hartner, Baer, Dodds).

Ettinghausen's conclusions or (as he would have probably agreed) working hypotheses can be summed up and slightly enlarged in the following manner:

There are in Islamic art certain themes such as the whirl, the lion, the bull, and the signs of the zodiac which are historically older than Islam and which, with vagaries of no concern to us presently, have been maintained in the new culture. Most of the identifiable symbols deal with secular themes or with what may be called "basic" religious symbols such as earth, fire, and life.

The one obvious new theme is writing; it is not merely an ornamental feature but either iconographic (E. Dodds, "The Word of God," *Berytus* 18, 1969, with the argument that it

replaces images) or vectorial (Grabar, *The Alhambra,* 1978, or "Dome of the Rock," *Ars Orientalis* 3, 1957; W. E. Begley, "The Taj Mahal," *The Art Bulletin* 61, 1979) in the sense that it charges neutral forms with concrete and sometimes very elaborate meanings. But—and this is a key point—the charge was of low voltage. The Dome of the Rock, the mosque of Damascus, the north dome of Isfahan's Friday Mosque, the Alhambra, and the Taj Mahal—buildings for which a highly intense meaning can be provided for the time of their creation—all lost their specific meaning soon thereafter. It is indeed as though Islamic culture as a whole consistently rejected any attempt to compel specific symbolic meanings in architecture comparable to those of Christianity and Hinduism (with their symbolic connotation in plan, elevation, and decoration).

It is precisely this low symbolic charge of Islamic monuments which made it so easy for them to be copied and imitated elsewhere (Ettinghausen's argument). A corollary would be that the same low charge made it possible for an Indonesian pagoda or a Roman temple to become a mosque. In reality there is a somewhat more complicated intellectual and methodological problem involved in this reasoning, as I have tried to suggest in several unsatisfactory essays (*aarp* 13, 1978; "An Art of the Object," *Artforum,* 1976; "Das Ornament in der Islamischen Kunst," *Zeitschrift der Deutschen Morgenländischen Gesellschaft,* Suppl. III, 1977). The problem is that a low charge of forms easily leads to ambiguity, and it is doubtful to me whether any culture can operate with an ambiguous visual system. Is it not, perhaps, once again a question of insufficient thinking and data gathering?

Let me try to sum up this rapid and probably incomplete survey of the most recent literature (there may be much value in surveying the texts and notes of the great scholars of old (like Herzfeld, van Berchem, von Kremer). No one has tried to identify an Islamic visual sign-symbol system in any serious way, with the partial exception of an Iranian and Sufi-oriented system. Part of the reason is the factual and intellectual underdevelopment of a field of study, but a more important reason lies perhaps in two aspects of Islam's historical destiny. First, it inherited many symbolically rich cultural traditions but could only preserve symbols which were not religiously charged and, to avoid the temptations of idolatry, preferred to restrict or even to stifle the growth of its own visual symbolism. Second, secular art was less affected by this restriction, but then secular art is by its very nature definable for the most part in social rather than cultural terms.

The hypotheses stated above are not fully satisfactory, in part for the very reasons I have used to criticise the opinions of others. They are abstract constructs for which archaeological data exist, to my knowledge, only from the seventh to ninth centuries, and I am not certain how far it is legitimate to generalise from a few references and monuments. Mostly these hypotheses lack contemporary evidence; they have not made Muslims speak. Finally, all these hypotheses lack a clearly stated methodological premise. In what follows, I try to provide the latter by suggesting three methods of approaching the question with which we began.

Approach One: Pure Theory. From Plato to Wittgenstein, philosophers have talked about symbols and signs, and it is difficult not to be fascinated with St. Augustine's uses of the word "sign" (T. Todorov, *Theories du symbole,* Paris, 1977) or with E. Cassirer's *Philosophy of Symbolic Forms* (3 vol. New Haven, 1953–57) and S. Langer's *Philosophy in a New Key* (Cambridge, Mass., 1953). These are all weighty and difficult works which rarely, if ever, attend to visual forms (music, literature, and dance predominate). Less intellectually compact and conceptually abstract are anthropological works which I have consulted: R. Firth's *Symbols* (London, 1973), M. Eliade's *Images and Symbols* (New York, 1961), and a few more concrete studies by C. Geertz or V. Turner (*The Forest of Symbols,* Ithaca, 1967), or semiological ones. For our purposes the most useful are the works of U. Eco: *A Theory of Semiotics,* Bloomington, 1979; "Semiotics of Architecture," *Via 2,* 1973; G. Friedmann, "Une rhetorique des symboles," *Communications* 7, 1966; R. Barthes, "Elements de Semiologie," *Communications* 4, 1964. A very interesting summary of several books is Abdul-Hamid el-Zein's "Beyond Ideology and Theology," *Annual Review of Anthropology* 6, (1977).

My overwhelming reaction to nearly all of these often brilliant and always fascinating works is one of despair. This despair has two components. The first is the noncommutability of abstraction; by this I mean that, even though specific observations and concrete reasonings about individual subjects led to the theory, I rarely saw an instance which would allow me to move backwards from the theory to some hitherto unstudied subject of Islamic architecture. The second component is that all these works hover between a requirement of nearly infinite and usually not available precision of information (particularly true of semiology; I dread trying to do a semiological analysis of a monument of architecture) and an obviousness of conclusions (the wall of a holy building is a symbol or a sign of the separation between sacred and profane, restricted and public spaces). In many ways the data of the anthropologist are too commonly spread in the segment of culture he studies to explain an accidentally preserved major monument, and questions of taste rarely appear in dealing with architecture as opposed to painting or objects (for example, see James C. Faris's *Nuba, Personal Art,* London, 1972).

How can these theories be useful even if they do not provide an automatic model or paradigm? First, there are certain semantic distinctions which are consistent enough that they can be used as premises for our purposes. For instance, a *symbol* is different from a *sign,* which indicates something, and an *image,* which represents it; a symbol defines something and connotes it but does not circumscribe it as does a sign or an image; thus a swastika can be anything from an ornament to a potential incitement to hatred and destruction. Then, while a symbol is physically identifiable, it is itself not clearly circumscribed. As a tower for the call to prayer, the minaret is but a

sign suggesting a function; it becomes a symbol when it reminds one of Islam, when it appears on stamps identifying a specific country (the spiral minaret of Samarra—its spiral quality is much more an Iraqi national symbol than an Islamic one), or when it serves to design a space (the Kalayan minaret in Bukhara, organising open space between a mosque and a madrasa redone several times). In other words, while the sign attribute is fixed, the symbol attribute is a variable which depends on some charge given to it or on the mood or feeling (Langer's terminology) of the viewer (referent). Theory, therefore, compels us to identify and isolate the triple component of sign, symbol, referent. Of the three, symbol is the one which depends on predetermined conventions, habits, or agreements which are not in the object but in those who share it. Our problem then becomes one of defining the semantic field of a symbol by finding the area in time or space of its contractual agreement with a social group.

Approach Two: Islamic Written Evidence. There are many different ways of imagining how written evidence could be used. Others with a better knowledge of texts than I will be able to provide examples or even answers to the following set of questions accompanied by brief and partial comments.

Is there an indication that visual symbols or signs were, at any time, accepted ways of identifying functions, defining one's own as opposed to alien aims, or providing qualitative judgements?

Looking over major classical and very different texts like Muqaddasi's *Geography* (see P. Wheatley, "Levels of Space Awareness," *Ekistics,* Dec. 1976), Ibn Nadim's *Fihrist* (tr. B. Dodge, 2 vols., New York, 1964), and Ibn Khaldun's *Muqaddimah* (tr. F. Rosenthal, 3 vols., New York, 1958, esp. II, pp. 233ff., 357–367), or Ibn Fadlan's description of the Volga Bulghars, my answer is negative. While alien lands are at times identified by the peculiarities of their visual expression (for instance, nearly all descriptions of India in classical times), I see no evidence of concrete visual symbols which would be considered as uniquely Muslim. The exception of the minbar in tenth-century geographical texts indicates a certain kind of administrative status rather than a reference to a concrete object. The only other exception is the Ka'ba which by definition is a unique monument. This is not to say that there are no Muslim symbols and signs, but they consist less in visually perceptible features than in memories of men and events: the place where something took place or where someone did something. The literary genre of the *kitab al-ziyarat* (guidebooks to holy and memorable places) which began in the twelfth century only strengthens the hypothesis that the Muslim tradition identified what is sacred or holy to it in a *denoting* rather than *connoting* fashion, i.e., in terms of memorable associations and generalised physical shapes (oval, rectangle) rather than of concrete visual forms. In other words, and with occasional exceptions (like the *abwab al-birr,* "gates of piety" in early fourteenth-century Iran), there is no symbolic iconography of Islamic architecture to be derived from texts, as there is, for instance, in Christian architecture.

Is there a Koranic or early Hadith symbolic system with visual associations?

This is a difficult question to discuss because it is difficult to develop an appropriate method of dealing with it. Should one simply analyse the Koranic frequency of use of certain passages over the centuries? For instance, one of the most consistently used verses both in architectural inscriptions and in depicting Divine Power is the magnificent Throne Verse (II, 256). But it is not the only instance in the Revelation of strikingly effective depictions either of Divine Might or of God's Throne. Some of them were occasionally used on monuments, as, for instance, VII, 52, in the north dome of Isfahan or LXVII, 1–5, found in the Hall of the Ambassadors in the Alhambra. In both instances the use of an unusual verse serves to explain the cupola's meaning, but can one conclude that these architectural meanings are inherent in the Koranic passage or that the monuments served to represent or otherwise symbolise the Holy Writ?

Another interesting passage is XXIV, 35–8, the "verses of light," which do suggest a symbolic physical setting reflecting Divine Presence. The passage was frequently used in mihrabs, but the later traditional Muslim mosque vocabulary hardly ever used the terms of the Koranic passage. This peculiarity does not preclude the existence of a Koran-based symbolic system; it merely questions its consistent validity for architectural history.

We know very little about the frequency and consistency of Koranic quotations. I propose the hypothesis that the symbolic or iconographic use of the Koran in Islamic art nearly always *followed* the development of a symbolic or iconographic need. Symbols, signs, or meanings were discovered in the Koran but, at least as far as the arts are concerned, do not actively derive from it; in other words, I suggest there is no "iconography" of the Koran. Matters are obviously quite different in theology or law.

How culture-bound is the rich Islamic literary tradition of opulent princely dwellings?

A story from the *Thousand and One Nights* such as the "City of Brass" reflects an unbridled imagination about a magnificent palace. It contains, no doubt, the esoteric meaning of a difficult quest for truth or reality through secret and mysterious doors (like the ubiquitous *ya miftah al-abwab*, "O Opener of Doors," in later Persian miniatures), but its details and its external mood are all of a brilliant secular world. Should one interpret such stories as simply stylistically Islamic, i.e., as universal archetypes which have acquired culture-bound details? Or are they key reflections of a uniquely Muslim vision of sensuous beauty—paradisiac perhaps, but more likely fruits of a unique imagination formed by the confluence of an egalitarian faith and the reality of rich and isolated dynamic centres such as Samarra or Topkapi?

How should we interpret technical and especially mathematical treatises applied to architecture or decoration?

Few of these texts have been properly published or translated. Where they are available, however, as in the very recent book by M. S. Bulatov, *Geometricheskaia Garmonizatziia v Arkhitektury* (Moscow, 1978), what is striking to me is that the subtle and complicated mathematical formulae are not presented as illustrations, symbols, or signs of a faith or even

of a cultural identity, but as practical solutions to architectural and ornamental requirements.

Hence, is it legitimate to suggest a culturally accepted symbolism for visual forms as long as, in the highly verbal culture of traditional Islam, written sources give it explicit mention so rarely and require an esoteric approach to literature for demonstration?

The obvious exception lies in the art of writing, where, thanks to the work of A. Schimmel and F. Rosenthal among others, it can clearly be demonstrated that a whole range of meanings, from direct sign to most elaborate symbol, had been developed, thought out, and accepted. I am far less certain whether such matters as theories of colour in mystical thought (Corbin), for instance, actually did correspond to the uses of colour in artistic creativity. But this, perhaps, is simply a matter of insufficient research.

To sum up these remarks on written sources seems fairly easy within the present state of our knowledge. Except for the Arabic alphabet, there was no coherent, consistent, and reasonably pan-Islamic acceptance of visually perceived symbols; there was no clearly identifiable sense, even, of forms considered to be one's own, culturally discrete. It may, therefore, be possible to propose that traditional Islamic culture identified itself through means other than visual: the sounds of the city, the call to prayer, the Word of the Revelation but not its forms, the memories of men and events. If valid (and it is, I am sure, subject to criticism), this conclusion would suggest for the contemporary scene that it is not forms which identify Islamic culture and by extension the Muslim's perception of his architecture, but sounds, history, and a mode of life.

To this statement intended primarily to promote discussion, I should like to attach three codicils. One is that there is some methodological danger in assuming too easily that written sources are the paradigms by which a culture saw itself; Written sources reflect in large part the world of the literati. For example, neither St. Augustine nor St. Thomas Aquinas provides much information about the formation of early Christian art or of Gothic architecture. The importance of written sources lies in the parallelism they provide for visual phenomena and, to a smaller degree, in showing a time's characteristic concerns which contribute to the taste and the will for creating monuments. My second remark is that written sources from the early Hadith onward provide an enormous amount of information in two related areas: the vocabulary of making anything from a textile to a building and hence the basic meaningful units (the morphemes) of visual forms, an area whose study has hardly begun, and judgements on changes of taste. For instance, a comparison between Ibn Jubayr (twelfth century) and Ibn Battuta (fourteenth century) describing the same parts of the Muslim world shows the same monuments and holy places in very different ways. Written sources do help in understanding the vernacular, the common, more easily than the unique in art, probably because the highest literati were most often visual illiterates or at best visual vulgarians, a phenomenon which is peculiar neither to the Muslim world nor to the past.

Finally, I have only alluded to written sources as essentially synchronic documents, with the obvious exception of the Koranic Revelation shown as a constant and consistent inspiration and justification of tastes, moods, and function. There could be a diachronic analysis of literary sources seeking to find common and repeated themes and motifs; it is a dangerous kind of analysis, for it can too easily find consistency by comparing features which are not true parallels (as, for instance, both Persian and Arabic poetry, where I have often wondered whether metric and thematic consistency over the centuries is in fact what was prized at the time of creation of a new work of art). Such diachronic analyses, which may have been attempted without my being aware of them, could be of great importance in identifying consistent cultural threads.

Approach Three: The Monuments.   Keeping in mind the broad questions raised at the beginning of these remarks, I would like to propose four points for discussion.

Proposition I. The Muslim world did create a number of monuments of art and architecture which are uniquely charged with symbols: the Ka'ba, the Dome of the Rock, the Taj Mahal, Fatehpur Sikri's throne of Akbar, and perhaps a few others (the mausoleum of Oljaytu in Sultaniyah, shrine of Lutfallah in Isfahan) once someone undertakes to study them properly. But, in all instances known to me so far except the Ka'ba (which is in a way an "uncreated" monument), the depth of meaning with which the monument was created did not survive the time of its creation or was modified, as with the Dome of the Rock, which grew in religious connotations as the centuries went by, or with the Taj Mahal, which lost them. Interesting though they may be to the historian, these monuments are of secondary significance for our purposes, because their uniqueness is more important than their typological set.

Proposition II. There are several instances of what I would like to call restricted symbolic cultural continuity in architecture. There is, for example, the large hypostyle mosque, a unique creation of the seventh century which solved several functional requirements of Iraqi Muslim communities. This type became a regional one in some areas (Fertile Crescent, Arabia, Muslim West) but it also became symbolic of the introduction of Islam into new areas. Early Iranian mosques (this is a somewhat controversial topic at the moment for complex archaeological reasons not pertinent to this discussion), early Anatolian ones, and early Indian ones tend to adopt a form identified with early and pure Islam. Another example is the classical Ottoman mosque, whose large dome flanked by minarets and usually preceded by a courtyard became a symbol of Ottoman cultural and political prestige and power from Algiers and Serbia to Egypt and Iraq.

The reason I used the word "restricted" for these examples is that specific historical and cultural conditions—the Ottoman empire or the Islamisation of new lands—led to the symbolic quality of these forms; it was not a matter of their intrinsic value. The Ottoman mosque can become a national or romantic symbol and the building today of a hypostyle mosque in Tunisia is merely continuing a regional tradition.

Proposition III. There are very few architectural forms which are consistently indicative of the presence of Islam. The most obvious one is the minaret, whatever actual function it has had over time and whatever reasons led to its creation. I must admit that I am not satisfied with any of the traditional explanations of the minaret and its appearance, not only in the skyline of Cairo or as the elegant framer of Iranian facades or Ottoman volumes, but as a single monument in the Iranian countryside, at Jam in Afghanistan or in Delhi. The study of Koranic quotations on minarets is very instructive, as they vary considerably from building to building or area to area. But in many cases both inscriptions and decoration lend themselves to a range of symbolic meanings which await their investigator. For instance, the use of the whole Sura Mariam (XIX) on the minaret of Jam identifies this extraordinary monument as a proclamation of Islam in its relationship to other religions, while the ornament of the Kalayan minaret in Bukhara can be understood as an expression of the central Muslim tenet of the Unity of God, since its different designs are in reality versions of the same motif.

Are there any other similarly obvious and constant forms? There are the mihrabs of sanctuaries, of course, but their symbolism is, with a few exceptions (Cordoba, some Fatimid examples in Cairo), an obvious one, and the object itself became automatically functional rather than emotionally or intellectually symbolic. There are traces of a symbolism of gates in cities or even buildings, especially palaces, but this symbolism expresses itself more frequently in the names of gates than in their forms, a few exceptions as in Jerusalem's Haram notwithstanding. And anyway, I am not certain that the symbolic meanings which can be attributed to the gates of Abassid Baghdad or Fatimid Cairo remained significant symbols much after their creation. I am hesitant in attributing a symbolic rather than a socially functional meaning to traditional physical constructs of the Muslim city like the mosque-market-maidan unit.

I have mentioned primarily architectural symbols, because the seminar deals with architecture. Nonarchitectural visual symbols certainly existed as well, but to my knowledge none has been investigated in sufficient depth to know which ones were simple signs (hand of Fatima) and which ones acquired the kind of range which is required of a symbol (colour green, the Crescent).

If the proposition of the previous section that self-recognition within the Muslim tradition was primarily auditory and social is acceptable, this difficulty in defining an overall Islamic visual system need not be considered as troubling. In fact, it may simply demonstrate two secondary propositions. One is that symbolic systems may indeed tend to be most easily perceivable in time rather than across time. The other one is that in the actual perception of the environment such items as clothing, objects used, and spoken accent are more significant than architecture.

Proposition IV. Symbolic and sign systems are to be sought not in architecture but in decoration, decoration being understood in its widest sense as those parts of a building which are not necessary to its physical utilisation or structural stability.

If my earlier suggestion of symbolic systems as richer synchronically than diachronically is acceptable, this proposition is strengthened by the fact that decoration could and did change in kind (continuous additions) or in meaning (the reinterpretation of the mosaics of Damascus by later writers). Furthermore, while nearly all architectonic units or even combinations and developments of units in Islamic architecture are easily relatable to the morphology and growth of other architectural traditions, this is much less so with decoration, whose motifs and combinations are nearly always culturally unique. To dismiss this decoration as "mere" decoration is a Western imperialist reflex from a society which equates meaningful decoration with representation and which for half a century has rejected decoration within its own so-called progressive architecture.

But how are we going to find meanings in it? There is something troubling, for instance, in looking at a series of thirteenth-century portals in Anatolia which are formally very difficult to distinguish from each other yet which serve as entrances to mosques, madrasas, hospitals, and caravanserais. Is this decoration unrelated to the purpose of a monument except in the very general way of beautifying, at best attracting to, an unexpressed function? Within the synchronic scheme proposed earlier, the answer may be positive, as one can easily argue that the contemporary did not have to be told by a facade whether a building was a warehouse or a hospital.

Yet it is unlikely that we will be satisfied with such an answer for three reasons. One is that a series of studies on objects and miniatures, for which similar explanations have been provided, tends to show that a close examination demonstrates in almost every case a complex iconographic and symbolic meaning. A second one is that it is hardly reasonable to expect enormous efforts on meaningless forms. And third, the study of major monuments of architecture almost always demonstrates great depth of meaning. In other words, we have not taken a proper look at these monuments and their decoration. Let me outline two possible approaches for dealing with this problem.

The first approach would be morphological, seeking to find such themes of decoration as have meanings. The most obvious one is writing, as monuments as diverse in quality and importance as the Taj Mahal, the Guyushi Mosque in Cairo, and Qaytbay complex also in Cairo are explained by the Koranic quotations on their decoration. One of the most striking "un-Islamisities" of contemporary architecture is its failure to make aesthetically appealing use of calligraphy. I should add that writing exists at several levels of intelligibility: direct quotation probably only available to the very literate in the past but to all in the future; rhythmic punctuation with litanic repetitions known to most, as in the clear *al-mulk lillah* (Power of God) which organises the lengthy and wordy inscriptions of Persian mosques from the fifteenth century onward; simple statements of God and His Prophet, known to all, which adorn the outside walls of madrasas in Khargird or Samarkand. I have elsewhere discussed and, I hope, demonstrated this use of writing as a vector of meaning in architecture (*The Alhambra*, 1978).

Next to writing is geometry. I am less clear about the actual perception of geometry and hesitate to accept in full the gestalt explanation proposed by Ardalan and others for Iran, but I am convinced that the geometry of Isfahan's north dome based on the pentagon or of Bukhara's minaret with several hypostases of the same basic design cannot be simply a designer's whim. But I am not sure how to approach the problem, just as methods should be devised for dealing with vegetal motifs or with a theme such as the *muqarnas*, which involves nearly all morphemes of decoration.

The second approach would be syntactic and would consist in studying and explaining whole ensembles. To my knowledge, no one has attempted to do this in Islamic architecture. One example may serve as a conclusion to this essay. I have long been puzzled by what seemed to me to be the arbitrary location of tiled panels in classical Iranian mosques of the fifteenth to seventeenth centuries. Yet, in the Masjid-i Shah's main dome, the progression to the burst of light at the apex of the dome seems to me to be an extraordinary attempt at symbolising the Revelation not as the static and learned order of a Gothic portal or of a Byzantine church but as the dynamic and sensuous illumination of a faithful praying. The symbolism of the decoration is not inherent to the design but is the result of man's prescribed action in the building.

Can one extend the point to propose that the true uniqueness of the Muslim visual symbolic system lies not in the forms it takes but in the relationship it creates, indeed compels, for its users? A celebrated Tradition is that wherever a Muslim prays there is a mosque. Symbolic or signifying identity lies in setting and man, not in form. Is this a possible challenge for contemporary architecture?

Afterword. What follows is a series of questions and concerns derived from the preceding pages which may in themselves merit further consideration.

1. Synchronic versus diachronic. I am suggesting that it is easier to identify a synchronic symbolic and semiotic system than a diachronic one which either becomes obvious and undifferentiated or requires the preliminary investigation of synchronic sets. Too few instances of the latter exist to justify many significant definitions of Islamic symbols. I should also add that the nature of a valid time frame is a very difficult problem which has hardly ever been addressed by historians of forms. I am not even sure that linguists have discussed the aspect of time in their consistent concern for semantic fields, but I may simply not be aware of some existing work.

2. Specific forms and archetypes. This is a delicate issue. If we were dealing with architecture in general, it would be perfectly appropriate to discuss and refine broad and universal human needs, feelings, and means of perception, as they are adapted to concrete ecological requirements. But I understand our concern for the architecture of Muslims to mean, when symbolism and signs are concerned, those aspects of architecture which are not universally meaningful but discretely significant to a certain culture. We *can* come to the conclusion that this discrete significance was minimal or merely cosmetic, that the contemporary world has made cultural discreteness obsolete, and that universal modes of judgement are the only valid ones. But, if we do come to this conclusion, we must be sure that we are aware of what it means.

3. Architectural symbols and functions. The greatest difficulty I had was in identifying those aspects of architectural creation for which it is justified to seek a symbolic significance. My answer is that the referent alone (user, viewer) decides on the symbolic meaning of an artistic creation. Hence architectural symbolism can only be demonstrated from nonarchitectural sources—written sources, opinion surveys, or whatever else may be developed. Theoretically it is possible to derive symbolic meanings from formal consistencies, i.e., the repetition over the centuries of certain forms (E. B. Smith, *Architectural Symbolism,* Princeton, 1953), but I am not sure whether consistency of form means consistency of symbols or convenience for functions.

4. Symbols and styles. Can one maintain a distinction between aesthetic and taste impulses (style) and a range of associative reactions (symbols)?

5. Visual and auditory perception. I may have overstressed the thought that Islamic culture finds its means of self-identification in hearing and acting rather than in seeing. But I am more than ready to be corrected on this point.

CONSERVATION OF THE HISTORIC ENVIRONMENT FOR CULTURAL SURVIVAL
DOĞAN KUBAN

The Aga Khan Award has been established to encourage the formation of a specifically Islamic architecture as an expression of modern Islamic civilisation. A natural concomitant to this objective is the preservation of the Islamic image in our physical environment. The continuity of our cultural identity throughout the process of modernisation can only be guaranteed by this act of preservation.

Industrial Ideology and Preservation.   The physiognomies of the cities in Muslim countries are rapidly becoming grotesque imitations of those of modern Western cities. This trend runs so counter to our aspirations that we must ask ourselves whether it is even possible to resist the hegemony of modern industry and communication and have a true Islamic image in a city and its architecture, as we were able to do in bygone centuries. This question is part of a larger one: will any historic culture, be it Islamic, Indian, Chinese, or any other, manage to survive as an entity distinct from the fabric of a uniform modern civilisation? Or will they all be consumed by the monopolising pressure of modern industry and mass communication? Is it conceivable to have Turkish houses or Muslim towns and at the same time to drive imported automobiles on bridges built over the Bosphorus by foreigners, to construct according to universal standards, to utilise universal electrical devices, to broadcast and to receive worldwide television programmes, and to promote tourism? How can one suppose that the maintenance of cultural symbols can withstand the onslaught of cost accounting and efficiency standards and yet be keenly aware of the fact that all nations are being used as arenas for opposing ideologies, that all markets are under the strangling influence of international corporations, and that all developing countries are subjected to the arm-twisting of international politics?

So many negative points bring into question the rationality of a proposal uniting modern industrial ideology with preservation. Support, however, is forthcoming in the enduring opposition of another group of universal—I might even say eternal—factors that determine the behaviour of men and societies. They are less often mentioned than the exigencies of industrial development, though no less relevant, since they are intrinsic to any human situation: language, religious attitude, geographical environment, race and, perhaps most important, the inertia of cultural behaviour. The last, which accounts for a great part of our real cultural differences, has amazing and recorded staying power; it is an eternal embryo of future diversities. Compared to all these factors, the homogenising effects of industrial civilisation may quite possibly prove to be superficial and temporary.

I cannot predict the future of the postindustrial Muslim man. At the moment, Muslim countries are so busy striving for economic development that the industrial factor in our everyday lives is greatly emphasised. On the other hand, throughout the modern world today, whether rich or poor, Western or non-Western, all countries are confronting all kinds of social, economic, and political evils, often with an encouraging optimism that suggests the ability to support a struggle against prevailing conditions. The battle for the defence of the environment is evidence of this. The fight is not so much one against industry as one against the domination of an ideology that allows industry, never yet an integrated element in any developed concept of society, to roam at will, a raging creature devouring the society itself. We are aware of its power, but we are also hypnotised by it. That is why the battle for a healthy environment, whether given by nature or wrought by man, often seems to be in vain. The enemy is identified, but is neither comprehended nor confronted head on. It is the same deficiency in our perception of the human environment that works against preservation and conservation. Our willing but dumb submission only increases the rapaciousness of industry, making a desolate wasteland of human societies. Industry has no organic relationship to human life, which is a process in time; modern urbanisation and architectural practice mutilate the past because they are the outcome of a process that is lacking in any real understanding of the time dimension in urban culture.

This is why conservation is generally thought of not as something organically related to the whole process of change in the human environment, but rather as something frozen, irrelevant to the future, and therefore utopian. But conservation is not an impractical attempt by nostalgic minds to see history preserved as an entity apart; it is a logical step in evaluating changes in the whole environment.

Because of the rapid changes taking place in our cities, a large part of the cultural continuity in our surroundings is thought to be tied up with the future of those aspects of the city that have an historical character, such as street patterns, vernacular architecture, and traditional building materials. If we were not looking for an Islamic city image—or, more simply put, a city that represented our culture—many of the issues raised here would not have great import. But they are of seminal importance.

Industrial Standards and the Obsolescence of the Physical Environment. When is a building old, and why do we destroy that which is old? Technically speaking, a building can be declared obsolete on a variety of grounds: structural, functional, environmental, economic. People usually assume that buildings are destroyed because they become too difficult to maintain. Technical failures or inadequacies of comfort, however, can almost always be remedied. The unfortunate destruction of our older buildings is more apt to be justified on the basis of cultural and economic obsolescence. Ordinarily, for example, we do not destroy mosques; instead we make them comfortable by adding heating systems. We preserve the minarets and install loudspeakers for the greater comfort of the muezzins. We are also able to maintain and even use the old palaces, the old khans, the old madrasas; we simply redefine their functions. The overriding consideration in the overwhelming majority of cases is economic, and it is argued as follows:

All of the conditions of the obsolescence are remediable by the expenditure of money. This expenditure will not be spent unless it can be adequately compensated by the returns to be obtained from a more effective use of the building in either its current use or some other use. If [the] expected would not be sufficient, then the building is also economically obsolescent. . . . If the potential value of a site for a new building is sufficiently high to justify its redevelopment, this might be called site obsolescence.[1]

Arguments like these are obviously based on simple profit. They are typical of the Western world, where "a great part of the preservation activity consists in creating, through the normal process of planning, a healthy climate for old buildings so that their economic life is prolonged."[2] One must realise, however, that a day will come when this conservation can no longer be economically justified. Following this logic, we are forced to conclude that upon the termination of its economical life, the cultural life of a building also draws to a close. Any idea of preservation based on this premise is, then, ultimately meaningless. We can preserve and we want to preserve old buildings only on the grounds of their lasting significance to our culture. Preservation is an act of volition. We must pay for it just as we pay for travel, entertainment, cultural activities, books, cosmetics, toys, cars, and arms. Nevertheless, we need an adequate theoretical rationale and a practical approach, so that our inherited environment is deemed worth preserving by all concerned.

By whom and how are the inadequacies of an aging building to be evaluated? This is now done by the industry-oriented culture and the industry-controlled media. As was noted earlier, the destruction of what is not new is clearly a side effect of the rate of consumption in an industrial society. It is the result of profit making through the plundering of human resources by an ever-growing demand for industrialisation. This should not be misconstrued as yet another romantic attack on industry, but we must analyse carefully what has become simply a conditioned reflex in many industrial societies. Industry assumed formidable power when it became habituated to the profit motive and to unscrupulous interpretations of efficiency.[3]

Under the avaricious influence of profit making the behaviour of industry turned aggressive; aggressiveness requires an outlet, and it has made itself felt in all areas of our experience. Nor are its victims only the old and obsolete. Its effects are all-pervasive; its multifarious demands on human beings and on the earth's resources are insatiable, limitless. This insatiable greed is not intrinsic to industry *per se*; it merely represents one particular type of institutionalisation of industry.

Industrial society has created a human being conditioned to evaluate everything according to industrial standards—but efficiency as defined by numbers alone can be a grossly inadequate yardstick. More cars and wider roads do not guarantee more orderly traffic. Improved safety rules and more careful driving are also needed: is it necessarily better, without any other qualifications, to go to work by car rather than on foot? Doesn't walking reduce the risks of ill health and danger and decrease the consumption of natural resources? Is it not better to shorten the distance between home and work, to live in smaller towns with less air and noise pollution, to create a denser social life, to counteract alienation, and to have more safety? These arguments, of course, are all well known, and while I do not intend to bring in a teleological argument, the mechanism of numbers is in itself inhuman.

In order not to be overwhelmed by the impact of the quantitative greatness produced by industrial societies, we must define efficiency in a manner that is consonant with our own conception of society. We ought not to introduce traffic chaos if our cities are still tranquil; we ought not to consider a project that brings pollution to locations where the air is still fresh and the water pure; we should abandon town planning theories (e.g., those elaborated in the United States) and housing projects devised for conditions in the industrialised countries. We have the obligation to counter profit making as the only motive in the development of our cities if we want to salvage our heritage. And we cannot—we should not—hastily accept standards of any kind for the regulation of our social and urban life. Nor can we complacently assign a viable age to a building, as is done in some Western countries, when a majority of our citizens lives in dwellings less comfortable than those destroyed by speculative developers.

Whether this kind of control is feasible is far from certain. But the possibility of urban planning that would express our cultural identity, whether through preservation, renewal, or new development, depends on our ability to decide for ourselves. The world at large will not offer to rescue our culture, except perhaps where extinction would have international repercussions, as in the case of the protection of an endangered species of wildlife in Africa.

The Change of the Physical Environment and the Meaning of Preservation.   As our goal I propose that a building should remain inviolate and be preserved as long as its form possesses meaning for us, and as long as its survival can be prolonged by technical means.

Laying down this principle at this point might appear to be premature, but if speculation and misguided industrial symbolism could be put aside, it would be practicable. The persistence of many institutions and many art forms and the perennial use of many artifacts are easily observable. Being thrifty with our building capital also seems to be eminently reasonable. Preservation can never hinder the development of the new, nor is it intended to; in all Islamic countries, population increases and social and institutional development will require more and more new buildings—but only their harmony with the old can possibly create an environment suitable for the continuity of our cultural identity.

In the transformation of our physical environment, what should the ratio of change to continuity be? How can one calculate the optimal proportions between economy, psychological balance, and cultural continuity? What is the real contribution of the inherited environment to our image of a city? In our city plans we supposedly direct and control a pattern of change. Does this pattern conform to a ready-made formula for change, or is it an abstract model consisting of our evaluation of the actual trends of development? It is my belief that most of what goes under the name of planning is simply the blind following of trends. Yet what is a trend, if not the expression of social demands sublimated and generalised through the mass media in terms of the dominant ideology?

Preservation and conservation as they have been commonly conceived should not find ready defenders among us. A rational approach must involve consideration of the man-made environment in its entirety. Its qualifications should provide for the fulfillment of our material, psychological, and symbolic needs.

The nature of material standards established through daily experience and propaganda can be debated, but it is evident that any old or newly built shell can be appropriated and adapted to satisfy them. On the other hand, psychological and symbolic needs must also be satisfied. These needs can be personal or societal. Some of our preferences may be obscure in origin, such as the concept of life space, the nature of which experimental psychology is only now attempting to decipher.[4] The hidden dimensions of our emotional field in our environment may regulate our demands upon it, although we may be unaware of those dimensions.

On the societal level, common aspirations are concerned with social status as well as with the whole world of forms. They are vital for the self-preservation of the individual within a society, and they are important for the sustenance of the society itself. The general aesthetic values we hold have taken shape over time: they are cumulative. The so-called tasteless-

ness of the modern environment is a product of its noncumulative character. Although opinions can be perpetrated on an international scale through propaganda, they create only fleeting values that may be temporarily powerful, but are easily replaced. The old is engraved on stone and is sometimes difficult to read; the new, although often sparkling and startling, is scratched on thin ice.

At this point the problem of historical continuity and integrity comes into our discussion. In reply to Lynch's questions "How far can we go in subsidising activities that are likely to survive in preserved surroundings? To what degree [does] contemporary utility, however discreetly provided, rupture the sense of historical integrity?"[5] we can only say that the questions themselves are remarkably misleading. When history is rightly viewed as continuous change, what kind of integrity can we speak of as being disrupted? We cannot excise a certain portion of the historical development and contend that only the old part is integral. On the environmental level, something completed has formal integrity. If left untouched, a building, for instance, can retain its original integrity. Another species of integrity has to be envisioned. What we should look for is not the integrity of the past, which exists only in the abstract and only in contrast to the modern period, but the integrity of aesthetic feeling revealed in a continuum of forms. This alone can provide justification for the preservation of an old street, for it bestows upon the viewer a feeling of continuity and allows us to construct a new house in a row of old houses, as long as it does not detract from them. This is the way the old can inform the new.

> In urban revival, we wipe out substantial areas of used environment at great psychological and social cost, to be replaced by new settings that lack many desirable features of the old. Having suffered the pangs of uprooting and saddened by the inhuman quality of much of the new urban development, many of us conclude that it is time to stop growth and change, or at least to leave the older areas alone and concentrate growth in empty fringes.[6]

These are the sad remarks of an urban planner who feels impotent in the face of the profit drive. The inhuman quality of new urban areas is the symptom of an as yet undigested industrialisation. The new would not be so destructive if values and the inducements of obsolescence were not based on industrial standards alone, and if we sought continuity, rather than constant innovation for innovation's sake. While this position might seem reactionary, I would contend that the dialectic of change in the human environment has always shown a strong element of continuity throughout history.

Relevant here is a further comment made by Lynch, who rightly criticises the present situation and in the process inadvertently discloses the inadequacies of the current concept of preservation. In Western countries, "under the banner of historical preservation, we have saved many isolated buildings of doubtful significance or present quality, which are out of context with their surroundings and without a means of supporting their meaning to the public."[7] Let us focus for a moment on these "isolated buildings of doubtful significance." Who ascertains the significance of a building? Can it be ascertained by a kind of consensus, or by a spokesman for the consensus? Upon what criteria is the evaluation based? What is a "significant" building? Is a new building *ipso facto* more significant? For whom? For how long a time?

This line of questioning unfailingly leads us to those buildings of art-historical value. Their fine aesthetic quality has been weighed by history; their very survival is proof of an approving consensus. For simple dwellings, however, history has withheld its assent. The focus of historical interest has always been on the expensive and the monumental; the recent attention given to simple dwellings is a noteworthy phenomenon. Since modest dwellings do not offer a wealth of forms or material, Lynch inquires in the manner of an ordinary citizen why this or that insignificant building should be preserved. Such buildings would lose the onus of "doubtful significance" if a consciousness of historical continuity carried the intellectual totebag of industrial man. The significance of a building would then be formed by its place in the continuity of its spatial and temporal environment.

Moving to the problem of a building's being out of context with its surroundings, we once again confront the common failure of the imagination of industrial man in devising new uses for buildings that are compatible with the buildings' changed surroundings. However, if he were to let go of the profit motive, he would not find it difficult to invent a new, meaningful use for any building. If a building has become incongruous with its surroundings, it is because change has occurred suddenly, without taking the older building into consideration, and with the subconscious intent of eventually doing away with it. If this were not the case, a formal and functional harmony would have been established from the beginning. Drastic change is a contemporary phenomenon, but so is purposeful preservation.

While it is true that many decisions for preservation have been made without consideration of the means of maintenance, this situation is the inevitable consequence of current priorities. The purse strings of speculators can hardly be expected to loosen for an allocation of funds to be wasted on the maintenance of old buildings. Furthermore, many preservation schemes are undertaken that are meaningless to a public conditioned to respond eagerly to the stimulus of the new because they are told it is better. Undeniably the new can often look attractive to the owner of the old, but is a new experience with an old building any less appealing for many millions of people? It has been shown in recent years that through a well-organised campaign such as the European Heritage Year, the attitude of the public can become favourably disposed toward preservation proposals. During the past few years, projects for both renewal of old and infill of new buildings into an old environment have proved successful for a variety of design purposes. "A world that can be modified progressively" is a powerful leavening ingredient in our discussions, and it might also prove useful for the psychological balance of society.

Town Planning and Approaches to Preservation and Conservation. There is no reasonable chance for our traditional architecture and townscape to survive modern changes and building activity if we do not consider the totality of the relationship between man and society, plus nature and the man-made environment, in terms of space organisation, existential time, and location in time. An assessment of the reciprocal relationship between the individual and his environment must be based on the perception of this environment as shaped by a specific culture and by nature. Unfortunately, in modern theories of city planning or architecture, nothing comes to mind that gives due importance to the individual as a cultural entity, a unit of irreducible originality, except the sharp criticism that brings his absence into stark relief. What diversity can be observed when five Turks and five Englishmen devise a social and physical theory of town planning? None. Their theoretical approach to preservation is essentially the same. But plans for the conservation of Ghent, Carcassonne, Isfahan, or Safranbolu cannot be approached with uniform and one-dimensional theories. Preservation promises to be a hopeless chapter in town planning practice if the current trends in modern city development—inflated land values, high-rise buildings, cars, and a general fascination with the new—continue to govern our decisions. Modern attitudes toward physical ambience should be reconsidered. We have to reject the impoverished standards of minimums, maximums, and even optimums that derive from oversimplified data and the interests of efficiency. The actual physiognomy of modern Muslim cities is painfully inefficient, not to mention its being irrelevant to present theory and practice.

Until we can arrive at at comprehensive theory of the physical environment that encompasses both past and future, both small and large dimensions, and in which the individual—the real user—takes his proper place, with everything else defined in relation to him, we should prefer the humane quality conferred by empirical methods. Until a certain cultural and economic stabilisation in our countries is achieved, numbers alone cannot constitute the mainstay of a theory of town planning. Conservation as the use and reuse of the existing environment is the field most appropriate for such an approach, because the quality to be dealt with and the quality sought are already there at our disposal. We would then have to deal only with the changing aspects of quantity.

In the West, where the modern theory of conservation took shape, the problem of historical continuity between the preindustrial and industrial city did not arise. History did not have to be denied or rejected before it could become modern. But in the Muslim and other non-Western countries, modernism was bought at the expense of the historical; a handy axiom was that the more conservative people are, the more of the historical environment they will destroy, because only through this sacrificial rite can they prove themselves worthy initiates of the modern world. Certainly there are deeper reasons for their behaviour, though it is a point worth remembering. That is why the Western approach to preservation in toto is unacceptable. We have to evaluate our environment as a function of our people, as the raison d'être of our history, and as a provision for historical continuity. While too great an emphasis on preserving the old can bring charges of chauvinism, my observations thus far have made clear, I hope, that conservation involves much more than just preservation.

Faulty conclusions in the problems or theory of conservation have their source in the premise that conservation is merely another, albeit more complex, planning problem that can be handled through the methodology of urban design. But conservation is not just another type of planning, nor can it be classified as nonplanning, although that is closer to its nature. If I were to give it a name, it might be "reverse planning." It must capture within it the dialectical nature of the changing environment; it must embody the struggle of the old and the new.

A planning process that incorporates the past as something living is not planning in the usual sense. If a house is kept intact, it has no need for a new plan; it is simply preserved. It is in this sense that, theoretically, total preservation becomes total nonplanning. But since we cannot expect to preserve everything, we must have some way of reaching decisions, and this is what I call reverse planning. Our starting point in conservation is what already exists, and our goal is to change it as little as possible. Our decisions merge with previous decisions, and that is why we cannot use normal town planning criteria. While this should not be taken to mean that conservation is unrelated to other aspects of environmental studies, we obviously lack a theory broad enough to cover decisions about the physical environment that encompass its past, present, and future simultaneously.

Future Conservation of the Historical Environment.   Conservation is essentially a cultural decision. Yet conservation specialists work hard to show that in practice it is also economically viable. Sometimes it is, but culture and economy do not necessarily share common aspirations. If the industrially-minded man proves that conservation is not economical, what kind of economy is he talking about? On the level of personal profit it might be uneconomical, but it could still be economical in terms of the economy of the country. Conservation must be viewed first and foremost on a national scale. Tearing down usable buildings is waste, to be sure, but finding proper ways to impede such waste is another matter. In socialist countries, conservation can be declared a general cultural policy and can easily be put into effect. In capitalist countries, private owners must be persuaded or paid to conserve the nation's heritage.

Here again we should not look to Western practice for guidance. In York, for example, acquisition, improvement, resale, lease, or anything else that improves the historical setting is not undertaken unless a profitable return is likely. If we proceed in the same way our cities will be doomed to destruction. York is in a good state of preservation and is well-maintained—it can afford the luxury of waiting. But if we cannot substantiate that conservation is economical in actual circumstances, we must demonstrate its desirability in other ways. Also, we should not overlook the economical assets of old housing stock, in view of the housing shortage in Muslim countries and the space needed for growing city populations. What further justifications are there for preservation and conservation? If the old quarters are preserved with all their formal characteristics, except for the addition of modern facilities, they will immediately become more attractive: cars will

not run through the streets, filling them with noise and noxious gases; houses will be surrounded by greenery; the environment will be favourable for social intercourse and safer for children.

There are clearly no grounds for expecting the private sector to involve itself in conservation except in special cases of public support or tourism. Public money will be essential, at least at the beginning, since direct financial profit is of no immediate relevance to the public authorities or the government. On the other hand, when we realise that the amount of public money allocated for these purposes is bound to be limited, large-scale conservation becomes impossible without the community's direct involvement. At this point we have to resolve the dilemma of cultural demands bound by financial constraints. If preservation depends on self-image, it cannot be called into being by laws; the support of the public is necessary. And while supportive public opinion can be generated through an active public-relations campaign, it cannot be sustained for long if it does not reflect some real demand.

Art historical, archaeological, and aesthetic interests are not commonly found in the majority. People may show interest in old buildings because they have some connection with historical events. But for large-scale conservation we have to devise a new methodology to educate the public. If they cannot be made to regard their history as part of their life, earnest efforts by an intelligentsia to save the historic environment will end in disappointment. The issues we are discussing are, then, ultimately ideological. The desire for a specifically Islamic character in our environment is no different in function from the modern ideology of industry, and promulgating it is simply another aspect of the struggle against the blind imperialism of industry. For some of us, losing this battle would mean losing any hope for a reasonably humane environment in a foreseeable future.

Conservation is not the ultimate stage in our expectations for our surroundings. It is the beginning. Since it is organically connected with the creation of the new, it is also a lasting aspect of environmental change. We can regard it as the physical basis of cultural identity: to get stability through change, we employ the past. Conservation offers motives for imagining new functions and embellishes the monotony of everyday life. Conservation will not only reconstruct history, but will retrieve for us its intrinsic aesthetic quality. What we preserve are not simply the relics of some class in some old society, but objects that are expressions of human effort. That a dichotomy exists between old and new is an assumption based on false premises; only their harmony can lead to better living conditions in our environment.

Some Practical Aspects of Preservation.   Preservation of the traditional building stock is no longer concentrated in the great centres of Turkey such as Istanbul, Izmir, Ankara, and other rapidly industrialising cities (although Istanbul still has a sizable stock of old dwellings) but in smaller cities, towns, even large villages. The traditional houses are, in most cases, two-story buildings with small courtyards or gardens. The restoration and reuse of these houses involves for the most part establishing structural soundness and setting functional improvements appropriate for modern living into the existing volume and floor area. This last usually presents no problem, because the floor space is almost always sufficient for modern accommodations. The structural decisions are determined by the goal of the preservation. If we agree to separate the exterior of the building, as public property and as the part that contributes historical continuity to the environment, from the interior, as private and flexible property, the structure can be radically transformed. It must be confessed, however, that the process can be rather expensive. It is occasionally undertaken, but structural intervention on a large scale should be kept to a minimum.

The distribution of the usable floor surface, redistribution of the functional organisation of the house, physical comfort, and safety are the concrete problems that most often need to be solved. Structural intervention is decided according to requirements in each particular case. At present the building market is short of materials for the maintenance or repair of old houses such as prefabricated elements to replace old floors, lightweight floor revetments especially designed for the purpose, and prefabricated modern equipment for service facilities. These are indeed severe problems, but they can be remedied in the long run. On the other hand, the inconvenience of old house plans has proved amenable to solution. Though design has been the least discussed aspect of preservation, for those involved, it has proved to be a most exciting one.

A study of the old house of Alanya, made by Şener of the Istanbul Technical University demonstrated that the organisation and dimensions of these houses were sufficient for modern housing requirements. All modern standards could be met with the existing shell, without even changing the extant distribution of space. The usable space is in fact larger than that required in the standards of social housing. Another example is a large house from Safranbolu in northwest Turkey, which will be used as a small hotel. A third is in Gaziantep, where three different uses for the same house have been proposed: a maternity hospital, a small library, and a student hostel. In finding new uses for old houses, finding a satisfactory use is of crucial importance. In Turkey obsolescence of houses and obsolescence of the environment go hand in hand. The percentage of owners who would like to build a new home on the site of the old one is never large. Until the idea of total environment takes root, the old building stock will have to house students, the elderly, and newcomers to the cities, or serve as social halls, maternity clinics, libraries, exposition halls, small hotels, and the like. In smaller towns, houses with gardens would be perfect for families moving in from rural areas. I am aware that uprooting the original population will elicit protest. But our cities are not like Bologna, where there is a stable population. In many recently developed cities the old quarters are inhabited by newcomers, but keeping the old social stratum in place is certainly of great importance wherever it can be done.

Conservation units should be kept as small as possible—a quarter, or better yet a street—since more flexibility can be obtained with smaller units. Obviously the size of the unit will be dictated by the characteristics of the site. A continuous landscape such as that presented by the Bosphorus is of a different nature, and other factors become very important operationally. In the plans for conservation an operational unit, whatever its size, should not exceed the size of an aesthetically or functionally continuous site. In practice, in town centres this unit can well be a street. The nodal points between units should not only unify but also distinguish. The spatial dimensions of the nodal points should be included in the unit under consideration. A nodal point will thus belong to two or more units and function as an element of transition and continuity in the city landscape.

Up to this point only the exterior aspect along the streets of the town has been considered, but the facade that is hidden from the street, as is the case in the uneven topography so characteristic of Turkish settlements, can have equal formal importance. The plan for a conservation area should indicate the link with the communications network, the preserved buildings, the operational units, and that third dimension of the preserved buildings, their facades and volumes. What remains falls within the province of architecture.

ISLAM, URBANISM, AND HUMAN EXISTENCE TODAY
MOHAMMED ARKOUN

My title is intended as a framework for research,[1] a framework inspired by reading the *Proceedings* of the first seminar.[2] In presenting "Architecture in the Spirit of Islam" the ideological or theological presuppositions may imply that the Islamic spirit is an immediate, simple, even atheistic notion. For me, within the framework of our research, it is problematic.

The title I have chosen avoids the implication of such presuppositions. It simply juxtaposes three main directions of thought in a particular order. Why have I placed "urbanism" between "Islam" and "human existence"? To the extent that urbanism is a physical environment designed by men, one in which their existence takes place, it serves to mediate between a projection of human existence, a general design, and real, concrete existence.

As a projection of human existence, Islam moves in two directions. The first is metaphysical, religious, spiritual, and therefore dynamic. The second is one which I personally hesitate to qualify with the adjective "Islamic." Here I react against what is presented as "Muslim" philosophy, "Muslim" politics, and the like. The second direction, the second level of signification, is the sociohistorical space in which human existence unfolds. This space should be restored to a real, positive signification. It should in no way be arbitrarily concealed by the term "Islamic." I wish to relate a personal experience in order to make this theoretical and analytical presentation less abstract. The example is that of Algeria, a unique laboratory for those who wish to reflect seriously on these problems. What I have to say about Algeria can be applied with proper correctives to any Muslim country, but owing to its recent history a number of problems appear there in extreme form. At the time of its independence in 1962, a unique upheaval occurred. An extremely active European community, a very mixed community, left the country. Entire towns were emptied of their inhabitants. An urban way of life conceived by and for the French and differing entirely from that required by a Muslim population was now vacant.

In terms of the Islamic definition of housing a significant problem arose. The colonial departure provoked an upheaval of the Algerian population. Apart from a few exceptions, the essentially rural population was unprepared to live in this physical environment. Consequently, the entire traditional semiotic universe was disrupted. Another framework for life was installed in its place, and this translated into all kinds of behaviour. For instance, people used their balconies to raise chickens. But there is more. All kinds of behaviour which are part of the Islamic way of life were uprooted and displaced. As it does not correspond to the functions demanded by the new population, the urban fabric deteriorates. There is clearly room for psychological and sociological research here. I am persuaded that much can be learned from this experience.

A second point to remember is that after independence, Algeria wished to break with its colonial past and pursue its own development. In terms of housing and urbanisation two phenomena had great impact: industrialisation and the agrarian revolution. In turning to heavy industry, Algeria installed complexes that rival those in Europe in terms of their impact on social structures such as housing and work. Consequently, we must now deal with problems identical to those faced by European industrial societies in the nineteenth and early twentieth centuries.

The problem is where to house the new workers. Should the most common type of urbanism be chosen, in other words, the low-rent housing development? There had been no well-developed tradition of urbanism. Nor was there any preparation at the architectural research level to accompany this great historical movement.

The leap into modern industry was a bold policy. At the same time it was deep-rooted in an ideology that calls for the remodelling of the Algerian identity. That is to say, national construction had as its first principle not only the recovery of an identity, but the remodelling of an identity, first, by regenerating its historical and cultural constituents, and second, by integrating new wealth and modern methods.

In the case of Algeria, for example, if we wish to identify the typical urban tradition, we should not look at those great monuments or mosques which engage the attention of the specialist and even amaze us. I emphasise that our approach must be pragmatic. When considering the history of Islam, Muslims as well as Islamicists usually take into account a fictitious historical continuity represented by architectural monuments or great philosophical works. In so doing the real social fabric is totally omitted. Classical Arabic historiography is the intellectual priest serving in the defence of dynasties. It celebrates works of civilisation which we continue to protect at the expense of local invention and creativity.

As an illustration, we turn to the architectural methods of the M'Zab. A religious minority within a social group extending far back, the M'Zab offers a particularly instructive lesson.

Taking refuge in southern Algeria for political and religious reasons, they built right in the middle of the Sahara. This is, in fact, Hassan Fathy's formula, "to build with the people." Their solutions met very precise ecological constraints before meeting the standard Islamic models which were certainly overlooked by the Berbers of that time.

Concerning the agrarian revolution in Algeria, socialist villages have been built. This is indeed an interesting phenomenon. A socialist village is one of those new villages built in the countryside to lodge the new agricultural workers. They adhere to what we call "modern" architectural models. Apartments are ordered in blocks; streets follow straight lines. The only sign of Islam's presence is, of course, the mosque, and this raises an important issue.

The mosque fulfills the function of mediation not as a building that has Islamic architectural attributes such as the mihrab or the minbar, but as a building with a functional semiotic system, a building in the midst of those smells, noises, and movements which characterise what we perceive as an Islamic milieu. The mosque mediates only when it is integrated into a lively system. But in a socialist village this system has practically disappeared. Here we are dealing with something different, with another language, a language of revolution which has nothing to do with the traditional Islamic language. The modes of relationship and of exchange are now different, and an entire system of signs has disappeared. Consequently, we must revise the Islamic language to adapt it to new realities. That is why I have chosen as my theme, "Islam, Urbanism, and Human Existence Today." The word "today" has considerable weight, for we must make our way through towns shattered by demographic pressures and a disrupted semiotic universe.

If we do not now seriously search for an Islamic language adapted to this new situation, we will find ourselves in the usual predicament of Muslim societies. When confronted by economic, demographic, and social pressures, they practice a kind of evasion. Always they resort to a Western technology which only further aggravates the problems of their interior universe.

What goes with this evasion? An Islamic discourse of an ideological nature which tries to legitimate these actions by referring to the authority of the Koran, the authority of Islam, which is supposed to function on a transcendental level. I make an appeal for a political philosophy adapted to the current historical situation of Muslim societies, a philosophy that would take up again the issues raised by the philosophers of the past—the relation between the authority of the Koran (divine, transcendental, religious) and that of the human powers and ideologies that seek legitimacy by referring to that authority.

I call your attention to the problem of signs and symbols. Here I cross paths with Professor Grabar. He began with an analysis of art history while I started with an analysis of the Koranic text. Both of us have independently employed the term "sign-symbol."

I prepared an essay, *"Peut-on parler de merveilleux dans le Coran?"* for a colloquium.[3] When people queried me on the notion of the supernatural in the Koran, I began to reflect on the semiotic status of the Koranic verses and wondered whether we should consider them as symbols or as signs. I linked these two words in order to indicate two possible directions which are continually manifested in Islamic life and in the relation of the Muslim to the Koran.

The first direction considers the verse as a linguistic sign, a linguistic expression referring directly to definable significations. This permits the definition of Muslim law and in fact indicates the direction of thought in the shari'a. The shari'a is inconceivable if we do not consider the Koranic discourse on this literal linguistic level where, according to lexicographic method, each word refers precisely to some referent. At this level the shari'a continues to influence Islamic discourse; for instance, it influences the decisions Muslims make in urbanism and economics.

In the second direction the verse functions as an opened space of projection; that is, a system of significations that materialises in the individual and collective experience of the community. Of course, you will tell me that these things are too complicated for an architect and he cannot follow all these directions.

What I emphasise is that thought is first of all an act of historical solidarity. Philosophers, ethnographers, architects, economists, and sociologists should consider things within the context of reality, the reality in which Muslim societies presently live. Then, if we find a path through all the confusion, horizons will open in which we can inscribe our thought and our action.

ISLAMIC ARCHITECTURE AND
THE POOR PEOPLE OF ISLAM
MAHBUB UL-HAQ

I wish to ally myself with the essential objectives of the Award, which His Highness the Aga Khan has enunciated so eloquently on a number of occasions. In his concluding remarks to the Istanbul symposium in September 1978 he said, "The Award will *not* be confined to architects competing with designs for a succession of prestigious public monuments. We are concerned with the Islamic world and, above all, *with the people of Islam.*" I have added the italics, for these are key words: *concerned with the people of Islam.* My main effort will be to highlight some of the policy implications of making Islamic architecture relevant to the people of Islam.

If Islamic architecture is to become more relevant to the people of Islam, we need to have some idea of their economic, social, and political conditions in the contemporary setting. The majority of people living in the Muslim countries—probably as many as two thirds—can be described as absolute poor: a condition of life so miserable as to defy any human description. They survive, if we can say survive at all, on 25 U.S. cents, or less than one tenth of a Jordanian dinar, per day. Their children are malnourished, they are largely illiterate, and they are often denied the very minimum of basic needs and public services. They live on the margin of existence, below any reasonable definition of human decency. In addition, the political and social environment in many of their societies is feudalistic, and the concepts of equality of opportunity and of peoples' participation in political and economic life are often mirages, not realities.

As an economist I live and breathe in the midst of these unpleasant truths all the time. Now, what is their relevance to Islamic architecture? Very simply, if Islamic architecture is to become a living reality in modern times, it must respond to the needs of the poor people who are the overwhelming reality in the Muslim world. It cannot afford to become an elitist concept. Islamic architecture must be unlinked from the popular image of kings' palaces and old castles and overflowing gardens and ornamental monuments. It can certainly borrow its essential designs, concepts, indigenous technology, functional features of drainage and cooling systems, etc., from the past, but it must translate them into a wholly new architecture that reflects the essential spirit of Islam and its values: equality, accessibility, mass participation, and cost effectiveness.

In other words, there are two fairly clear choices. We can proceed from a study of architecture to the needs of the people, or we can reverse the relationship and proceed from the needs of the people to the relevance of Islamic architecture to those needs. My own preference is for the latter course, though both routes can be made compatible if we remember that they are essentially linked. I do not believe in art for the sake of art; I believe that art must be for the sake of life. And I certainly do not believe in Islamic architecture merely for the sake of Islamic architecture; I believe that a revival of Islamic architecture must correspond to the needs of the poor people in Islam. Let me not overdraw the contrast. It should be possible to engineer a happy blend, a proper fusion between the functional needs of our poor people and the aesthetic needs of an architecture that truly reflects our Islamic culture, traditions, and history. But this remains an open question: we have no final answers yet.

The real question is the social, economic, and political context within which all of us—architects, economists, everyone—must work. We simply cannot shirk our broader social responsibility and pretend that poor societies have no alternative choices. For instance, the lights that shine so brightly on individual objects in the Tehran Museum of Glass and Ceramics could also have lighted a poor village. The 140 million Jordanian dinars that the first phase of Yarmouk University may cost can also be spent on alternative needs and less costly designs. The water that saturates the lush gardens and trees of the high-income Clifton and Defence Society and along the main highway to the Karachi airport is water denied to at least two million poor inhabitants of Karachi's low-income areas who do not even get adequate drinking water. Architects may admire the beauty of these buildings and the symmetry of their designs, but economists will bemoan the wasted resources and the denial of the very basic needs of the poor.

Let us face the honest truth. Poor societies have scarce resources, and they confront some cruel choices. There is no use shrugging off our social responsibility under the convenient label of "client-architect relationship." The architects must point out the different options and alternative choices to the policy makers, and must be prepared to be overruled. I welcome the emphasis on an architect's broader social responsibilities as a breath of fresh air.

My architect friends may be looking somewhat unhappy, but I assure them that I do not expect them to be the final decision makers in the system. None of us technocrats is. But at least we can point out a number of alternative policy options and designs, to ensure that the people making the final decisions have a reasonable range of choices.

I have proceeded so far at a certain uncomfortable level of abstraction. Let me come now to a few practical examples, to illustrate how architecture should respond to the essence of the Islamic value system. Islam teaches equality. A building that does not embody the concept of equality cannot be regarded as a very illustrious example of Islamic architecture. I once saw a presentation for a government building in Ta'if, Saudi Arabia. The design showed separate gates for the king, the ministers, public officials, and ordinary mortals. The entire building was described as a "fortress," a word that summarises the conception of the architect regarding the proper distance between the public servants and the people whom they supposedly serve. To cite another example, any city that is built along hierarchical lines and that consciously segregates different income groups in different locations can hardly qualify as a noble example of an Islamic city, regardless of the architectural excellence of its individual buildings. To show my impartiality, let me say that Islamabad, the capital of my own native country, falls within that category. You can decide for yourselves how many others also do.

A corollary of equality is unrestricted access to public buildings and monuments. Monuments that do not reflect the national pride of a people, or that are seen only as symbols of personal glory, can become objects of public indifference regardless of their unique architectural style. Islamic architecture cannot be just a geometric form, a poetic mosaic, a marvel of symmetry: it must also respond to the aspirations of the people. It must embody traditions they can touch and feel and with which they can identify. Even the Taj Mahal has been ridiculed by a popular Indian poet, Sahir Ludhianivi, in a verse in the local Agra dialect that, loosely translated, means:

> Millions of poor people have loved and died; who says their love was not sincere? But then there came a great emperor with his great wealth, who built a great monument to his personal love, and thereby made fun of the daily struggle and the daily love of us poor people, whom he freely exploited.

Let there be no misunderstanding: I am not campaigning against the Taj Mahal. The real question is: Do the monuments of the future symbolise the aspirations of a whole nation, or only the personal ego of an individual?

It is important to remember that the much admired urban fabric of many older Muslim cities was not the result of any grandiose vision of individual architects. Rather, it represented a multitude of decisions made by the members of the community, through a subtle social interaction that struck a balance between the rights of individuals and their neighbours and the larger community.

Another essential feature of Islam is to place man (and woman) at the centre of the universe. Islamic architecture must therefore be built around people, rather than herding people around architecture. We economists have learned a bitter lesson during the last few decades as we have belatedly recognised that the real end of economic development is not increase in production but increase in human welfare; not worship of the goddess of GNP growth, but satisfaction of basic human needs. Of course, the two objectives are linked, but the perspective is important: Do we go from production to people or from people to production? Let me pose the same question to the architects: Do you go from buildings to people or from people to buildings? I hope that the architects are much wiser than the economists, and that they do not get lost in form and design and forget to put people and their needs and aspirations at the centre of their creations.

Islamic architecture must be economical and cost-effective if it is to be at all relevant to the needs of the poor people of Islam. Islam resents conspicuous consumption; it preaches austerity and simplicity. However, architects and economists are too often prisoners of their own disciplines. Architects, fascinated by the beautiful symmetry of design and form, feel uncomfortable when reminded of financial costs. Economists, on the other hand, are far too lost in their economic calculations to appreciate beauty, which is also an integral part of life. I hope for a happy marriage between the two, or (if that is an unrealistic expectation) at least a quiet coexistence.

I wish to ask seven specific questions to which I think we must seek convincing answers.

Can Islamic designs and forms be incorporated into low-cost housing, which is targeted for poor people with an income of less than one quarter of a U.S. dollar per day? Can Islamic architecture be blended with the public services of education, health, and water supply where standard costs must be so low as to be affordable to the poor without requiring huge and perpetual government subsidies?

What is our choice when confronted with the conservation of an historical building or the preservation of people? Take for example the walled city of Lahore. This is an historical site that architects romanticise but that its half million poor residents bitterly resent and would gladly leave if given an alternative to such a miserable slum. I recall that when environmental concern arose in the rich societies, the developing countries argued that preservation of human life was far more urgent for them than conservation of wildlife. What would be the architects' answer if given the same choice between people and buildings?

We must pause and ask ourselves whether we are getting too preoccupied with buildings, too little with people; too much with form, too little with substance; too much with physical realities, too little with socioeconomic objectives. For example, in the presentation of educational building models, the very objectives they are supposed to serve are scarcely mentioned.

How much of a stress are we to place on indigenous technology, local materials, indigenous architects? Many projects built in Muslim communities are designed by non-Muslim, nonindigenous architects. While it is an eloquent tribute to the infinite tolerance of Islam to let non-Muslims interpret Muslim architecture and Muslim culture for Muslim societies, and while I am a great believer in the interaction of varied cultures and religions and architectural designs, I would plead for some balance. There must be more self-confident development of indigenous architects and increased recognition of them by their own governments and by outside aid agencies. It is a sad commentary on their own intellectual colonialism that many governments are still reluctant to recognise the talents of their own nationals, even when they are seeking a revival of national pride and culture.

While I have freely used the term "Islamic architecture," I am still a little confused about what it really means. Many attempts to define it have tended to obscure rather than sharpen the distinction between Islamic and non-Islamic architecture. I am left with no clear or generally accepted definition of Islamic architecture except that the relevant buildings are all located in Muslim countries. I am sure we agree that this is not much of a definition. Is Islamic architecture that which embodies the essential value system of Islam, or is it a triumph of form and colour, or is it some unique synthesis of the two? I, at least, am not very sure. In a way I am glad that Islamic architecture is not rigidly defined at this time and that its definition is evolving gradually and pragmatically. But there is also a danger in keeping it too open-ended.

Let me go on to an even more ticklish question. Much of the Islamic architecture we admire today is the product of a feudalistic age in which the will of the people hardly mattered. It reflected elitist decisions, although not always elitist value systems. Its adaptation to contemporary needs must take peoples' aspirations and voluntary choices into account. But do we really know these needs? Have there been any careful surveys? Are the poor people aware of what we are doing here? Do they really care? Should not some of our projection and dissemination be aimed at those people who will be the final arbiters of tomorrow?

Let me add a final series of questions. Can Islamic architecture develop in those Muslim countries that still deny equality of opportunity to their own people, that still violate every principle and the very spirit of Islam, and that are still run by vested interests? Isn't the revival of Islamic architecture part and parcel of a much larger movement, a much wider struggle for a real renascence of the true spirit of Islam?

These are troubling questions; they are not the sole concern of the architects. I raise them with great humility, aware of my excessive ignorance. But I have faced many of them as a national economic planner in Pakistan, and some I still confront in dealing with problems of mass poverty at the World Bank. If I may make a concrete suggestion, I believe it would be extremely useful in future seminars to structure the workshop discussions around a set of specific predetermined questions, so that there is more focus in the final results.

It is unrealistic to expect that we will find all the final answers tomorrow. What is important is simply that we keep searching. And what is of even greater importance is that we involve more disciplines in this search, since we have a tendency to get wrapped up in our own individual disciplines.

I believe we are all on a journey of discovery, a voyage of the spirit. We have a proud culture, a glorious heritage. Let us follow its spirit, not merely its form. Let us distill the very best from it, not the worst. Let us not turn a nostalgia for the past into costly monuments for the future. Let us build for tomorrow's generation and for all our people, not only for a few. And let us do it with candour, with honesty, and with humility, for the task is immense and the process has just begun.

Let me conclude with a few of my favourite lines from T. S. Eliot:

> *All our knowledge brings us closer to*
> *our ignorance;*
> *O, where is the knowledge we have lost*
> *in living;*
> *O, where is the wisdom we have lost*
> *in knowledge.*

URBAN HOUSING IN THE THIRD WORLD: THE ROLE OF THE ARCHITECT
CHARLES CORREA

The architect practicing in the Third World faces the unique and formidable challenge of using his skills and resources to alleviate the dehumanising conditions of the urban poor around him. Obviously, the area to which he most often directs his efforts is that of housing. Right away, the architect must confront two mind-boggling facts about the problem. The first is the scale of the demand; the second is the totally inadequate income of the urban poor.

In several Third World cities (Dacca, Ibadan, Karachi, and Bombay, for example), pavement dwellers might constitute anywhere from twenty-five to fifty percent of the population, and their numbers are increasing at a faster rate than in the rest of the city. In contrast, income per household is abysmally low. In Bombay, one third of the households earn less than Rs. 250, or thirty dollars (U.S.) per month; another third earn less than sixty dollars each month. If fifteen percent of this income is applied toward housing rental, a high figure for this income level, we will find a capital budget per housing unit of $450 and $900, respectively. In Bombay today, the sale price of new buildings ranges from $300 to $600 per square metre. Just calculate how much space each family can afford through the market process! Even if we totally ignore the cost of land and other components and count only the construction costs, a simple four-storey walk-up tenement of brick bearing walls and reinforced concrete slabs will cost about seventy dollars per square metre. This price does not leave the poor much better off.

The architect finds that, despite his most persistent efforts, he cannot bring the cost of housing anywhere near the level of what the urban poor can actually afford. What this group *can* afford are the simple single-storey structures that they so skillfully and beautifully build for themselves. They use local materials like mud and bamboo, recycled tin cans and palm leaves, and succeed in harnessing their own resourcefulness and experience.

But if this housing solution exists, why do so many people continue to live on the pavements of our cities? There are two crucial reasons. First, the scale of the demand dictates that most prime urban land has already been preempted for other uses, a circumstance forcing the vast majority of these self-help housing efforts onto unwanted land at the city's edge. Situated far from the major transport arteries and other urban infrastructure, and without access to public transport, the poor have no mobility, no job choice, and often no job at all.

This is why, in a great many cities, the squatters resist any well-intentioned attempts to transfer them to sites and services schemes far away from the city's main infrastructure. Too often these areas become mere ghettos of cheap labour, at the mercy of local entrepreneurs (can this perhaps explain their increasing popularity with the financial establishment?). Naturally, the poor—at least the smart ones—move back to the pavements at the centre of town. Housing is a relatively low priority on their survival list, after such items as food, clothing, and health care. More important than adequate shelter is direct access to the nerve centres of the city.

This brings us to the second reason that a seeming housing panacea is not implemented. Although many planners and decision makers in Third World cities will readily acknowledge the advantages of self-help housing, they feel that when you add the cost of using prime urban land at such relatively low densities, the economic savings vanish. This negative view is compounded, as in the case of Singapore or Hong Kong, by the notion that there is an upper limit to the total city area available and that it should not be squandered on single-storey housing.

This is a widely held opinion and one that merits serious consideration. Urban housing is not a discrete problem; its total cost to society is much greater than the construction cost of the unit itself. It is the product of a series of other locational decisions involving job distribution, desire lines, transport arteries, and so forth. What we are looking for, in effect, is the optimal trade-off between construction cost (which varies with density) and the opportunity cost of urban land.

To discover the optimal balance in this trade-off, we will need to define housing precisely and determine how it actually functions. Housing involves much more than just houses. The room, the cellular unit, is but one element in the whole system of spaces that people need in order to live. In an Indian urban setting, there appear to be four such necessary spatial elements. In hierarchical ranking, these are the space needed by the family exclusively for private use (cooking, sleeping, storage, and so forth); the areas that foster intimate contact (e.g., the front doorstep, where the children play or one chats with his neighbour); the neighbourhood meeting places (e.g., the city watertap or the village well), where one becomes part of his community; and finally, the principal urban area, perhaps the *madina*, used by the entire city. In other societies the number of elements and their interrelationships may vary, but it is clear that human settlements everywhere—from small towns to sprawling metropolises—have some analogous system. This analogue will vary according to the climate, income levels, and cultural patterns of each society.

We may discern two important facts about these systems. The first is that some of the elements consist of covered spaces and/or open-air spaces. This is of fundamental significance to developing countries, since almost all of them are located in tropical climates where a number of essential activities take place outdoors. For example, cooking, sleeping, entertaining, or children's play need not transpire indoors; these activities can occur just as effectively in an open courtyard. Suppose that, in the context of a particular culture, we estimate that perhaps seventy-five percent of the essential functions of private urban living can occur in an open-air space. After accounting for climate constraints (monsoons and the like), we find this capacity still viable for at least seventy percent of the year. This then gives the courtyard a usability coefficient slightly greater than half that of an enclosed room. All vernacular housing, from the casbah in Algiers to the paper house of Tokyo, is the result of an adroit trade-off between the production cost of building and the cost of land for open-air spaces. Each society, and each household within it, finds its own balance.

The second important fact about this hierarchy of living spaces is that the elements are interdependent; insufficient space in one area can be offset by providing more in another. For example, the compensation for small dwelling units may be larger neighbourhood community spaces, or vice versa. Sometimes glaring imbalances do exist: in Delhi, for instance, there are about seventy-five square metres of public open space per family. Would the distribution of public and private space work better if, as in Isfahan or Benares, a fraction of this public space were traded for a small courtyard (of perhaps ten square metres) for each house?

To identify the hierarchy and to understand the nature of these trade-offs is the first step in the provision of housing. Without such an evaluation, one is in grave danger of formulating the wrong questions. This is why so many low-cost housing solutions deal with the problem as a simple one of trying to pile up as many dwelling units (cells) as possible on a given site, without any concern for the other spatial requirements of life. The environments that result are quite unusable: as the surrounding buildings get taller, the open-air spaces get more and more restricted in function. A courtyard flanked by single-storey buildings is for sleeping; with two-story surrounding buildings you can still cook in the courtyard; when five stories surround a courtyard, it is suitable only as a children's play area; a ten-story surrounding structure relegates it to the role of a parking lot. The old indicator of so much open space per 1,000 persons is too crude; the space must vary, both qualitatively and quantitatively, according to the nature of the building in relation to where it stands.

If a functional balance is maintained among all elements in the spatial hierarchy, how do densities relate to costs? In India, with a built-up area of twenty-five square metres per housing unit and a community area of about thirty square metres per family, ground floor housing accommodates about 125 households per hectare. Five-storey walk-ups double this figure to about 250 households; twenty-storey buildings will double it again, to about 500 households. As the building heights increase twentyfold, gross neighbourhood density increases about fourfold.

If we view the larger context, what impact does variation in density have on the overall city? Contrary to popular belief, only about a third of a city is devoted to housing. Actual housing sites usually account for less than twenty percent of usable land, a surprisingly low figure when compared to transport (twenty-five percent) or industry (fifteen percent), for example. Therefore, doubling the densities in the residential areas does not halve the overall size of the city; indeed, it would make only a marginal difference. (This fact was amply demonstrated two decades ago in planning concepts developed for Hook New Town.) What needs to be emphasised here is that any variation in residential density makes a crucial difference to the life style of the inhabitants. This is particularly true in the warm climates that prevail in most of the Third World. In exchange for only a marginal decrease in overall city size, increased density drastically reduces the amount of open-air space and hence the usability of the housing. Furthermore, it sharply escalates the construction costs of the individual units much more than would be the case in the developed Western countries.

In the Third World countries, the specifications for one-, five-, and twenty-storey buildings vary dramatically. A multi-storeyed building (whether of five or of twenty floors) must be built of brick and reinforced concrete, not because the weather demands it (as is the case in Europe), but for structural strength. In contrast, low-rise structures can be made of a wide variety of local materials—from tiles and earthen brick to mud and bamboo—at a mere fraction of the cost. "Low-rise" may be defined not only as self-help housing, but as traditional vernacular architecture in general—that wonderfully rich idiom created by people all over the world without the benefit of professional architects. Not only is the traditional vernacular solution apt to be more successful in economic, aesthetic, and human terms than the professionally designed and constructed architecture, as any reasonably honest architect will admit, but also far more appropriate socioeconomic processes are involved in its production. Sprawling, multistoreyed housing projects can be produced only by a limited number of builders and developers who can handle the technology and finances involved. In contrast, money invested in vernacular housing is pumped into the economy at the bazaar level, just where it generates the greatest amount of tertiary employment.

One can list other significant advantages of low-rise housing in the Third World. First, the houses can grow, a possibility that is becoming imperative in developing countries where current goals yield other priorities. Second, low-rise edifices as opposed to high rises are far more sensitive to the social, cultural, and religious determinants of our environment. Such a building pattern makes it relatively easy for people to adjust their spaces to their own preferred life styles. To cite an example from the world of Islam, one has only to contrast the courtyard housing in Isfahan with the inflexible high-rise development around the Tehran airport.

If we look at the major concerns of humanists and environmentalists today—balanced ecosystems, recycling of waste products, people participation, appropriate life styles, indigenous technology—we find that the people of the Third World have already formulated responses to these concerns. From the Polynesian islands to the Mediterranean villages to the jungles of Bangladesh, marvelous shelter has been built for thousands of years. In fact, the wonderful thing about the Third World is that there is no shortage of building materials and construction skills. What *is* in short supply, of course, is the urban context in which these worthy solutions are viable. The real task and responsibility of the Third World architect is to help generate this new urban fabric.

The creation of an adequate urban context requires an increase in the supply of desirable urban land on a scale commensurate with the dimensions of the demand. This newly created context would accommodate the housing backlog in addition to the growth that lies ahead. It will probably involve the redistribution of jobs of greater or lesser desirability and hence the redistribution of the pressure points of the city. A total restructuring of our cities is likely to result. This is the strategy behind New Bombay, the growth centre for two million people currently being developed across the harbour from the old Indian city. In the existing metropolis the densities are extraordinarily high, reaching over 3,000 persons per hectare in many areas. These densities are not a product of building heights, but result primarily from high occupancy per unit (ten to fifteen persons) and an almost criminal paucity of schools, hospitals, and other social infrastructure. As compared to the fifteen square metres of open area per person in Delhi, on Bombay Island the figure is about one square metre, and this includes the green of the traffic islands. Even roads constitute only eight percent of total land usage, a fact that may explain why they always look so crowded.

Such unimpressive statistics are found in a hundred other cities throughout the Third World. In this context, the improvement of housing conditions is first and foremost a matter of readjusting the land-use allocations. Can this really be done within an existing city structure without modifying the pattern of job and desire-fulfillment lines?

In studies undertaken during the planning work for New Bombay, we tried to determine, in the context of the city's income profile and resources, what optimal residential densities would be. We found that for most land values the trade-off with construction costs suggested that the ideal densities involved low-rise living patterns from 250 to 1,000 persons per hectare. Exceeding residential densities of 1,000 persons per hectare puts the Third World city into serious trouble. An analogy with body temperature is very tempting: we are ill when our temperature exceeds 98.6° F.; might there be a similar indicator for cities? One suspects that this is true for developed countries as well. For instance, the difference in overall population density between London and Paris is small, but overall density makes a great difference in the kind of accommodation available to the average resident in each city.

Other areas of participation for the Third World architect concerned with housing range from large-scale site planning to the grouping of a particular cluster. The key word in that sentence is "participation." In the past, the prototypical architect in these societies was not the beaux-arts prima donna, but the site *mistri*, an experienced mason/carpenter who helped with the design and construction of the house. The practice continues even today in the small towns and villages of India: owner and *mistri* go together to the site, and with a stick scratch into the earth the outline of the proposed building. There is usually some argument about the relative advantages of various window positions, stairways, and so on, but the important thing is that the two share the same aesthetic; they are on the same side of the table. This fact has been behind all the great architecture of the past, from the Alhambra to Fatehpur Sikri.

Would modern architects be willing to participate in building in this manner? Probably not, since all our training encourages us to con the client into building *his* house *our* way. Alternatively, we go to the other extreme: we move among the poor as if in a terrible disaster area, fancying ourselves Florence Nightingales among the wounded. What the architect must bring to bear on the situation is neither the prima donna performance nor the Red Cross bit; he must bring what the site *mistri* has always brought, which is compatibility, experience, and a high visual sense.

In order to improve our environment in the Third World, we must have a strong visual sensibility. The poor have always understood this. With one stroke of a pink brush a Mexican potter can transform his product. It costs him almost nothing, but it changes the quality of the purchaser's life. It is not a coincidence that the best handicrafts and the finest visual sense come from the world's poorest countries. What is so beautiful about the Arab house, as Hassan Fathy has often pointed out, is that the builders have had only the simplest materials at their disposal: sand, earth, and sky. These builders have had to be inventive. Fathy's own work is staggeringly beautiful; he does not patronise the poor by forgetting about aesthetics. On the contrary, he participates with all his passion, intelligence, and visual sensibility so that everyone comes out a winner.

To summarise the role of the architect in the Third World, we acknowledge that the poor are not coming to the cities for houses; they are coming for work. Thus to ask *how* to build is also to ask *where* to build. Sites and services schemes are part of the answer, but they are not in themselves a panacea. To be viable, they will have to plug into key points in the city infrastructure. Because of the scale of the demand, this effort is going to require a major restructuring of our cities. It is the primary responsibility of the Third World architect to conceptualise and help catalyse such a restructuring. On a small scale, the architect should participate, as did the old *mistri*, in such matters as site layout; he should always remember that he and the people are on the same side of the table. If he has performed these two tasks effectively, all the architect really has to do when it comes to the houses is get out of the way.

CHANGING ROLES AND PROCEDURES IN THE DESIGN OF PUBLIC BUILDINGS
MONA SERAGELDIN AND FRANÇOIS VIGIER

In the built environment, a public building does four important things: it stands as a landmark, it transmits a message, it performs a function, and it fulfills a need. The designer shapes the performance of the building by creating its visual expression, organising the use of its spaces, and articulating its programmatic requirements. But in the end, it is user response that spells the difference between success and failure. As a landmark, the building must generate a sense of pride, the message it conveys must be comprehensible to be understood, its functions must be coherent to be efficiently discharged, and the need it fulfills must be one that the population actually feels.

The process of modernisation has created a growing alienation between the users of public buildings and the procedures by which the buildings are provided. In essence, the provision of these facilities has become programmatically routinised. Their function tends to satisfy a bureaucratic interpretation of the public's need, their location within the urban fabric is based upon specified planning standards, and their architectural form has become standardised. These tendencies can be found in all countries, since government has assumed a broader range of responsibilities and replaced the religious authorities, community associations, and charitable individuals who traditionally provided such public facilities as places of worship, schools, hospitals, parks, and fountains.

In the West, the institutionalisation of public facilities began in the late eighteenth century, and was essentially completed by about 1900. In the Middle East and other Islamic areas, this process began later and is still occurring to some extent. Western countries developed building prototypes suited to their institutions and culture as part of this institutionalisation process. Most developing countries, including Islamic ones, have adopted these Western prototypes or adaptations of them, either as a result of the direct influence of colonial governments or as part of the process of technology transfer from more to less advanced countries.

The extent to which these imported building types have satisfactorily met the needs of their users has lately been subjected to a growing scrutiny. Some of their deficiencies are obvious, such as their unsuitability to local climatic conditions and disregard for such prime requirements as the provision of communal prayer areas in certain public building types. Other deficiencies are more subtle, insofar as they relate to the user's perception of the public building and his willingness to make full use of the services housed there. This relationship between user and building is complicated by the cultural stratification of societies whose populations present a full range from illiterate to highly educated, from traditional to modern. The manner in which public services are offered may thus be understood by some strata and not by others. Furthermore, Islamic cultures are highly dynamic. Education and modernisation are altering traditional concepts, in particular those affecting social and geographic mobility as well as the use of space within the neighbourhood and city. These changes in turn affect the relationship between the user and the many public services provided by government.

This paper argues that the widespread use of Western prototypes for public buildings has to some extent prevented their full and proper use by the population they are intended to serve. The institutional factors that led to the selection of Western models in the delivery of public services are examined and the consequences for the indigenous building process analysed. Finally, an evaluation of the adequacy of selected public building standards leads to suggestions for the revitalisation of the participation of users in the design process.

Changing Roles in the Supply of Public Services in the Near East and North Africa—Institutional Evolution. The modernisation of Near Eastern and North African institutions started in the early nineteenth century as traditional trade relationships with Europe were transformed. The advantages of the Western model were clearly demonstrated by the profusion of inexpensive manufactured goods that flooded the eastern Mediterranean area, as well as by the military superiority of the European powers. A few countries launched major institutional and economic reforms in order to compete with the West. Others succumbed to European colonialism. Still others, though able to retain their independence, became increasingly subject to the economic dominance of the West. In any event, Western institutions, whether they were adopted willingly or were imposed by force through colonial rule, proliferated throughout the region, starting with a reorganisation of the central administration.

Development programmes, regardless of when they were initiated or under what circumstances, entailed fundamental changes in the role, functions, and operations of the state. The necessity to muster resources and technical capabilities on an unprecedented scale mandated the establishment of an administrative framework capable of implementing these programmes. The traditional concerns of the *diwan al-saltanat*—the army, the collection of taxes, the appointment of high officials, and the administration of the public treasury—proved totally inadequate in a world dominated by modern industrial powers.

Inevitably, the process of economic development led to increasingly centralised decision making in the provision of public services, and gradual expansion of government functions through new, specialised line ministries and executive departments. The sequence and scope of this state takeover of the service functions traditionally provided by community associations, kin groups, and wealthy citizens were dictated by the path and rate of development and by the nature and urgency of the problems encountered rather than by ideological considerations or resource availability.

The transfer of responsibility from the private to the public sector and the concomitant decline in the role of community associations can be traced back to the economic impact of the West, the early attempts at modernisation, and specific colonial policies. It was spurred by three convergent forces.

First were the resource requirements of economic development. The infrastructure needed to support production activities increased in complexity at an unprecedented rate, as technological innovations rendered older facilities functionally obsolete while still physically sound. The human resources needed for the development effort required a panoply of educational facilities to provide skilled manpower.

Second were the political exigencies created by the development process itself. Development opened avenues for upward mobility based on a new factor: the acquisition of skills and knowledge required by the modern economic sector. Islamic social principles of equity demanded that the means to acquire these skills be made available to as wide a spectrum of the population as possible.

Third was the welfare function of the Islamic state. It is, by law, the responsibility of the state to supply basic needs to those unable to secure them on the open market. The definition of what constitutes basic needs expanded beyond medieval concepts of mere sustenance to encompass an array of goods and services once thought of as privileges but today recognised as fundamental rights.

The emerging bureaucracies either incorporated older institutions or paralleled them. In both cases the result was the same. The ascendency of the state undermined the role of the community groups and associations that had formed the basis of the traditional structure of society. These associations were extremely diverse and offered the population a full range of participation in their activities. Some were formal, like guilds; others informal, like groupings of relatives, friends, and neighbours. They could be geographically defined, like the administrative *'arafa, shiakha, hara, khitta,* or *mahalla*; or undefined, like Sufi associations. Some were restricted by lineage, like the ashraf, while others had looser membership criteria, like provincial affiliations. Their common feature was a clear economic, social, or religious bond that permitted a complete identification of the individual with the group. People belonged to one or several of the associations and defined their roles, rights, and responsibilities accordingly.

Erosion of this social structure resulted from changes in the outlook and way of life of the local elites, a natural consequence of constant exposure to the Western world. Colonialism accelerated this trend, as economic and political domination created an incentive for emulation, and even vehement nationalism could not altogether prevent ambivalent attitudes. Traditional community associations were thus deprived of elite leadership, patronage, and protection. Physical dysfunction became evident as new patterns of urban expansion followed Western design standards and were totally unrelated to the traditional Islamic urban fabric organised around *khittas, haras,* and *suqs*.

The final disintegration of the community associations occurred mainly as a result of the expansion of the state bureaucratic machinery, which gradually took over their administrative, fiscal, and regulatory functions. Government came to regulate all key services through licensing, taxation, and pricing policies. The expansion of governmental functions through line ministries and executive departments terminated the public service role of the *awqaf,* and dealt a severe blow to similar functions undertaken by community associations. Their roles became sharply limited, although they continued to build and administer mosques, *zawiyas, kuttabs,* and various charities.

With national independence came a determined effort to embark on large-scale development programmes. Forceful state intervention and the transfer of Western technology were deemed crucial in bridging the economic development gap. The use of imported Western institutional models met with varying degrees of success, but in any case hampered a possible revitalisation of traditional community associations. These were left to redefine their roles and coexist as well as they could. The imperatives of development today dictate an expanding scope for government action in the provision and delivery of public services. In light of this, it is difficult to envisage the role of community associations extending beyond the provision of specific personal services, mutual aid, and charities.

Sources of Public Building Prototypes. In expanding the public-service functions of the state, Muslim countries have looked to the West for physical standards, building models, and organisational frameworks. This demanded planners, architects, and engineers capable of designing new types of facilities, contractors capable of undertaking large-scale projects involving new building techniques, and administrators capable of managing a new functional apparatus.

The adoption of a prototypical plan for institutional buildings has certain clear advantages. It permits the development of functional spaces interrelated to ensure efficient utilisation. Moreover, the limited range of uses for each space, the uniformity of usage regardless of where the building is situated, and the need to build a large number of buildings with similar, if not identical, programmes are pervasive arguments for the standardisation of design norms. For example, in European countries where the central government had assumed responsibility for education and had established uniform curricula, school buildings were rapidly standardised. The size of the school, its location within the community, and its plan and elevations had to conform to national norms.

The standardisation of other public building types occurred more slowly, but was also essentially complete by the end of the nineteenth century. Their design was determined largely by technological and economic factors. Hospitals were shaped by considerations not only of medical care but of construction costs and ease of maintenance. Public housing embodied hygienic norms of ventilation and space per resident, as well as budget constraints that required a dense grouping of four- to six-storey walk-up blocks. In most instances, adherence to bureaucratic norms dictated the plans and the selection of specific building materials and gave little leeway to designers to search for more innovative solutions.

The extent to which the public building types that evolved in Europe were satisfactory solutions has been the subject of some debate. In spite of their stylistic modernisation in the last few decades, their programmatic durability seems to indicate that they have adequately met institutional needs. The minimal involvement of users in their design has been symptomatic chiefly of social structures that have rarely stressed the participation and collective responsibility of communal groups since the centralising of government functions started to gain strength after the fifteenth century. It was thus accepted that the provision of new public services and the extension of governmental responsibilities to include community facilities previously provided by religious and charitable institutions would take place in what had become an expected "governmental style," characterised by centralised decision making and little concern for user participation.

Though the standardised European public-building prototypes may have been suitable for their indigenous conditions, at least insofar as they were part of a stylistic and institutional tradition, their transplantation to the Islamic countries of the Near East and North Africa was culturally traumatic.

User Needs in the Design of Public Buildings. State control meant equal access to services. It also meant that the processes by which these services were provided and administered, as well as the standards for their physical plant, were formulated by government and could be altered at any time in the public interest. While services had traditionally been provided to fulfill a need commonly defined by provider and user, the relationship between people and public services was henceforth regulated by the statutes of administrative law.

The government replaced the user as the client for whom public buildings were produced by an array of architects, engineers, builders, and procurement contractors. The staff providing the services became government employees, while users were categorised as general, prospective, or actual beneficiaries. This classification offered little guidance to the providers of public facilities, whether ministry officials or design professionals, since users rarely constituted a homogeneous group. As an added complication, Islamic societies are today in a highly dynamic phase of their evolution. The process of modernisation has complicated the economic stratification common to all countries by superimposing sharp differences between the educated and the illiterate, urban and rural populations, men and women, and modern and traditional occupations. This is reflected at all levels of society. The best indicator of this dynamism is a growing generation gap in attitudes and life styles, which has overshadowed the ancient cultural gaps between social classes.

The implications of these trends for the programming and design of public buildings are evident. User attitudes towards public facilities differ widely among various segments of the population. Therefore, the adoption of uniform standards for service areas, building prototypes, and building plans is totally inappropriate. The concept of social space for men and women provides a dramatic example of these differences in all three categories of standards.

The service areas of schools, mother and child clinics, and welfare centres used by women are markedly smaller than those of comparable facilities for men. In the more traditional Islamic countries and among less educated, older, urban women in general, there is a marked reluctance to venture alone out of the immediate neighbourhood. Recent experience has shown that facilities for women fail to reach the outer bounds of their targeted service areas where they extend beyond the maximum distance a woman is willing to walk alone. Inadequate public transportation and the inability to keep facilities open at times of day when male family members can accompany their womenfolk have compounded the problem. The siting of public facilities must therefore take these conditions into consideration, rather than follow the more usual international criteria based on an efficiency formula for maximising utilisation ratios and minimising construction and operation costs per unit of population served.

Building prototypes accommodating various facilities, particularly multiservice centres offering a broad range of social services to all segments of a population, have had uneven success. Modelled after European examples that have demonstrated the economy of sharing expensive facilities, they have failed to recognise the deeply ingrained reluctance to come into contact with members of the opposite sex in unfamiliar surroundings. Separate facilities, from schools to health and social-service centres, are still required for certain social strata, even though mixed facilities may be acceptable for others.

Building plans must also recognise the desire for a separation of men from women or of families from single youths in common areas. Thus, separate waiting rooms may be required in clinics, hospitals, and facilities such as railroad and bus stations, which are used by all social strata. It is worth noting that common waiting areas have been readily accepted in airport terminals, which until the large-scale interregional labour movements of the 1970s were used primarily by the more affluent and better educated. Where only one waiting area is provided, it is not uncommon to find a de facto segregation of the common space, with men congregating at one end and women at the other.

In general, considerable reprogramming of Western prototypes for service facilities is required. This does not seem to be easily comprehended either by Western-trained designers or by the technocrats of national and international agencies that provide funding. Moreover, the programming and design effort must recognise that different expressions of user needs are evolving. With education and exposure to different life styles, traditional attitudes are changing. The formulation of standards is thus complicated by the need to anticipate change and accommodate it. This is not an easy task, as the rate of social change varies not only among countries and between urban and rural populations, but also according to education and economic upward mobility. It is clear, however, that the mechanical application of uniform standards, whatever their origin, is a disservice to users of public facilities.

Changing Nature of the Commissioning and Building Process. The Institutionalisation of the Contract System of Labour Recruitment. Paralleling the case of *mi'mar* officers whose functions were taken over by the ministries of public works, trade guilds—the most formal of all community associations—proved unable to supply government with the manpower needed to execute large-scale and technically sophisticated projects. By the end of the nineteenth century, colonial administrations unwilling to tolerate a labour market regulated by noncodified rules had already decreed the abolition of the guild system. The disappearance of geographic and labour recruitment monopolies changed the complexion of the building trades. Persons were now free to enter and practice any trade, and clients were free to select the *mu'allim* to supervise the construction work and to recruit whatever workers were needed without resorting to the guild sheikhs, who had been the intermediaries in the older system.

The disappearance of a regulated labour market led to the emergence of the contract system of labour recruitment. Contractors replaced guild sheikhs as suppliers of construction labour and formed a class of foremen and trade bosses in the different job activities. These contractors were middlemen, supplying large foreign or local employers with the labour they needed. As such they were very different from the guild sheikhs they replaced, few of whom were able to adjust their role to fit the new conditions and become contractors.

Without the protective institutional framework of the guild system, only a severe labour shortage could prevent the exploitation of workers. Until the 1970s, when ambitious development projects created a labour shortage on the regional scale, demographic pressure and rural-urban migration had saturated the construction industry with a pool of unskilled labourers ready to work for minimal wages. No *esprit corporatif* could survive under these conditions, and no institution developed to replace the guilds.

The contract system effectively cut off labour engaged in the building trades from the client (public or private) and the designer (foreign or local), both of whom found it far more expedient to deal with contractors. Small-scale developers can still secure building materials and deal directly with an array of individual skilled workers and craftsmen operating in the locality. However, since even for simple residential construction no fewer than ten different trades are involved, for any project of significant scale this process quickly reaches

unmanageable proportions.

Commissioning Procedures and the Adoption of the Bidding System. The dissolution of the guilds and the institutionalisation of the contract system of labour recruitment led to the adoption of the competitive bidding system for the award of public-works commissions. Engineering and contracting firms developed to undertake the larger contracts for both government and the private sector, including construction of public buildings and public works. Foreign dominance of the field during colonial times was a natural extension of foreign control over the financial and land markets and over the technical professions. The dissolution of the colonial empires brought an end to open discrimination against native professionals and entrepreneurs and permitted the emergence of large local firms that have adopted Western bidding, management, and construction techniques. Thus, the duality that pervades the whole economy extends to the construction sector, where large-scale enterprises with modern machinery and equipment contrast sharply with small-scale builders relying mainly on manual methods of construction.

Impact of Standardised Building Types. The decision to use Western building prototypes for the public facilities required by efforts to modernise and become more economically competitive with Europe was to have significant consequences for the process of design and building construction.

One important consequence was the abandonment of local architectural traditions. Some of the governmental service functions that were adopted in emulation of European countries had no easily traceable indigenous style; they represented the importation of a new technology or of functions that in the Near East and North Africa had never become sufficiently institutionalised to generate a specific architectural form. Transportation terminals, factories, and communications centres are examples of the first category, while the second includes hospitals, paramedical and welfare centres, and government offices. Therefore, foreign designs were adopted in the absence of an appropriate indigenous building type. This is perfectly understandable, particularly since these functions were frequently introduced into the region by colonial governments or by foreign concessionaires. Other governmental functions, however, particularly schools and housing, had a long indigenous architectural tradition that was systematically discarded in the modernisation effort. There seems to have been little justification, for example, for using European school prototypes rather than a type of building derived from the traditional madrasa. One-story classrooms disposed around a courtyard would not only have ensured an easily understood continuity in style, but would also have been better suited to local climatic conditions and would have allowed the use of local construction materials and labour.

A second consequence was the gradual disappearance of traditional building skills. The very modernity of European building types, the building materials employed and the technology required to produce them, and the ways in which they were assembled were sufficiently alien to the local building industry to reduce its participation in the construction effort to a minimum. The reliance on skilled foreign construction workers—chiefly Italians, Greeks, and Maltese—to undertake the masonry and stucco work, the plumbing and electrical work, and the carpentry and finishing, relegated local labourers to menial tasks. The situation was exacerbated by the outright favouritism that colonial administrators and concessionary companies showed to contractors from their own countries. In addition, the very scale of government construction projects discriminated against local contractors, whose small scale of operation, lack of education and managerial skills, and inadequate financing excluded them from competitive bidding procedures. Large foreign firms were thus again at an advantage wherever governments adopted the more efficient bidding procedures used in the West.

The local construction industry languished as government contracts were denied it and the better private sector buildings increasingly emulated new European fashions. Traditional skills were devalued and lost within one generation or so, because skills better suited to the new building types which were being constructed had to be learned by local craftsmen and labourers.

A third consequence was a growing Westernisation in the design profession. Architects, engineers, planners, and other professionals studied Western models and entered their professions imbued with ideas and precepts that inevitably promoted the use of the Western building types that were quickly becoming the symbols of progress. The young professional found himself in a position somewhat analogous to that of the traditional building craftsman. He had to perform as a professional judged by Western standards if he wanted to compete with the foreign firms that had cornered the more lucrative public and private building contracts. Thus in the 1930s a number of highly competent and competitive designers started to emerge; their very success was due to their ability to design in the international style.

The rapid growth of this group, whose scope of activity expanded with their countries' independence, has done little to promote the development of Islamic contemporary architecture, since its members' views are strongly permeated by international influences. They are, in fact, largely indistinguishable from their colleagues the world over. They follow the dictates of the same architectural schools of thought, emulate the same masters, share an identical preoccupation with architecture as "built form." In other words, they are part of the same professional culture. Much of the work of these designers has clearly responded to the Western taste of the minority of the population from which their wealthier and more sophisticated clients are drawn, and for whom they design modern luxury housing, hotels, office buildings, and government ministries. However, they have generally been no more able than their Western counterparts to respond to the needs of the majority of the population, whose life style is still imbued with traditional values.

The Adoption of New Programmatic and Design Standards.   The spatial organisation of the Islamic city reflects social and institutional structures based on well-defined groups sharing a common interest in a specific geographical area—*khitta, hara,* or *suq*. The failure of Western observers to recognise this relationship is amply demonstrated by their persistent description of the Islamic city as lacking order, resembling a rabbit warren, or consisting of a confused jumble of narrow alleyways. In planning, as in architecture, the European model was deemed superior, and new districts that started to be laid out in the nineteenth century introduced unfamiliar features to the region: wide streets to accommodate vehicular traffic, the rectilinear street plan, and the free-standing structure. These became the physical planning norms accepted by local professionals and government officials alike. Though undoubtedly suited to the evolving tastes of a Westernised elite, they failed to take into account the traditional life styles of the majority of the urban population.

The design standards used in public housing projects illustrate the lack of sensitivity to user needs. The wide streets have been planned to accommodate nonexistent automobile traffic. Hot and dusty, they do not provide the shade required for comfortable pedestrian usage, and their unnecessary width quickly becomes a wind tunnel and an ad hoc refuse dump. The walk-up apartment blocks are closely modelled after those of European public housing projects. These accommodations are ill-suited to the traditional keeping of poultry and small domestic animals, which are a main source of protein for the poor. Moreover, corridors and stairwells do not fit traditional notions of individual responsibility for communal space: their usage leads to tenant conflicts, they are not maintained or kept clean, and they deteriorate rapidly.

The planning standards that have shaped large government projects have consistently ignored the fact that a majority of the population still prefers a spatial organisation that fosters community interaction. The sharp contrast that exists between the planned developments and the informal settlements clearly reveals the continuance of a traditional organisation of space, one that is meaningful and well-adapted to the life style and priorities of the largest and most rapidly growing segment of the urban population. Thus the spontaneous division of large settlements into small, identifiable groupings of streets and buildings provides an intimate human scale and creates social neighbourhoods responsive to overriding concerns for privacy, the social space of different population groups, and community cohesion.

In spite of the lack of public services, the atmosphere prevailing in settlement areas where the environment is shaped to respond to the needs of the users contrasts sharply with the sterile atmosphere of large-scale public housing projects based on intensive design standards. Moreover, it should be noted that although recognisable expressions of traditional building, such as courtyards, do appear in these settlements, there is little effort to recreate traditional architecture either in the use of materials or of design motifs. On the contrary, given a choice, settlers have shown a marked preference for materials and forms which are urban, functional, and modern, such as concrete, cement, or fired brick instead of mud, and slab roofs instead of domes.

The Reintegration of Users in the Design Process. User participation in the design process is vital to the successful delivery of public services. Local needs, concerns, and life styles must be taken into careful account and the use of unsuitable, unfamiliar building styles and programmes avoided.

Current development programmes in the Islamic countries emphasise the adoption of Western technology without its cultural and social forms. The sheer scale of investment in public works usually entails a continued reliance on large Western professional and contracting firms which have the technical and financial capacity to undertake the volume of work. This conflicts with the desire to revitalise indigenous cultural traditions and to decrease the dominance of foreign influences. Spurred by the attractiveness of high technology solutions to technocratic elites and by the marketing of technology irrespective of need, suitability, or cost, governments often undertake large public investments without considering alternative solutions more in keeping with indigenous skills, resources, or traditions.

Reliance on skilled foreign technicians and labourers is not in the best interest of the host country except on a temporary basis. To counteract this one-way relationship, governments now require the formation of joint ventures in which foreign firms associate with local partners. Yet, little critical evaluation of standards occurs, and large projects continue to be constructed with little consideration of local conditions.

In the area of housing, the inability of most governments to provide a sufficient number of units has resulted in the proliferation of informal settlements where the user has considerable latitude in shaping his environment. In these situations, public investment tends to follow development rather than determine it. In public buildings, on the other hand, the relationship between user and physical space is predicated on rigid standards rather than on the expressed needs of users.

While there may be some rationale for not involving users in the appraisal of design solutions, their non-participation in the identification of needs—a trend that grew out of the dynamics of the development process—should be deplored. Lack of information all too often results in legitimate needs being ignored. Lack of sensitivity makes it easy to dismiss issues as being unimportant. Lack of concern leads to regarding negative social impacts as "unavoidable" costs.

The indifference of users toward public buildings provided by government, and considered as belonging to government, is well known. It breeds abuse and vandalism and creates an unjustifiable drain on resources for maintenance. An alien landmark cannot promote community identification, and the message it conveys will not be understood. A building whose functions do not serve the community's needs and respond to its priorities will fail to be adequately utilised.

It is clear that a revitalisation of the participation of users in the design process is essential. This will require the involvement of the ministries responsible for programmatic decisions and of the designers of public facilities, in addition to the users themselves. Yet experience in most countries has shown that it is difficult to convince government bureaucracies to relinquish their prerogatives and pay more than lip service to broadening the participatory process in decision making. The current administrative decentralisation policy in most countries of the region reflects principles of centralised planning and decentralised implementation through a hierarchy of governmental administrative bodies, rather than an intent to involve the local level in the decision-making process.

Local authorities have been delegated powers to administer directly or participate in the administration of public utilities and services. However, their actions are subject to central review and approval, and their activities burdened by cumbersome bureaucratic procedures. Furthermore, local authorities generally lack adequate professional and technical personnel, budget appropriations, or both, and have little choice but to continue to rely on central government for the planning and design of public buildings.

An important objective of decentralisation is to involve citizen councils in the administration of local affairs. However, it is often difficult for these councils to fulfill their intended function. Most users or beneficiaries have little understanding of administrative law and limited ability to deal with an impersonal bureaucratic machinery except through the familiar patronage system. Under these conditions, citizen participation tends to be unrepresentative when mandatory, and inadequate when voluntary.

Designers may be able to play a catalytic role in the development of a more sensitive approach to the delivery of public services. Their current inability to fulfill this role is due largely to the nature of the education they have received. Whether obtained in their home universities or abroad, the professional training of planners, architects, and landscape architects has not only stressed Western solutions but has relegated the Islamic tradition in art and architecture to history courses. Little attention is paid to the social and economic determinants of design, and the studio problems given to students assume educated, Westernised, sophisticated clients. Although successful in training professionals to compete with Westerners on their own terms, this pedagogical philosophy has effectively cut off Muslim professionals from their own culture and stylistic background. It is therefore not surprising that an interest in their own culture is almost invariably manifested in a superficial use of traditional forms, rather than in a search for solutions responsive to life styles and concepts of private and social space that are still influenced by Islamic traditions.

Certain themes are recurrent. Outer shells using such pseudo-Islamic motifs as pointed arches, domes, and *mashrabiyya* barely disguise floor plans of Western inspiration. At times, the sole justification for this approach is the desire to express nationalistic sentiments. Similarly, elaborate Islamic decorations are thought to be symbolically appropriate for buildings with religious functions, or for those somehow associated with Islam—a ministry of pious foundations, for example. Conversely, there is a pervasive tendency to enrobe in the Western-style buildings that are intended to house functions that are strongly influenced by sociocultural traditions— housing and education, for example.

If this misinterpretation of what is "Islamic" in architecture is to be remedied, professional curricula will have to undergo major reforms. Architectural history courses must stress the social, cultural, and ecological factors that gave rise to specific architectural forms rather than treating these forms as purely plastic art. The evolution of institutions and their influence on the spatial organisation of cities must be understood. The growing body of socioanthropological work currently being undertaken by the universities of the region must be integrated in professional education, both to increase the sensitivity of young designers to the varied life styles of the population and to equip them to formulate solutions that will better fulfill the needs of their users.

The professional's influence in promoting designs that are appropriate to indigenous conditions can be significant. As a designer, he can demonstrate that there are better solutions than to reproduce building types originally developed in a totally different context. As a member of his country's educated elite, he will participate in the determination of standards used for public buildings. As the local partner of international architectural and engineering firms undertaking projects in his country, he can make known to foreign consultants the needs peculiar to his country and, through his informed participation, help ensure better solutions.

The process of economic development entails constant innovation. The introduction of unfamiliar concepts and designs is bound to be controversial, as it implies some degree of disruption of existing attitudes and organisations. Communication must be established between designers and users if public buildings, particularly those involving functional, technological, or organisational innovations, are to be successfully integrated into the structure of the Islamic community.

Professionals, rather than bureaucrats, should take on the responsibility of ascertaining user needs and desires and incorporating them into the design process. The ability to show that local concerns have been considered is the first step towards acceptance of and satisfaction and identification with the buildings. The demonstration to users of the usefulness and usability of new building types is the single most important factor in overcoming the innate fears, expressed opposition, and secret apprehension that are so easily generated by the process of modernisation. Independently or as local associates of foreign partners, professionals in their roles as practitioners, officials, advisors, or consultants must demonstrate that the value of the Islamic cultural heritage is of substantive, not merely symbolic, importance.

ON RECREATIONAL AND TOURIST COMPLEXES
YASMEEN AND SUHAIL LARI

As defined today, recreation tends to mean self-indulgent amusement. However, the history of Islam suggests a different connotation. Recreation was taken in the literal sense to signify "re-create," to refresh or rejuvenate oneself mentally and physically. Traditionally is has meant a journey into self-knowledge, a removing of oneself for spiritual transformation by retiring into a saint's *khangah* or *zawiya*. Often outside the city walls, these structures were also considered abodes, sanctuaries, and resting places for travellers. Recreation also meant leaving the crowded and often unsanitary environment of the city to avail oneself of the specially created paradise gardens, where arrangements for amusements were often made.

The difference in meaning and attitude between recreation as self-indulgence and recreation as spiritual rejuvenation is not only a problem of old versus new interpretation; it is also the difference between the Third World and the technologically advanced world. To the latter, affluence has brought new kinds of recreation directed toward purely personal pleasure, a kind of art for art's sake. This is a luxury that we in the Third World cannot afford. Our great recreational gatherings are therefore linked with some functional or spiritual purpose. For example, the horse and cattle show in Lahore provides entertainment in the form of folk dances, musical bands, and dancing animals, but at the same time it fulfills the practical purpose of displaying the various horses, camels, and cattle.

The advent of capitalism, militarism, and mechanisation and the conquest of the world by Western science and technology heralded the emergence of a new era. Western superiority was never seen by the West as merely a matter of technology; it was a total superiority. Livingstone, Manchester, and the Bible went hand in hand. It was the acceptance of the total superiority of European culture, not force alone, that held non-Europeans in lengthy psychological and political subordination. It induced in the conquered a sense both of inferiority and of dependency, and the natural correlation of these feelings: a belief in the inevitability, even the rightness, of the Western rule.

In the area of tourism, it was felt that no efforts must be spared to provide facilities to amuse and indulge Western tourists, in order to attract them in ever greater numbers. The newly built tourist facilities were therefore based on concepts and standards of recreation in the affluent Western societies. The high-rise hotel became one of the most distinctive features of our emerging cities.

The majority of Westerners have acquired their perceptions of Islamic architecture from buildings like the Brighton Pavilion, films about the Arabian Nights, and nightclubs with an "oriental" atmosphere; all of these rely heavily on images of arches and domes. The perceptions of the Western-educated elite are heavily coloured by the popular Western media; they are sadly lacking in any but a superficial knowledge of our Islamic heritage. It is not surprising, then, that our cities are dotted with buildings designed by both foreign and local architects that are at best called "instant Islamic." Their impression is created by the mere application of certain elements on the facades. In every other respect they are poor imitations of buildings found all over the Western world.

Since tourism is a substantial foreign exchange earner, great emphasis has been placed on international tourism. It was felt that, in order to attract foreign tourists, gambling houses, nightclubs, and bars had to be built. Little attention was given to domestic tourism, to the development of places of cultural importance, or to traditional centres of pilgrimage.

The latest developments in our countries, however, point towards a return to fundamentalism and populism, and towards a new awareness and assertion of self-identity. Strict new laws on drinking, entertainment, and sex require that new directions in tourist recreational facilities be sought. These regulations have disrupted plans developed for the promotion of tourism, since they are diametrically opposed to those facilities planned for the pleasure and convenience of international tourists. Thus the beach resorts, casinos, bars, and many new hotels, either built or in the planning stages, have become superfluous in their present social unacceptability. Gadani Beach near Karachi, once promoted as a haven for tourists and including an ambitious project for a beach hotel, has now been taken over as a shipwreckers' junkyard. A casino in Karachi, planned after the civil war in Lebanon to make Karachi a new magnet for tourists, now lies deserted by the sea, soon to become a magnificent ruin. Similarly, the structural skeleton of the Hyatt Regency Hotel in Karachi stands unfinished, a mute reminder of the "good" days of the past.

The result of the back-to-Islam movement could have been a rediscovery of the moral and intellectual traditions of the past, coupled with the pursuit of spiritual growth and equilibrium, but in terms of architectural manifestation the results leave much to be desired. The real need was for a different orientation, a change in direction and attitude, but architectural solutions have responded by putting an even greater reliance on arches. In one hotel being constructed by an international chain, there are so many different forms of arches that one wonders whether this adaptation has not become a deformation, whether the whim of the client has not become stronger than the architect's own judgement.

For example, all hotels built in Pakistan for international chains have been designed by foreign architects. For practical reasons the design operation was carried on outside Pakistan. Since Western standards and Western models were used, it was not considered important to involve local architects in the design process. It is not surprising, therefore, that despite the number of hotels being built, Pakistan still has not produced any hotel experts; it will continue to rely on foreign expertise for this building type. But can any architect, local or foreign, design a hotel building that is relevant and appropriate when the models are exclusively Western ones?

We ought to question the validity of so-called symbols of progress, particularly in the context of high-rise buildings and comparable engineering feats: they abound in the West, but are they suitable, appropriate, and relevant to us? In the context of economic development, emphasis should be placed on the evolution of life styles that save energy, time, materials, and foreign exchange; efforts should be directed toward moving away from those symbols of progress that are important only because of their high visibility and their supposed allusions to success. Instead of emphasis on only science and technology, we need to direct ourselves toward humanisation of the environment and balanced cultivation of our natural and social resources.

While many aspects of the Islamic heritage are important to us, the following are of particular relevance in the context of building for tourism:

1. Places for travellers and for tourism once were in abundance, and hostelries for all types and income groups of travellers were available. There was special emphasis on gardens as places for entertainment.

2. Islam teaches humility, so buildings were kept low to denote a rejection of luxury and ostentation. The construction of big buildings was considered synonymous with pride and arrogance.

3. The secular and religious life are not separated in Islam, and buildings for trade and travel have formal and functional parallels in religious architecture. The same plan could be used for a number of different functions, and it was difficult to distinguish between a mosque, a madrasa, and a caravanserai. In the words of Oleg Grabar, "the main concern of Islamic architecture did not lie in the maintenance of certain forms, but in the expression of certain activities."

4. Islam discourages excessive expenditure on buildings and encourages the judicious use of resources. For both hot and dry and hot and humid climates, architecture was used as a means of controlling the environment. The insulation properties of various materials were exploited and a range of ventilation systems developed.

5. The outward form of the building is not considered important. The buildings are self-effacing, and the exterior gives no indication of the importance of the building nor of its interior spatial organisation. Even an important monument like the congregational mosque is usually obscured by buildings of secondary importance, like the bazaar, suq, khan, or *hammam*. The grandeur and the beauty of a building are revealed only when you enter its portals. The inward-looking character, the focus on enclosed space, and the element of surprise are used in buildings, in gardens, and as an important feature of city design. These aspects are still visible today in the *madinas* and casbahs of ancient towns like Lahore and Peshawar.

In designing buildings of importance, and particularly in designing buildings for tourism, certain issues demand consideration:

1. The Western model is not appropriate because it requires sophisticated technology and conspicuous consumption of resources. A model that exploits indigenous solutions for controlling the environment must be developed.

2. Expenditure on buildings must be realistic. Excessive

stress on standards and exorbitant expenditure in order to create political and status symbols in the race for modernity must be resisted.

3. The clients, private developers as well as government agencies, must be made aware of the advisability of seeking other solutions. It is important that decisions not be taken purely on the basis of optimum utilisation of land, or because on a visit to Europe or America the client has been dazzled by beautiful edifices.

4. A partnership on an equal footing between local and foreign consultants is important. Such a partnership could seek to avoid unnecessary expenditure on materials and undue emphasis on high standards, and could develop local expertise and self-reliance.

5. Research on traditional forms and techniques is essential, so that professionals may be aided in the production of more appropriate buildings for the future based upon the architectural inheritance of Islam.

ON EDUCATIONAL FACILITIES
ISMAIL SERAGELDIN

We have been looking at buildings, but one should not forget that education is, fundamentally, a process that involves people. It is not the building but what goes on in it that spells out the success or failure of an enterprise. Accordingly, I think it particularly relevant at this stage to look back at the character of the traditional Islamic universities and compare this to the character of contemporary universities. Out of this brief comparison may come some guidelines, or perhaps the criteria which may aid in identifying points of strength in architectural schemes for education.

One point I would like to mention is that the mosque was central in the traditional Islamic university largely because the university was dealing mostly with shari'a and the law. If that religious function has been somewhat marginalised in the role that it plays in modern universities, we should not forget that the mosque has a very major social function today. This social function is reflected in different buildings, sometimes referred to as campus-life centres, which provide a focus for social interactions within the universities. Whether these indeed need to be isolated from the mosque, and the mosque turned into a religious monument or a central landmark within an architectural scheme, is a question I leave unresolved for now.

University life is what concerns me. University life has three components: the life of the students, the life of the teachers, and the interaction between student and teacher life. In the old times the students had a sort of commitment to the university. They usually came from afar, stayed on campus, and educated themselves over a long period of time. With the presence today of regional university campuses and large numbers of people living off campus, this may no longer be true. Whereas enrollments were formerly small and identification between classmates possible, today's very large enrollments frequently make this difficult. Student interaction used to be extremely strong; conflicting bonds exist today, and it is

weak. Student organisations tended to be all-inclusive; they were affiliative, and had few layers. Today they tend to be exclusive and have many layers, with some associations for political purposes, some associations for professional purposes, and so on. Some very real changes have taken place in the development from traditional to modern universities; it would not be fair to yearn for a return to the past without adequately reflecting on the meaning of these changes and the demands they place on the architecture which should serve them.

The same differences apply to teacher life. Teachers were previously committed to the university completely, but today they are partially committed—they serve on many boards, they consult outside, they have to do research, they have other activities. Teachers used to reside on campus; now many of them live off campus. Their numbers were small and now are large; relationships between teachers used to be very rigid and structured, while now they tend to be much more fluid and sometimes even absent. Teachers move from university to university with great ease, which they did not do in the past. Again we have a series of differences that are worth a good look in deciding, for example, such questions as the location of faculty housing, the location of faculty offices, the relationship of those offices to student facilities, and the like.

As for the core of the pedagogic process itself, the student-teacher interaction, this too used to be completely different. In effect traditional education was customised, with each student learning up to his level of ability; today we have much more of an assembly-line operation. It is geared toward previously specified standards and norms, whereas the earlier one was looser—students learned various subjects from various people, then moved away to learn from other people in other places. The motivation for learning was different—not so much seeking satisfaction in the job market as learning for a career and learning for itself. It seems to me that the concrete interpretation of these kinds of changes should be the main function of architectural design for universities.

I suggest the following bases for the design of universities. A first step is to identify how the three functions (student life, teacher life, and student-teacher interaction) are generally conceived in Muslim societies today, and particularly conceived wherever the project is being considered. This fundamental conception must go into the architect's brief.

Second, one should define criteria that will both guide the design and help judge alternatives. The key criterion is whether a given design nurtures the desired pattern of social interaction or whether it makes it difficult to happen in the first place. Beyond that point a use of architectural vocabulary is fine, but it should not supersede the earlier point. After all, one does not use words in a sentence simply because they are nice if they do not also make good sense in that sentence. I think the same is true of architectural vocabulary—choosing

the right expression and the right location will definitely enhance the architectural statement, but using an architectural element that has a nice ring somewhere else, without adequate concern for whether it is really suitable, yields artificiality at best.

Finally, I suggest that, out of concern for the people who use these buildings and for the functions within them, perhaps we should avoid our predilection for large-scale unified geometric designs. Let these designs grow out of a microanalysis of each part related to an analysis of its function and relations. One courtyard may be six modules wide, the next may be eleven, and another seven, depending on the nature of each specific part. They should not all look the same simply because such a configuration looks elegant on a large-scale plan. After all, the magnificent urban environments of great Islamic cities were seldom designed on the basis of geometric grids and were not built as a unit.

ON MOSQUE ARCHITECTURE
NADER ARDALAN

As a practicing architect in the Islamic world, I hold views that reflect the concerns of one who has practically and philosophically encountered the issues of traditional architecture and its potential integration within the contemporary context. My fifteen years of experience in this field have taught me that Islamic art and architecture traditionally place the highest value on the achievement of beauty. This is a natural outgrowth of the Koran, the fountainhead of the Islamic perspective, which emphasises goodness, truth, and knowledge while placing the primary concern upon *ahsan al-'amala* (Beautiful Deeds). Another example of this emphasis, the ninety-nine Holy Attributes of God are referred to as *asma' al-husna* (Beautiful Names). Therefore, it is understandable that in Islam the fundamental mandate of architecture, apart from fulfilling necessary functional requirements, should be to manifest a purposeful sense of beauty. Meaningful beauty in Islamic architecture requires both a quantitative dimension of concern, achieved mainly through a process of pragmatic environmental adaptation, and a qualitative dimension, expressed principally through Islamic aesthetics.

This paper concentrates upon a few major themes of the aesthetics of Islamic architecture and is intended as a complement to the more quantitative considerations expressed by others in the seminar. In particular, it offers a preliminary survey of the visual language of symbolic forms found in the architecture of the mosque. The mosque has been selected

because it occurs in varying shapes and sizes as a fundamental part of city planning in all Muslim cultures from Spain to China, and because it possesses the most charged set of visual symbols. An important reminder of the pivotal role of the mosque in Islamic thought is the saying of the Prophet inscribed upon the gateway of the Qutb Minar: "He who builds a mosque for God, God will build for him a similar one in Paradise."

To achieve an understanding of the visual language of mosque design, a two-part methodology has been employed. First, by analysing the origins of mosques and studying the transformation of ancient pre-Islamic building types into mosques, it is possible to discern a distinct set of generic Islamic forms and typologies of spatial organisation. Second, a comparative survey of the major mosques of the Muslim world makes it possible to catalogue the occurrence of these generic forms and typologies over the last fourteen hundred years. The results of this preliminary study, while still incomplete, indicate the existence of a definite visual language possessing both a vocabulary and a grammar. The vocabulary basically deals with the aesthetic concepts and models of the parts of the mosque. It concerns such issues as constituent forms, surface pattern, colour selection, and modes of material usage. The grammar, on the other hand, relates to various systems of organising these parts into a coherent whole within the framework of Islamic concepts of place making.

Some qualifying remarks are, however, necessary. First, while there seems to be a distinct visual language that is uniquely Islamic, there exists a multiplicity of dialects related to various ecological and cultural regions of the Muslim people. Second, some parts of the vocabulary and grammar have achieved, through accretion and evolution, highly charged symbolic meanings upon which there may still be a general societal agreement, while other parts of the language are very regionally bound. An example of this is the dome, which receives a high emphasis in the zone of Persian culture but is rather undeveloped in the African, Saudi Arabian, and Indonesian cultural zones. Third, the visual language to be presented is only a "kit of tools" related to a mode of architectural expression. Just as a dictionary and a handbook of style do not by themselves guarantee a masterpiece of literature, the different levels of aesthetic beauty depend upon the creative excellence of the user. Nevertheless, documenting the parts and structural systems of this visual language is necessary for building a bridge to the historical traditions of Islamic architecture that unfortunately have fallen into a state of obscurity. Our work supports the position that art in Islam is rooted in the principle of Divine Remembrance and that the value of true creativity lies in the ability of that art to resonate with a profound accord between man, nature, and the Absolute.

Visual Characteristics of Mosque Architecture.   It is possible to deduce a basic list of recurring generic forms as well as some principles of spatial organisation. There is a definite concern for orientation in space expressed both in the cosmic orientation of the Ka'ba (set with corners to cardinal directions) and in the terrestrial alignment of mosques toward Mecca. The architectural device for this purpose is the mihrab. A second principle is introversion, characterised by courtyard and central dome planning. This concern is also reflected in the gateway and portico, important parts of a "positive space" design attitude.

The domical, mandalic form highlights a third principle of centrality and symmetry. The dome, when in evidence, normally provides the special sacred space within which the *mihrāb* is located. In Southeast Asia and other forest ecologies, this sacred space often takes the form of a pyramidal roof with wooden rafters. Regardless, the idea of centrality remains constant. From the ritual of daily and congregational prayer, two other generic forms have evolved: the minaret and the place of ablution. The plinth has emerged as a necessary consequence of single plane courtyard designs set upon land with minimum topographic slope. The symbolic value of a raised place is further in evidence in the placement of mosques on hilltops as in many Turkish and Indo-Pakistani examples.

To reiterate, the following recurring forms of mosque architecture constitute the major elements of inclusion that have evolved over the centuries: mihrab, minaret, gateway, courtyard, portico, place of ablution, plinth, and dome. Acts of exclusion are relatively few and are primarily restricted to the removal of specific imagery that would limit the transcendent unity of the Divine. This aspect is most telling of the eclectic and integrative nature of Islamic architecture.

In surveying 113 mosques by region, some definite patterns are observable. For example, the Arab cultures of Arabia, Iraq, Syria, Egypt, North Africa, and Moorish Spain are heavily represented by the hypostyle mosque with a flat roof or a flat roof with dome accents. In East and West Africa the flat hypostyle type seems to predominate, although great dynamics of design, which could in time alter this trend, are evident. The Indian subcontinent (including Pakistan and Bangladesh) represents a unique cultural identity, although ecological variations have influenced the design of mosques there considerably. Mosques in Iran, Central Asia, and Afganistan show strong affinities of type. Predominantly of the four-*eyvan* variety, they rely heavily upon the *chahar taq* concept of place making. Turkey is also one of the more homogeneous areas, having evolved the central dome plan within its own regional borders and being basically of one ecological zone.

Despite the preliminary nature of the survey, it is important to note that all eight generic forms were found in each of six geographic zones (which include the Far East) and that they appeared in no less than eighty-three percent of the mosques surveyed. The incidence of courtyards was ninety-three percent; minarets, eighty-nine percent; domes (pyramidal also included), eighty-three percent; gateways, 100 percent; porticos, eighty-six percent; plinths, eighty-seven percent; places of ablution, ninety-seven percent; and, of course, mihrabs, 100 percent.

In the mosque typologies, the results are for the most part regionally bound, but there is also a spread of cultural types beyond the regional borders. Turkish central dome plans in North Africa and Egypt are the product of Ottoman stylistic imperialism. The presence of the Iranian four-*eyvan* plan in Iraq and the Indian subcontinent reflects similar historical processes.

One overpowering question for further inquiry arises as a result of this study. Is the prevalence of these eight generic forms a mere coincidence, the result of autocratic impositions, or does their repetition represent a natural Islamic language of visual forms for mosque design? Our preliminary evidence points to the latter.

Moreover, what can be learned from the study of mosque typologies of spatial organisations? Assuming that an ecological imperative is at work with cultural identity, do the adaptive forms thus produced have applications beyond the mosque? A fruitful direction for future action lies in the development of a complete inventory of major Islamic buildings. If systematically undertaken according to the various ecological and cultural zones of the Muslim world, other building types such as the madrasa and caravanserai can be analysed for their generic forms and ordering typologies. A compendium of such studies would provide a useful road map to the more relevant forms appropriate today for each of the ecological/cultural zones of Islam. With greater refinement, the study could address other architectural dimensions which have been forgotten. This much needed remembrance could help make explicit the multiplicity of expressions inherent in the world of Islam and, through an understanding of the generic nature of transcendent forms, surfaces, and patterns, create a new sense of visual beauty worthy of Islamic culture.

STATEMENT OF
THE MASTER JURY

As members of the Master Jury, we have carefully considered the nominations for the first Aga Khan Award for Architecture during our meetings in Geneva from June 30th to July 5th, 1980. Our deliberations were greatly facilitated by the thoroughness and technical competence of the nomination, review, and evaluation process conducted under the supervision of the Steering Committee for the Award over the last two years, and by the high level of discussion in the five seminars on architectural concepts and designs.

In our task, we were guided by the terms of reference for the Award which stress recognition of those projects "which demonstrate architectural excellence at all levels"; which respond to their "social, economic, technical, physical, and environmental challenges"; which nurture "a heightened awareness of the roots and essence of Muslim culture"; and which "have the potential to stimulate related developments elsewhere in the Muslim world."

We found our task a difficult one. The difficulty arose from the prevailing reality that Muslim culture is slowly emerging from a long period of subjugation and neglect in which it had virtually lost its identity, its self-confidence, its very language—those characteristics which, after all, are what relevant architecture does and should express. The present is a period of transition—a period when traditional heritage is being rediscovered, when new experiments are being made to combine modern technology with cultural continuity in both richer and poorer countries, and when there is urgent search for socially responsive forms of architecture for the poor majority.

Considering the fact that this is the first time that an award of this kind has been instituted, the sustained effort and imagination that went into the nomination, review, and evaluation process were remarkably thorough. An impressive effort was made to review projects in as many as thirty countries. However, there was a somewhat restricted coverage in the projects we reviewed, and certain areas of architecture were not fully represented, such as educational buildings, mosques, community centres, and public offices. We hope that a much larger sample of projects will be made available to future juries once the objectives of the Award are better understood and firmly established. Thus, the projects presented to us reflected the present stage of transition, experimentation, and continued search in Muslim societies.

In most instances they represented not the ultimate in architectural excellence, but steps in a process of discovery, still an incomplete voyage towards many promising frontiers. Although we have selected some of the projects for their excellence in architecture, many of them stand as accomplishments in this continuing search for relevant forms and designs that has already started and which must be supported. For this reason we have deliberately chosen a fairly broad sample of projects for the Award, rather than up to only five projects, since few projects really meet all the criteria for a creative and socially responsive Islamic architecture, though each presents an important facet of the ongoing search for an ideal. For this reason too, we have allocated the prize money with the intention of striking a balance between need and encouragement, keeping in mind the use to which this money can be put by those receiving it.

In the process of our independent review and selection of projects for this Award, we have become deeply conscious of the need for future evolution of Islamic architecture to meet the urgent needs of the impatient masses. The search for appropriate forms of low-cost housing is one such area of urgent crisis in many Muslim societies. A good deal of intensive research and analysis is needed to identify cost-effective, indigenous, and innovative solutions to the architectural forms which are most suitable for the economic, cultural, and technological needs of the Muslim world. No responsible architect can ever afford to ignore the socioeconomic environment in his legitimate pursuit of excellence of design, nor is it necessary to sacrifice architectural excellence in finding socially responsive solutions to the difficult problems of these societies. We faced this dilemma time and time again in our discussions, but on closer examination the dilemma proved to be a false one. What is really needed is a redefinition of architectural excellence in a socioeconomic context.

We believe that it is necessary to support continued research on appropriate forms of architecture for Muslim societies when only limited financing is available. The study of architecture should be encouraged in schools as part of a broad movement to train future generations for practising and disseminating relevant concepts. We urge that special efforts be made to provide adequate financing for research and training in this area.

We would like to place on record our deep appreciation for the visionary initiative taken by His Highness the Aga Khan. We also value highly the major role played by the Steering

Committee in piloting the entire process for the Award, the high calibre of technical review, and the substantive organisation by the Convenor and his staff. The Award has started a new dynamic process towards a contemporary architecture that meets the evolving needs of Muslim societies.

Within this broad perspective we present our unanimous recommendations for the Award.

Social Premises for Future Architectural Development: Kampung Improvement Programme, Jakarta, Indonesia; Pondok Pesantren Pabelan, Central Java, Indonesia.

Search for Consistency with Historical Context: Ertegün House, Bodrum, Turkey; Turkish Historical Society, Ankara, Turkey; Mughal Sheraton Hotel, Agra, India.

Search for Preservation of Traditional Heritage: Sidi Bou Said, Tunis, Tunisia.

Restoration: Rustem Pasha Caravanserai, Edirne, Turkey; National Museum, Doha, Qatar; Restoration of the Ali Qapu, Chehel Sutun, and Hasht Behesht, Isfahan, Iran.

Search for Contemporary Use of Traditional Language: Halawa House, Agamy, Egypt; Medical Centre, Mopti, Mali; Courtyard Houses, Agadir, Morocco.

Search for Innovation: Inter-Continental Hotel and Conference Centre, Mecca, Saudi Arabia; Water Towers, Kuwait City, Kuwait.

Search for Appropriate Building Systems: Agricultural Training Centre, Nianing, Senegal.

Members of the Master Jury: *Professor Titus Burckhardt, Mr. Sherban Cantacuzino, Mr. Giancarlo DeCarlo, Dr. Mahbub ul-Haq, Mr. Muzharul Islam, Professor Aptullah Kuran, Dr. Mona Serageldin, Mr. Soedjatmoko, Mr. Kenzo Tange.*

RECIPIENTS OF THE FIRST AGA KHAN AWARD FOR ARCHITECTURE 1980

Rustem Pasha Caravanserai
Edirne, Turkey

Turkish Historical Society
Ankara, Turkey

Ertegün House
Bodrum, Turkey

Restoration of the Ali Qapu,
Chehel Sutun and Hasht Behesht
Isfahan, Iran

Sidi Bou Said
Tunis, Tunisia

Courtyard Houses
Agadir, Morocco

Water Towers
Kuwait City, Kuwait

Halawa House
Agamy, Egypt

National Museum
Doha, Qatar

Medical Centre
Mopti, Mali

Inter-Continental Hotel
and Conference Centre
Mecca, Saudi Arabia

Agricultural Training Centre
Nianing, Senegal

Mughal Sheraton Hotel
Agra, India

Kampung Improvement Programme
Jakarta, Indonesia

Pondok Pesantren Pabelan
Central Java, Indonesia

AGRICULTURAL TRAINING CENTRE
NIANING, SENEGAL
COMPLETED JULY, 1977

Classroom block (north elevation). In the foreground,
the social hall; in the background, the main classroom.

Main classroom.

Experimental garden plots
(student dormitories in background).

AGRICULTURAL TRAINING CENTRE.
Sponsor: CARITAS, Frère Romuald Picard; Architects: UNESCO/BREDA, Kamal El-Jack, Pierre Bussat, Oswald Dellicour, Sjoerd Nienhuys, Christophorus' Posma, Paul de Walick; Master Mason: D'Iallo.[1]

In 1975 a vault supported on low, bearing walls was built in an open lot in the city of Dakar, Senegal. It was built by D'Iallo, a mason, using sand and cement alone, without the addition of expensive imported wood or steel elements. The idea of introducing the vaulting technique to Senegal had been promoted by a group of architects from a United Nations agency. For them this prototype represented the successful first phase of developing inexpensive building systems. Placing it on an accessible lot in Dakar as a demonstration piece was the beginning of the second, implementation, phase. A resident of Nianing, Florentin Diouf, saw the model and envisioned an application of the prototype for the housing of an agricultural school he was planning for Caritas, a social-welfare organisation.[2] Diouf contacted the prototype sponsors, BREDA (a UNESCO Regional Bureau for Education in Africa), and thus Caritas and BREDA joined forces in the making of the Nianing Agricultural Training Centre. It was to become an experiment in regional self-sufficiency.

1. The Nianing region. Near the Atlantic shore, the centre is surrounded by its fields and gardens and adjacent to the village of Nianing.

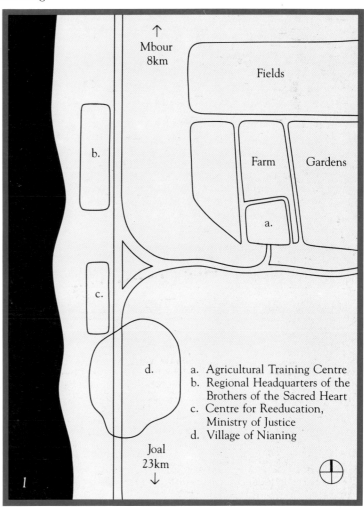

a. Agricultural Training Centre
b. Regional Headquarters of the Brothers of the Sacred Heart
c. Centre for Reeducation, Ministry of Justice
d. Village of Nianing

BREDA's Dakar experiment was stimulated by an allied UNESCO organisation, UNEDBAS (UNESCO Regional Bureau for Education in the Arab States). In 1973 UNEDBAS had published the results of their survey on constructing educational buildings. The survey held as its basic premise that the architectural and social gap between school and society should be reduced. In order to realise this goal they recommended regional and local self-reliance in school construction. Three components determine self-reliance: scale, labour, and materials. The scale of the project must correspond to a community's level of organisation. The labour force should be local, and organised by technical leadership that promotes on-site training, thus developing a community's base of skills. And the construction should maximise the use of indigenous building materials—an economic and cultural consideration.

The Dakar prototype promised to fulfill all these objectives through a short-span masonry structure. Working with the Dakar masons and suggesting new procedures, the BREDA architects developed a simple construction sequence. This building process was labour intensive, the materials local and inexpensive, and the enclosure sufficiently simple to serve a wide range of programmatic needs. The Agricultural Training Centre offered the first opportunity to apply and refine the system.

The Agricultural Training Centre.   The Agricultural Training Centre sits on two hundred acres (160 square metres) of land just to the east of the village of Nianing and less than a kilometre from the ocean. The site, like most of the Sahel region, is mainly flat, dusty savannah, dotted with hearty baobab trees. Subject to dry spells, the area was ravaged by a four-year drought beginning in 1968.[3] Although droughts in Sahel-Sudan countries are cyclical, this drought was exceptional in its geographic extent and severity, and, consequently, in the number of people and livestock it affected.[4] Starvation could be countered by widespread foreign-relief efforts, but soil erosion and desertification, unstopped, have long-term effects on the agriculture of a region. Caritas Senegal, the sponsors of the centre, have been committed to developing agricultural

2, 3. A shaded courtyard has been defined by classroom block, student dormitories, and teachers' housing.

capacities. Accordingly, they responded to the 1968–72 drought with plans for a training centre.

The objective of the Agricultural Training Centre is to introduce new agricultural methods to youths throughout Senegal in order to bring the region closer to agricultural self-reliance. At the school, every two or three hours of classroom theory is coupled with five or six hours in the actual practice of farming and allied skills. For this purpose the school developed a sixty hectare demonstration area on an adjacent farm. Though facilities at the school were intended for fifty, as many as eighty students have been enrolled at a time. Graduates return to their villages after two years of training in agriculture, animal husbandry, hygiene, and first aid. In this way, model farming methods taught to a few can be widely introduced for the benefit of many.

The school complex is organised into three basic units according to function: the teaching block, the student dormitories with adjacent sanitary block, and the teachers' housing. The entrance to the centre (the main teaching block) leads through a portico and hallway which then opens into a large open hall, the focus of all social activities, used variously for meeting, instruction, and dining (there is no actual dining room in the programme). Connected to the hall by passageways and organised around an interior garden court are the single large classroom and school library. To the left of the entrance, enclosing a second courtyard, are the director's office, kitchen, and service area. The open space between the teaching block and the student dormitories behind it is sufficiently protected to be used on occasion for teaching.

All student rooms open onto a common courtyard, closed at one end by the sanitary block and at the other by a block of faculty housing. Each of the six student houses accommodates twelve students, two men to a room. The sleeping rooms are arranged around a shared common room. When enrollment swelled to eighty, some common spaces were appropriated for needed sleeping rooms. The two large blocks of the instructors' houses define still another courtyard to the west. Units are of two sizes, one or two bedrooms, each with living room and shower/water closet.

An Architecture of the Vault. The architecture of the Nianing centre is based on a structural system of barrel vaults supported by parallel bearing walls. As this is a compression system, no imported steel or expensive timber is required. Rather, locally available masonry materials are used for construction.[5]

The structural capacity of the materials—sand and cement—is the major determinant of the vault span; however, the length of the vault can be any dimension desired. For the sake of expedient construction, vault spans were standardised to either 301 or 141 centimetres (the 141-centimetre vaults cover service spaces). The vaults are constructed parallel to

each other with the outer walls of any group buttressed to compensate for the outward thrust of the vaults they support. When the programme needs called for a space wider than a 301-centimetre span, arched openings were made in the bearing walls to extend the space. As many as three vaulted spaces are combined into a single room through arching.

The infill end walls are the major source of light and air. The openings filled with claustra work soften the light as it enters the building. They also permit the free circulation of air—no glass is used for windows—while being sufficiently deep to prevent rain from entering the building. Although the client initially feared the low nighttime temperatures in winter would require greater insulation, the 20-centimetre thick sand-cement brick walls and the cement vaults offer reason-

4. Site plan, plan of classroom block, partial section through classroom block. The centre is organised into three blocks—classroom, student dormitories, and teachers' housing; the space between forms courtyards and open walkways. The architecture of the Nianing Agricultural Training Centre develops a simple structural theme into a rich composition of light, texture, and colour within a clearly ordered community of spaces.

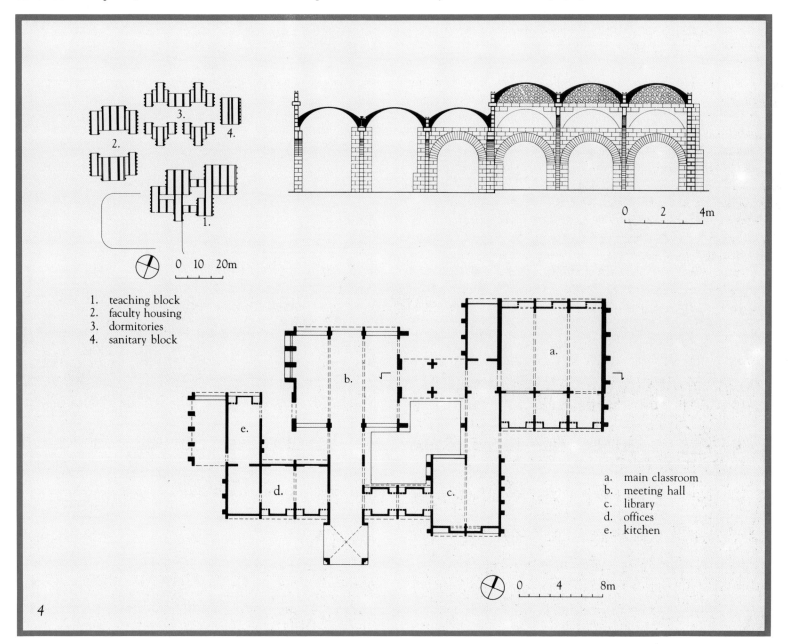

1. teaching block
2. faculty housing
3. dormitories
4. sanitary block

a. main classroom
b. meeting hall
c. library
d. offices
e. kitchen

4

able thermal protection. The walls proved to retain sufficient daytime heat which was then radiated at night to ensure satisfactory nighttime temperatures in the dormitories.

The school's plan is realised with a limited number of elements, using the span of the barrel vaults as the primary measure of space. By varying the vault length, combining vaulted spaces into groups, connecting parallel spaces with arched openings, and clustering groups to create interior and exterior courtyards, a spatial hierarchy is created.

As a complex, the architecture of the Nianing Agricultural Training Centre develops a simple structural theme into a rich composition of light, texture, and colour within a clearly ordered community of spaces. And it accomplishes this end within a limited economic, material, and constructional framework. The architecture is a remarkable exercise in the discipline of constraint.

Construction.   In giving the BREDA team complete freedom, Caritas made it possible for them to experiment with the building system. This was particularly valuable since BREDA could realise its two goals: to construct a good building; and to develop a building process which would offer the maximum investment in the community economy (here seen as reducing the investment in materials in favour of increased labour expenditures). The BREDA architects, along with third-year students and professors at Dakar's Ecole d'Architecture, planned the project in the first half of 1976. Two students were then hired to elaborate the initial drawings before construction began. During the thirteen months of work on the

centre, the initial plans and details were changed, construction techniques and training and management of labour were improved, and various systems for paying worker wages were tried. From their experience in Nianing, the BREDA team are convinced that allowing for a period of experimentation and training during construction is essential for developing self-reliance in building.

The first construction phase—building the student dormitories—brought about the greatest number of innovations.[6] With priority given to developing masonry skills, the BREDA

5. *Classroom courtyard. 6. Main classroom. 7. Social hall.*

architects supervising the work found it necessary to reject inadequate workmanship. Some walls were demolished and reconstructed to assure quality. Contrary to local practice, the masonry was left exposed, free of all finishes. This was done not only to reduce costs, but to encourage quality in the production of the bricks and in the bricklaying.

The building process of the centre was characterised by successive refinements. There were adjustments to the structural system and its construction technique; and gradual improvements came in the quality of masonry craftsmanship, efficiency in execution, and development of an increasingly effective method of labour management.

Brickmaking. The first step in the construction process was producing the bricks. The materials for brickmaking, sand and cement, were obtained locally; sand is a material found in abundance in and around Nianing. Two types of sand were used: sea sand, which was taken from the upper sand layers along the beach and desalinated naturally by the rain; and dune sand, scraped from beneath the upper earth layer. Added to equal portions of these two sands was a small amount of local cement comprising eight percent of the total mixture weight. Formed into masonry units, this mixture can withstand 175 kilograms per square metre of compression stress (more than necessary for the centre's structure), and is resistant to erosion. Since the structure was subject only to compression stress the exclusive use of local materials was possible.

The sand-cement mixture was formed in metal moulds by a brickmaking crew. Bricks of three sizes were moulded; a

8. *Constructing vaults at Nianing. For this experiment in regional self-sufficiency, both skilled and unskilled labour were recruited from the area. Construction provided the workers with training. Several men who began as common labourers rose to the status of mason during the project.*

9. *From right to left, the sequence of constructing arches for the main classroom.*

10. *Axonometric illustrating construction sequence of the Dakar prototypical vault. A movable wooden form is seated on the bearing walls. On the form is placed a shuttering of millet stock (a) followed by a layer of sand/cement (b); wire mesh (c) is incorporated at the apex of the vault; and a second layer of sand/cement (d) completes the construction process.*

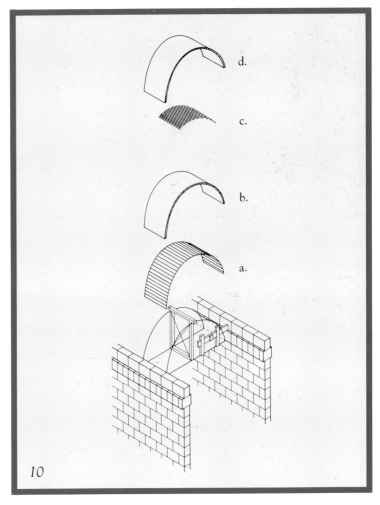

fourth brick size was made by cutting down the largest brick.[7] The bricks were made with a single metal mould that could be compartmentalised according to the desired brick dimensions. Partway through the project, a second mould was added, eliminating the need to cut bricks.

Once in the mould, the sand-cement mixture was shaken and tamped with a wooden mallet to compress it. The bricks were turned out and cured on a cement slab for a period of six days. During the drying period they were sprinkled with water and at times covered with plastic or straw to prolong the drying process. The brickmakers patterned a number of bricks with relief designs. The masons then used these special bricks as decorative elements in the walls.

The workers made two types of brick claustra: trapezoidal and triangular. Also cast in metal moulds, these units were made of the same sand-cement mix, and were cured using the same methods.

Building Bearing Walls.   Construction of the short-span structure began on rammed earth foundations, stabilised by laterite. The bearing walls supporting the roofing were made of solid blocks in order to ensure homogeneity and to counter the horizontal forces of the roofing units. Outside walls were buttressed to absorb the thrust of the barrel vaults. All the bearing walls were topped with a protruding course of brick that served as a shelf for the form work used during the erection of the vaults.

In constructing arches, a brick "forming" wall was built without mortar to the shape of the desired opening. This wall could then be dismantled upon completion of the arch. To help shape the semicircular forming wall, a plank was placed at the center of the desired opening and used as a compass to draw the construction form. This technique proved to be an easy one for the masons to use, and made it possible to span wall openings of 7.2 metres using only masonry.

Forming Vaults.   Vaults were built with plywood struts to support a shuttering of millet-stalk matting; installing this frame-

11. Construction components of building system: end infill wall, decorative brick details, claustra, vaults, scupper. Sand, the primary building material, was obtained locally.

work required no special skills. A layer of mortar was then applied in the same way as for slabbing. Wire mesh was included along the centre of the first vault layer to stabilise the mortar. The subsequent mortar layers were laid after the shuttering had been removed. When completed, the thickness at the vault's summit was 4 centimetres. Making such a vault presents no particular difficulty, although a strict order of working is necessary to ensure good stability during the process of construction.

Labour.   There were two major divisions of labour: brick producers and masons. All labour came from local sources, since there was an abundance of unskilled workers in the region at the time the project began. The construction system was designed to require a minimum of specialised skills; the only specialists on the site were the few masons who were required to assure quality in bricklaying. Thus, the number of tasks to

be mastered by any one person was limited, enabling the unskilled labour force to develop the necessary skills.

Work on the site was begun by the master mason and his assistant, both of whom had built the short-span prototype in Dakar. At the end of one month, the team consisted of six masons and twelve unskilled labourers. Regular supervision was carried out by the BREDA architects two or three times a week. A few months after the work had started on the site, the team consisted of ten masons and twenty workmen. As the work progressed, the master mason trained teams consisting of one mason and one workman; it was estimated that half of the unskilled labourers were trained as masons during the construction period. It was the duty of the site foreman to recruit the necessary labour, and it was he who proposed the composition of each category of workers. The workers were paid by the local Caritas representative, at the rates laid down in the Collective Agreement for Buildings and Public Works.[8]

Important training was also acquired during this period by the BREDA team. From the construction of the first small experimental vault to the school's completion, the team improved the design and implementation of the system, so that other projects built subsequently were built quickly, without constant supervision, and more cheaply.

Economics.   Per metre construction costs—expenditures for labour and materials—declined as the project progressed. The student dormitories, where the system was first introduced, were built at a cost of 12,400 CFA per square metre. Costs were later reduced more than 30 percent due to simplification and modifications made in the construction process and to experience acquired by the masons. Overall, construction costs averaged 10,000 CFA per square metre, the figure stipulated by the client at the outset.[9] And labour expenditures accounted for a full sixty percent of the total 17 million CFA cost of construction.

When the BREDA vault system was compared to other roofing systems, only undulant cement roof proved to be less expensive.[10] Only slightly more costly, the BREDA vault system offered the added benefit of training the local population to build for themselves.

Replicability.   A series of eight projects, based on the short-span system, were built following the construction of the Nianing centre: chicken coops for the Agricultural Training Centre, grain silos built in Ndiarao, a private school in Nianing village, a chapel at Sandiara, a nursery school in Dakar, an intermediate technical school at Nguekohe, a centre for Intermediate Practical Education in Koubanao, and a Koranic school in Melika.[11] These projects testify to the adaptability of the short-span masonry construction system for a variety of programmatic needs. In each of the projects building costs were considerably lower than those of conventional modern construction methods. By the use of entirely local labour, with wages comprising sixty percent of the total building cost, these projects made optimal use of community resources. Self-reliance in construction was realised, and in terms that are architecturally gratifying.

Subsequent applications of the Nianing building system in Senegal. 12. Grain silos, Ndiarao. 13. Chapel, Sandiara. 14. Classroom of Koranic school, Melika. 15. Private school, Nianing. In addition to the four projects shown here, four other buildings based on the short-span system followed the construction of the Agricultural Training Centre.

15

MOPTI MEDICAL CENTRE
MOPTI, MALI
COMPLETED MAY 1976

Looking down the main axis of the centre.

The small openings, rounded forms, and discrete massing
are part of the architecture's naturalised idiom.

The buildings of the centre nestle at
the base of the Great Friday Mosque.

The pedestrian is invited into the sheltered
yet public areas of the centre.

MOPTI MEDICAL CENTRE.
Client: Ministry of Health; Ministry of Planning and Development, Mali; Sponsor: Fonds Européens de Développement (F.E.D); Architect: André Ravereau.[1]

The Mopti Medical Centre is the result of a national plan whose goal is to make modern medicine available to citizens throughout the country. The Mopti Medical Centre, promoted and funded by the Fonds Européen de Développement (F.E.D.), was developed by the Mali Ministry of Health, and constructed under the supervision of Mali's Direction Nationale de l'Urbanisme et de la Construction (D.N.U.C.) as a regional facility to serve both the surrounding rural area and the immediate urban population.[2]

The Site. Sited in the city of Mopti, the centre serves a district of 9,340 square kilometres supporting a population of nearly 150,000 (at the time the project was initiated, Mopti itself had 34,000 inhabitants). The city is significant as a commercial centre whose vitality revolves around an active river port on the Bani River.

The land the government provided for the centre is on the bank of the Bani, and adjacent to the port.[3] Significantly, the centre is on the city's main avenue, Avenue de l'Indépendance, facing the Friday Mosque. The mosque exemplifies a sculptural quality that characterises the townscape of the city: plastic forms of smoothly moulded earthern walls which appear to grow out of the ground on which they rest. The design of the centre was to develop these forms and the technologies underlying them, and to enhance the pattern of pedestrian and vehicular movement that existed on the avenue before ground for the new facility was broken.

1. Mopti lies at the confluence of the Bani and the Niger Rivers.

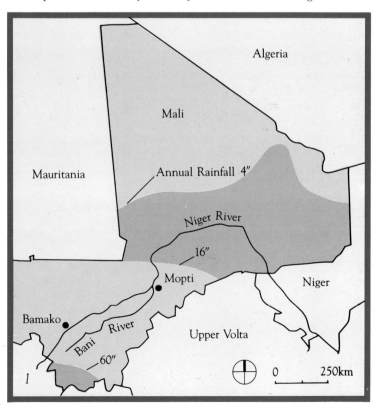

The Architectural Response. The Fonds Européen de Développement selected André Ravereau to design the centre. Their decision was based on the architect's work in housing and institutional building in the M'Zab valley of Algeria—works marked by culturally attuned technological responses to the architectural needs of a specific site. Confronted with the the facility's needs and the social, climatic, and economic constraints. As he stated later, "I responded more with an task of designing the Medical Centre within a constricted time frame, Ravereau was able to understand, without delay, intuitive impulse than with an elaborate process of design." The functional objective being an integrated maternity and health centre to serve the needs of the greater Mopti community, Ravereau identified his architectural goals: to adequately relate the facility to the site's sensitive environment which included the Friday Mosque, the River Bani, and a consistent urban tissue; to create a structure that would not interfere with the traditional customs of families visiting and cooking for patients; to construct the project in a manner inspired by the local traditional techniques of building with natural dark clay called banco; and to achieve a high level of thermal and lighting efficiency without relying on sophisticated systems. The result was a building that performs its main functions, enhancing the community of buildings in which it stands through the use of related materials and forms.

The design the architect developed is articulated along a central axis that forms an interior street parallel to the busy Avenue de l'Indépendance. The street is accessible to pedestrians through two entrance gates, one located at the northwest, the other at the southeast end of the centre. Along the avenue side of the street are the two clinics: a general clinic at the western end, and a child care and social service clinic to the east. Between the two clinics is a two-storey house with an enclosed yard used by the resident doctor. Access to the clinics is from the pedestrian street. To the river side, away from the noisy and dusty avenue, are those functions that require more privacy: at the eastern end are the delivery and operating rooms, directly adjacent to an ambulance entrance. They are connected to the two wards, one for male patients and the

other a maternity ward. The two wards define a U-shaped semiprivate courtyard which opens onto the river. Various support facilities, including a house for the head nurse and a previously existing administrative building, are located at the western end of the site along the river where they are easily reached by a side access road.

The spatial qualities of the central axis are greatly appreciated by pedestrians; many people prefer walking through the centre's street rather than taking the more direct path down the Avenue de l'Indépendance. Narrow, covered passageways alternate with open spaces and planted courtyards to connect various structures and to interrelate private and public activities. In the shaded areas, people wait for medical attention, gather to talk, and prepare food for hospitalised patients. The constant and easy contact with the community and families of patients blends the centre into the urban life of Mopti and removes much of the apprehension often associated with medical centres.

Banco, a dark, abundant, indigenous clay, is used as the primary construction material in the Medical Centre, in conjunction with cement and reinforcing steel through techniques that constitute an upgraded version of the building technology common to Mopti. One aspect of the project's "ameliorating" technology is revealed in brick manufacture. The standard brick manufacturing process of the region uses wooden moulds for shaping. However, for the Medical Centre the bricks were made in a hand-operated press—a cinva-ram block press. Bricks from this process have two advantages over bricks made from wooden moulds: first, the compressive force the press exerts on the banco makes a denser brick that is more resistent to compressive stresses; second, with the press, more bricks can be manufactured by fewer men in less time. The banco mixture itself was fortified by adding concrete to the clay and sand combination in an amount of thirteen per-

2. Architect's sketch of the site, showing the centre's relationship to the river, the mosque and other urban features.
3. Ravereau studied the arrangement of windows to assure protection from direct sun and to provide for ventilation.

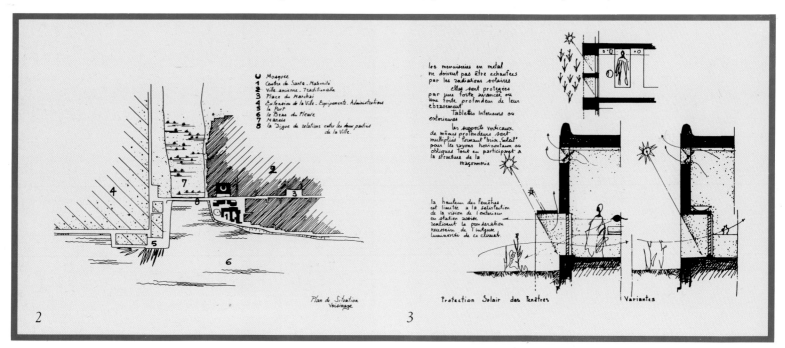

2

3

cent of the mixture's overall weight. Another innovation in the local technology is the use of reinforced concrete for spanning (spans in Mopti are typically reinforced banco, with wood serving as the reinforcement). Concrete and steel permit longer spans that are easily maintained.

Many aspects of the centre's configuration and detailing were designed in response to climate. Mopti, in the Sahel region, is hot and dry most of the year (there is a late summer rainy season marked by squalls).[4] The thick banco walls are excellent insulators against the searing Sahel heat. Window

4. The architect's section through the maternity block showing the use of the porch and windows for ventilation, section through the central axis, and layout of the centre with its main areas indicated; the dispensaries, maternity, surgery, administration, staff housing and ambulance entrance.

openings are not glazed, but are provided with metal shutters for privacy and for filtering the light. These openings are either deeply recessed or designed with overhangs and brise-soleils which protect the metal shutters from the direct rays of the sun. Window and door openings are positioned to assure cross ventilation. Ceiling heights vary to permit high louvred windows to vent warm air. (To counter dust infiltration when windows are open, some openings have been blocked or covered with handmade screens.) Though the Medical Centre, like other buildings in Mopti, has the same outer aspect—the dun-coloured soft, heavy planes of banco, a series of small and larger innovations was introduced by the architect in the building process itself. There was a need to reduce the costs of construction, to extend the lifespan of the structure, and to ensure climatic comfort. There was also a need to integrate the centre into the life of the town.

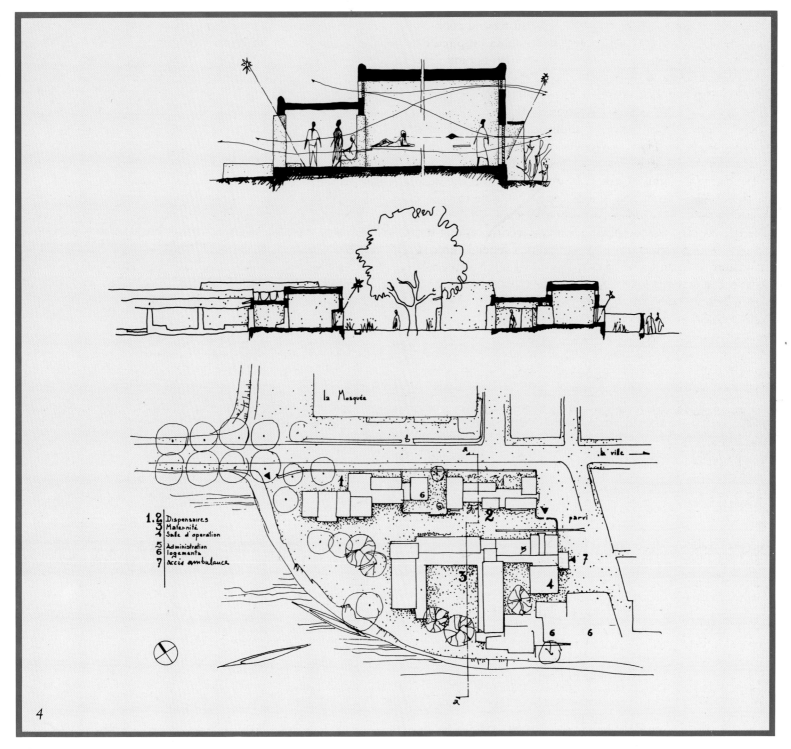

4

COURTYARD HOUSES
AGADIR, MOROCCO
COMPLETED DECEMBER, 1964

During the reconstruction of Agadir, the architect
Jean-François Zevaco designed economical
housing suitable for middle-income families.

An entrance court. The threshold to the house
proper lies deep within the building plot.

COURTYARD HOUSES. Client: Ministry of the Interior, Morocco; Architect: Jean-François Zevaco.[1]

Agadir today spreads out along the shore of an Atlantic bay, renowned for its sandy beaches and mild year-round climate. It is a completely new city; the old Agadir disappeared on February 20, 1960, when a fifteen-second earthquake shock demolished the town. Agadir was totally unprepared, as common knowledge had insisted that earthquakes never happened there.[2] Eighty percent of its buildings were destroyed and tens of thousands of lives lost. As disaster-relief efforts were completed, Agadir began reconstruction under the direction of the Ministry of the Interior. A master plan was conceived by the Service de l'Urbanisme and the High Commission for the Reconstruction of Agadir, and within five years, seventy-five percent of the new Agadir had been built.

A wide range of public and social services was provided for the new town. Its new urban centre expands upon the old, and contains the city hall, a main mosque, a commercial shopping area, offices, major public institutional buildings, and residential blocks. Hotels, the principal commercial attraction of the city, are sited along the shoreline some distance from the city's centre.

Jean-François Zevaco, an architect from Casablanca, was one of several architects awarded building commissions during

1. Agadir as rebuilt after the earthquake of 1960.

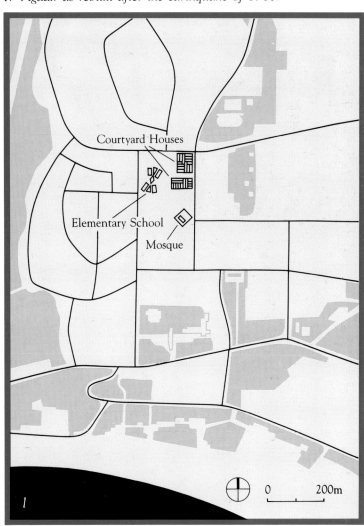

1

the reconstruction. In addition to a number of public buildings, he was asked to design and construct economical, easily maintained housing suitable to the life style of middle-income urbanites and to the climate of Agadir.

The project's brief and design were formulated between December 1962 and April 1963. Construction began in December 1963, on a site of 5200 square metres of flat terrain in the urban centre, just behind a mosque, next to an elementary school, and within walking distance of major public buildings and the commercial shopping district. Construction was completed in December 1964, and the housing occupied in 1965.

Zevaco used his design experience with the Mediterranean patio house in planning the dwellings. For reasons of economy and density he created an ingenious row-house design which, despite the closeness of the units, served the need of families for privacy and comfort.

The seventeen single-storey dwellings are of two types arranged in two blocks, one consisting of four Type A dwellings and six Type B, and the other consisting of three Type A and four Type B. The Type A dwelling has three rooms, a

kitchen, and a bathroom. Type B, which is very similar to Type A, was created by the extension of a Type A bedroom into the adjacent patio and the partitioning of this extended room into two bedrooms in the place of one. Hence the Type B dwelling consists of four rooms, a kitchen, and a bathroom.

Standing at the end of a long access garden, each house was designed with five patios and a service court. Each rectan-

2. Unit house plan (Type B). Because of the central location of the houses and because of their private, single-family character, the courtyard houses are highly prized.
3. Plan and street elevation of one housing block.
4. An entrance court. The entrance garden complex with the side and back courts provides each unit with excellent cross ventilation.
5. The seating alcove, the heart of the Moroccan home, has been placed in the main room.

2

0   5   10m

3

0 5 10   20m

0 10 20m

4

gular lot contains two L-shaped structures comprising the enclosed volume of the house. This allows the double orientation of each living room and bedroom towards gardens or patios. Each unit is surrounded by walls the height of the house itself, so that families can use outdoor areas as private extensions of indoor living space.

The private character of the dwellings is enhanced not only by the high wall surrounding the units, but also by their layout and interior design. One enters the house through the long courtyard leading to a vestibule that leads into the salon or European-style living room, which can be partitioned to create a Moroccan salon with low benches and cushions as well. While one side of this partitioned room is opened to guests, the other may be kept closed. To the right of the vestibule is the kitchen, and on the other side of the kitchen is the traditional Moroccan family room, the focus of family activity. Here meals are served, children play and sleep, and television is usually installed. The other bedroom is for parents or, in Type B, for older children. The design of the house is such that as one moves away from the street and the salon, one moves into the areas of the home devoted to the more intimate aspects of family life.

The physical comfort of each room is assured by the double orientation towards the patios. This orientation provides

6. *A back garden, showing a view of the kitchen door and sitting room window. Each unit is surrounded by walls the height of the house itself so that families can use outdoor areas as private extensions of indoor living space.*

good cross ventilation in warm weather.[3] The amount of sunlight penetrating into the houses' interiors at different times of the year can be controlled by a system of adjustable shutters.

The basic dwelling block is a reinforced concrete frame (poured on site) that meets the rigorous antiseismic codes legislated after the 1960 earthquake. The frame supports a reinforced concrete slab roof. Infill is composed of cement block partitions, wood and metal joinery, and glass. Floors are terrazzo. Walls and ceilings are covered with vinyl paint. With the exception of steel for concrete reinforcement and glass, which were imported, all materials were locally produced.[4] In addition to the use of local materials, the project involved construction by a domestic labour force. The entire project was constructed in a year's time; such a timetable was, of course, related at least in part to the extraordinary circumstances of the destruction of the major portion of the city.

The land on which these houses were built was and is the property of the government, which retains the title to them.[5] Intended for middle-class civil servants, rents are calculated according to income. Because of the central location of the houses and because of their private, single-family character, they are highly prized. It is for this reason, it appears, that the dwellings have been maintained in good condition. The plan has also provided some opportunities for modifying individual dwelling spaces to changing needs. For example, interim living spaces have been made by covering patios, which, though limiting open space and altering patterns of lighting and cross ventilation, has been done in keeping with the character of the houses.

6

SIDI BOU SAID
TUNIS, TUNISIA
ONGOING SINCE 1973

Sidi Bou Said from the southeast.

Simple geometric forms and the use of similar building
materials and colour result in a harmonious townscape.

A view to the sea from the minaret of
the mosque and shrine of Sidi Bou Said.

SIDI BOU SAID. Client: Municipality of Sidi Bou Said, Tunisia. M. Baly, Mayor; Planners: Technical Bureau of the Municipality, Mme. Sanda Popa; Conservator: Abd El-Aziz Ben-Achour.[1]

The conservation of the built environment and of cultural heritage has become particularly important within most countries of the Islamic world where the physical and social landscape has undergone rapid changes in recent decades. The normal decay of the urban fabric has been hastened by the pressures of larger populations and poor services. It has become quite clear that the strategies for restoring and rehabilitating a single building or even a group of buildings are inadequate when applied to a built environment. There must be major administrative decisions enforced through a period of time; there must be a collective will and a viable economic base to preserve and to maintain a special environment.

Sidi Bou Said is such a special environment. On the municipal and the national level decisions have been made to safeguard it. It is a small village perched on a cliff-top site overlooking the Mediterranean. The quality of its narrow streets, lined with whitewashed dwellings and refreshingly planted with trees, shrubs, and vines in many places, is all the more significant due to the minimal intrusion of the twentieth century. The village is located on Cape Carthage, near the classical site of the same name, overlooking the Bay of Carthage. Tunis, the capital city of Tunisia, is situated a short distance to the south.

History. The site of the village has been occupied for thousands of years, as surviving archaeological evidence demonstrates. During the ninth century, under Aghlabid rule, the seacoast of Tunisia was fortified at strategic points, including Cape Carthage. Here on the site of the present village was built a ribat and a lighthouse (*menar*). During the peaceful Hafsid dynasty in the thirteenth and fourteenth centuries the ribat became a Sufi religious centre. Shaikh Abu Saʿid Khala-

1. *Tunis region. Sidi Bou Said was founded as a shrine and pilgrimage town and developed into a place of retreat and resort for the inhabitants of Tunis.*

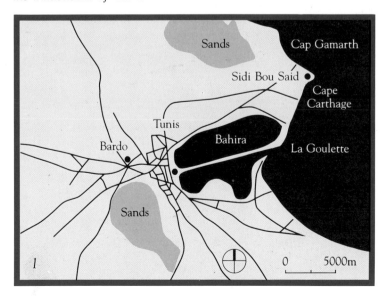

fa b. Yahya al-Tamimi al-Badgi (1156–1231) settled on the site, and his tomb subsequently became a major pilgrimage spot. By the seventeenth century the settlement of Sidi Bou Said (then called Jebel al-Menar, or Jebel al-Marsa) had begun to develop and a marketplace was built, mainly for serving the increasing number of pilgrims.

In the eighteenth century wealthy inhabitants of Tunis, seeking refuge from the city during the hot summer months, discovered the favourable seaside climate. Tunis's political and religious dignitaries, rich artesans and merchants constructed summer residences in the village; some clustered in the immediate vicinity of Abu Sa'id's shrine, others in outlying areas amid large and elaborate gardens. In time a seasonal service population, which operated small shops and stands catering to the summer residents, became established. By the mid-nineteenth century the village was well known both as an important religious center and as a fashionable summer resort.

At the end of the nineteenth century the village was declared a Commune Musulmane and was offically named Sidi Bou Said. At about the same time the village became a year-round intellectual center, and a place of permanent retirement and exile for many foreign artists and intellectuals. Here, far from the censorship of intolerant government, debates were held on poetry and particularly on music. In response to this influx of a more permanent resident population and the physical development that accompanied it, the settlement was officially declared a village in 1915. With this declaration came the first legal efforts to conserve Sidi Bou Said's unique cultural and architectural heritage. The twentieth century has seen the recognition of the outstanding qualities of Sidi Bou Said, recognition which has helped stimulate pride and interest in preserving the essential characteristics of the village. Along with this recognition on the part of residents and scholars there has come a different kind of recognition, largely by the national government, of the village as a major tourist attraction.

Conservation. Throughout this century many important steps have been taken to ensure the continued survival of the historic fabric of Sidi Bou Said. From the first decree of 1915 through the Management Plan of the 1970s the town has set precedents in the Islamic world in establishing guidelines for its preservation.

In the early years of the twentieth century the increasing popularity of Sidi Bou Said threatened the built form and the architectural character of the village. Through the influence of Baron d'Erlanger, a retired banker, a decree was passed in 1915 which was designed to preserve the beauty of the village and to provide guidelines for growth and change. The text outlined policy on the following points in particular: the modification of building facades, and the disposition of public spaces; the character and massing of new buildings; owner obligations regarding repairs and restoration; building permis-

2. Street plan. The village character emerged from the organic growth of dwellings, mixed with shops and other business buildings, keeping the community mosque as the focal point.
3. Current land-use plan. Recent escalation in real estate values, erosion of the village's cliff face, and development pressures accompanying a burgeoning tourist trade threatens the social balance and physical integrity of the community.
4. Partial street elevation leading to the suq.

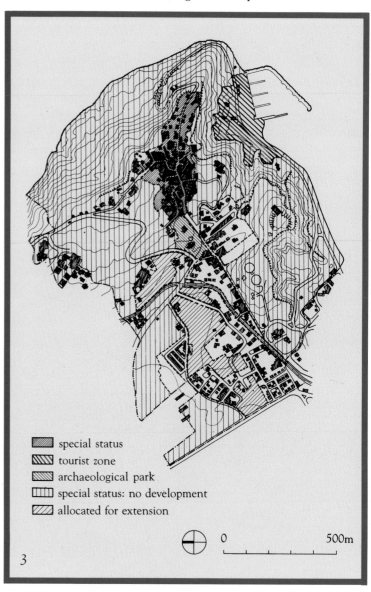

special status
tourist zone
archaeological park
special status: no development
allocated for extension

2

3

sion procedures; and penal measures.

This restrictive approach has been the main legal base for public authorities to control the existing physical structure of the village. Since the institution of the decree, there have been some alterations of facades and some exuberant new buildings; some buildings have deteriorated or been destroyed because of vacancy or lack of maintenance. There have also been some major alterations on a number of old houses.

Until very recently, documents defining the physical structure of the village, such as measured drawings of plans and elevations, and physical checks of registered buildings were not available to the municipality or other public authorities. The rise in the value of land and speculative trends have been major threats to the integrity of the village, increasingly so after the 1950s. The outskirts of the village were invaded by new construction and alterations were made to some of the large old houses. The crucial problem of erosion of the cliff-face could not be dealt with within the limits of the 1915 decree. Finally, the decree had never taken into account social issues such as the impact of tourism or new land uses. These could only be included within a more comprehensive planning policy and not in a restrictive and small scale approach to conservation.

Despite those negative points, one can consider the result of this first conservation phase to be relatively successful. The alterations did not change the scale and structure of the village, and thus the basic morphology and pattern was preserved. Even the new construction generally did not exceed an acceptable massing or othewise overwhelm their neighbors. The municipality tried to exercise control, and users generally maintained their houses and neighborhoods. Also very important to the process has been the fact that there has always been the image of a self-preserved village called Sidi Bou Said.

The decree of 1915 has been updated many times, and has been complemented by further legislation such as the decree of 17th September 1953 (Decret de Protection des Sites). This decree concerns the protection of sites all over Tunisia, placing the case of isolated villages in a wider legal context. This further legislation has had only a slight impact on the existing situation. The need for broader action has always been felt, especially since the 1960s after the rise of mass tourism, the change in the population structure of the village, and the acceleration of the erosion of the cliff, which had already reached the first old structures. Furthermore, it should be kept in mind that Sidi Bou Said is adjacent to the archaeological site of Carthage. The historical, physical, and contemporary contextural relationships and the problems of the two sites could well be brought together, and both conservation plans included in a single programme.

These considerations led to the present conservation project, called Projet du Parc National de Carthage—Sidi Bou Said. In 1973, a first master plan was prepared. This plan has since been developed and was approved in 1978. The responsible authority for the plan was the District of Tunis. The physical layout and drawing was assigned to an architect and all analytical work was done by the district staff. This plan analyses the demographic and social structure of the village, as well as its economic potential, and predicts future development. It defines a perimeter which includes the Sidi Bou Said village, as well as a portion of the archaeological area of Carthage, which remains in the municipality. Furthermore, it takes into account the geological features and their problems, which are integral to the conservation of the site.

The Management Plan proposed five major zones for the village: housing extension zone; existing housing zone, with special statute (the special statute aims at safeguarding and promoting the historical character of the village); green belt zone, for public use (between the preceding two zones), defined within the framework of safeguarding archaeological resources, also dealing with the delicate issues of vehicular and pedestrian traffic, and amenities; tourism zone, linked with all

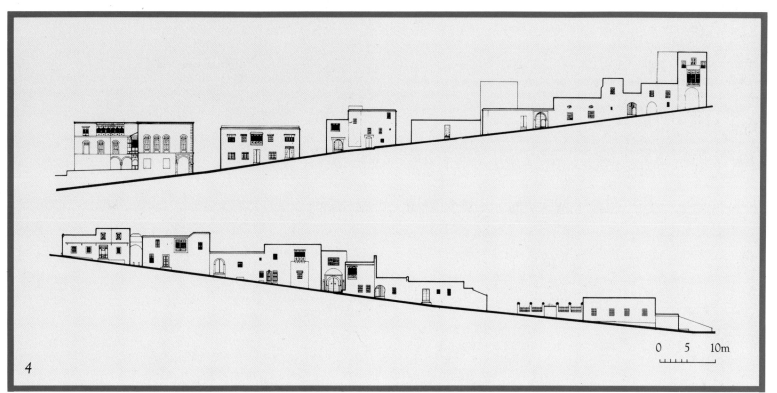

4

0   5   10m

possible uses of the port; and natural park zone, which involves the safeguarding of the site and includes a landscaping program. The implementation and detailed works of the plan were to be completed by the municipality.

In May 1979 a further development occurred when the joint Tunisian government/UNESCO Projet du Parc National de Carthage—Sidi Bou Said was announced. The subject was again the conservation of the sites of Carthage and Sidi Bou Said. The aim of the project was to accomplish all the necessary analytical studies and the plans for the creation of a national park, and to carry out some excavation of archaeological sites and some geotechnical operations for the control and protection of the cliffside areas where erosion was a problem. The municipality of Sidi Bou Said was in charge of carrying out all the physical and social surveys and studies and for supplying all the graphic documents required in the project specifications.

One of the main efforts of the municipal authorities has been the problem of locating parking lots and of limiting vehicular traffic. The present achievement is seen by the authorities as insufficient and incomplete. They also want to be able to return the suq to its original function of local shopping, replacing the present tourist shops. The new portside tourism unit is one way of accomplishing this without removing the tourist trade. The municipality also attempts to restrict alterations on existing houses. With few exceptions they do not issue new building permits within the conservation area; they try to ensure that proposed restoration projects respect the original form and appearance.

Fortunately there is no lack of skilled labour for maintenance, repairs, and restoration work. The traditional skills exist, since the technology of new building in Tunisia has not yet obliterated them with industrialised methods. Even some new houses are built with techniques similar to those used for the traditional houses. Building permission given in new

5. Café des Nattes.
6. View from the café. The café overlooks the suq. Streets, squares, and the semipublic spaces between buildings provide areas for encounter and play.

housing development areas takes into consideration the density, massing, exterior appearance, and relation to the streets of the immediate neighbourhood. Each request to the municipal council gives rise to detailed debate.

Further evidence of the municipality's interest in the conservation of the village was displayed when the electric power lines were placed underground in the 1960s. It is also interesting to note that visitor accommodations in Sidi Bou Said are extremely limited: tourists are welcome to visit the village, but are reminded that it is a living community when they find they cannot spend the night.

The villagers are the real backbone of the conservation effort in Sidi Bou Said. The owners of old houses do not have any financial support for restoration—neither loans nor contributions from national housing organisations or banks. Credit loans can be obtained only from the Caisse Nationale d'Epargne Logement (CNEL) and are restricted to new construction. For restoration, people must go to private banks. The current residents are very concerned about their homes and their village, and are generally conscious of the fine qualities of their surroundings. Combined with the legal measures and the support of the municipality, this social structure is a positive element for the actual conservation process.

Architecture. The importance of the conservation victories in Sidi Bou Said would not be so great and influential if the vernacular buildings of the village did not remain in such im-

107

pressive condition. The architectural fabric of Sidi Bou Said is justly renowned for its authenticity and unity of scale, form, and colour. The village is made up of public space and private enclosures, all representative of Islamic Mediterranean prototypes. The former consist of open squares and narrow, winding streets, the latter of introverted courtyard houses. Houses are generally two storeys high and feature the same general features: whitewashed masonry walls, vaulted and domed roofs, narrow windows with iron trellises, and balconies with wood railings and screens. All exterior woodwork, including

7. Entrance to a private home. 8. Window grill. The twentieth century has seen the recognition of the outstanding qualities of Sidi Bou Said, recognition that has stimulated legislation and financial assistance for preserving the essential characteristics of the community. However, the pride and interest of villagers are the strongest forces behind the conservation effort.

doors, window frames and lattices, are painted sky blue. Many portals are outlined in ochre, and wall corners are frequently curved and adorned with ceramic tiles. Despite the different origins of some of these elements, the integrity of the whole is apparent. Both the elegant and the modest houses, and also the mosque, are in perfect scale. The simple geometric masonry forms and the use of similar building materials and colours result in a harmonious village architecture. There are ingenious solutions for some types of urban elements such as the public seats in front of some houses that are perfectly integrated with the masonry of the exterior wall, or the refined iron work of the street lamps.

Taken together, the humble streetscapes and carefully detailed houses create a characteristic picture of a traditional urban community, a picture particularly demanding of careful conservation and protection in the late-twentieth century.

The preservation of Sidi Bou Said is of widespread importance and has come about by the efforts of both residents of the village and of public authorities. The physical and architectural value of the houses, monuments, and townscapes, as well as the high spiritual and symbolic significance related to the history of the village, gives it a continuing interest and makes the care and attention given to its conservation eminently worthwhile.

Sidi Bou Said is a unique example of self-preservation which should be a prime example in promoting and encouraging initiative in other Islamic countries and in similar small-scale participatory programmes of conservation.

HALAWA HOUSE
AGAMY, EGYPT
COMPLETED APRIL, 1975

Massing of living room, bedroom,
belvedere, and sitting room.

Courtyard. Architectural elements, traditional
in Egypt, incorporated into the courtyard
include: fountain, *liwan,* and *mashrabiyya.*

HALAWA HOUSE. Client: Esmat Ahmed Halawa;
Architect: Abdel-Wahed El-Wakil; Master Mason: Aladdin
Mustafa; Plasterer: Mu'allim Attiyah; Carpenter: Hassan El-
Naggar.[1]

The Halawa house is located in Agamy, a seaside town in
Egypt, near Alexandria. With miles of sandy beach and cooling sea breezes, Agamy offers a splendid natural setting for a
summer resort.[2] Its main coast road is the locus of commercial
activity, while the area between the main road and the beach
has been divided into plots set in a grid of sandy roads. The
town has developed gradually since the 1940s, and now few
unbuilt plots remain. The first homes built in Agamy were
bungalows of rough stone masonry with low pitched roofs.
Most homes now have flat roofs and reinforced concrete
frames, with concrete-block infill. The interiors of typical
homes are hot, and the exteriors, especially when damaged by
the climate, are generally unattractive.[3]

The Halawa house sits on a narrow plot, bordered on three
sides by sandy roadways and on one side by two other plots,
one of which is being redeveloped. Between the site and the
beach is a single-storey house. Design of the Halawa house
began in 1972 with the client's desire for a secluded resort
environment. The project's architect, Abdel Wahed El-Wakil, added to that desire his concern for developing a contemporary architecture based on traditional forms and indigenous
materials. The architect states that the house was "a long
awaited opportunity to realise the study and research I was
undertaking in vernacular architecture . . . showing the external aspect and inner significance of traditional architectural heritage and its use in contemporary design."[4] The result is
an imaginative design, highly successful structurally, climati-
cally, and functionally.

*1. Agamy, Egypt. Agamy is a summer resort on the Mediterrane-
an near the port of Alexandria. This coastal town has been a popular summer retreat for many decades.*

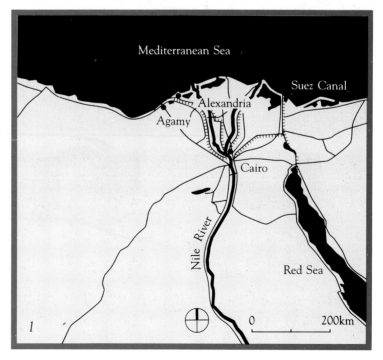

Spatial Design. The narrowness of the plot on which the house is built could have been a major disadvantage, particularly when combined with the building code restrictions (one-third plot ratio, 5.5 metres maximum height, and 2.5 metres setback from neighbouring houses). By skillful development of a courtyard design, these constraints have been turned to advantages. Neither the courtyard nor the vaulted loggia has been included in the calculation of the plot ratio. Yet the courtyard has become the focus of all activities within the house, as well as having provided for their basic segregation and guaranteeing privacy from the outside world.

The two-storey house is built around three sides (north, east, south) of the open courtyard. On the ground floor on the north side is a beach entrance leading to the living area, which is paved in marble and includes an alcove (*liwan*) and a fireplace. A vaulted loggia with wind catcher and a guest bedroom and bathroom are also on the ground floor's north side. On the east side of the house are the work yard, kitchen, and servant's quarters (bedroom with bath). The servant's quarters open into the backyard and the kitchen is conveniently positioned between the work yard and courtyard. To the south are a double garage and a storage area. There is also a terrace with a small garden within the boundary wall.

Open stairs lead up from the south side of the courtyard to a loggia on the first level. This is the entrance to a pair of

bedrooms with shared bathroom above the garage. A belvedere (*maq'ad*) overlooking the beach leads to the master bedroom. Beyond the master bedroom is a private terrace. Beside the master bedroom door and at the top of the stairs is a ladder giving access to the flat roof above the master bedroom, with a low parapet around it and a bench constructed against the barrel vault for sunbathing and viewing.

The articulation of space throughout the building is handled with great sensitivity. There are no awkward transitions. On the contrary, the eye (and foot) is led on by a series of "invitations": a canted corner, where one turns from the entrance lobby towards the courtyard, another where the stairs turn towards the belvedere. Similarly the perspective of the

2. View into the courtyard. The circulation zone around the courtyard connects bedrooms and services.

3. Vaulted sitting room with courtyard beyond.

4. Sitting area of master bedroom. Features of traditional craftsmanship include: a built-in cupboard, typical for Cairene homes; mashrabiyya screens on windows; and a ceiling of wood beams and battens, which is very effective insulation.

courtyard from the living area is framed by a pair of arches, the further of which is displaced slightly to the right of the nearer. The same attention to detail has also gone into the handling of changes of level in the paving of the courtyard, stairs, and belvedere. A flight of eight steps leads from the courtyard to a half landing (still visually within the courtyard), then five more steps to the first floor. On the left is a parapet (the first), on the right two bedrooms one step higher and under the archway (symbolic threshold). Further steps announced by a rising plane in the passageway beckon to the left, into the belvedere. A final farewell to the courtyard,

three more steps and a half turn to the left lead at last to the door of the master bedroom. All of this, done in such a natural manner that its essential theatricality is hardly apparent.

The Use of Tradition.   Agamy, formerly part of the local bedouin territory, did not have an indigenous architectural tradition on which El-Wakil could draw. Hence, the architect sought another Egyptian tradition, not specifically identified with this region, in which he could work and whose idioms he could use in order to create a suitable style.

The technological basis of the design is the ancient Upper Egyptian tradition of masonry construction. Made of undressed local limestone, burnt red brick, and mud mortar, the closely set bearing walls are opened with arches and spanned with barrel vaults and domes. Masonry renderings, inside and out, consisted of three coats of traditional sand-lime plaster

5. Transverse and longitudinal sections, ground and first floor plans. In the Halawa house, the timeless art of the mason and carpenter articulates spaces designed with great sensitivity, endowing the architecture with a profound beauty.

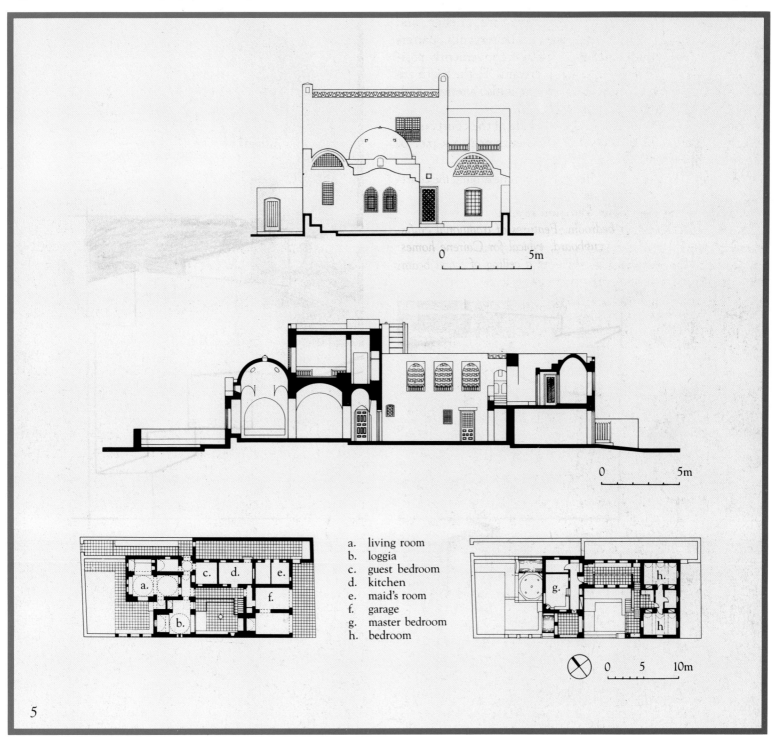

a. living room
b. loggia
c. guest bedroom
d. kitchen
e. maid's room
f. garage
g. master bedroom
h. bedroom

5

known as Alexandrine plaster.[5] Innovative to the tradition is
the use of reinforced concrete for footings. A concrete slab
was used over the kitchen and garage, where flat undecorated
ceilings were called for, but not over the master bedroom,
where it would have provided insufficient insulation. (This
insulation was provided by a ceiling of treated wooden beams
and battens with a special layered composition.)[6]

The project's master mason, Aladdin Mustafa, who had
participated in building the village of New Gourna using mud-
brick construction methods, taught local unskilled labourers
to construct vaults and arches using the inclined vault system,

6. *Masonry construction. The technological basis of the Halawa
house is the ancient Upper Egyptian tradition of masonry construction. Clockwise from right top: a) Walls were laid with rubble masonry followed by the springing of the major arches. b) The walls of
the first level are capped with a variety of superstructures: concrete
slabs on the right, vaulting on the left. c) Master mason Aladdin
Mustafa constructing an inclined barrel vault. d) The house before
a rendering of Alexandrine plaster was applied.*

6a

6b

6d

6c

which requires no shuttering. Together with the plasterer and the carpenter, both skilled Egyptian craftsmen, the house took form with many traditional features: an octagonal fountain in the courtyard; the loggia *(takhtabush)* and wind catcher *(malqaf)*; the alcoves *(liwan)*; masonry benches *(mastaba)*; the belvedere *(maq'ad)*; the oblique entrances; and architectural decoration (windows with patterned brick claustra, *mashrabiyya*, and stained glass; woodwork; tiles; and brass lamps and door handles).

The architect's stated goal of using traditional forms and indigenous materials cannot be seen as an imposition of out-

7. Mashrabiyya screen. The craft of wood turning and carpentry is revealed in all the screens in the house.
8. South facade detail. The window is closed by a heavy wood shutter with small openings for ventilation. The claustra in the vault above assure a continuous flow of air.
9. Living room windows soften the light from the courtyard.

dated designs and means, but rather as a solution to some of the problems imposed by climate, town plan, and typical house structure in Agamy. The traditional Islamic feature of the courtyard with a fountain in it, for example, serves practical as well as aesthetic purposes. By orienting the house to catch the sea breeze and by providing an open courtyard, the architect has provided a physically comfortable and private area that dispenses with the need for circulation corridors and hence serves as the centre of activity for the whole house. The courtyard is particularly comfortable because it lies in partial shade and draws fresh air down through the wind catcher. It is paved with Muqattam sandstone, noted for its thermal properties, on which one can walk in bare feet even in the height of summer.

The traditional forms and materials similarly answer the demands for a sense of privacy, openness, and comfort. Marble floors keep the living areas cool. The circulation of air, enhanced by the wind catchers and the courtyard, obviates the need for air conditioning. Because most seating and cupboards are built in, the house seems to be larger than it actually is. The wall and roof structures give good insulation, and the rendering withstands the effects of the climate better than standard gypsum cement plaster, which would have required annual repainting. The play of light on the structures, created by the filtering of light of varying intensities through *mashrabiyya*, eliminates the need for extensive decoration.

RUSTEM PASHA CARAVANSERAI
EDIRNE, TURKEY
COMPLETED AUGUST, 1972

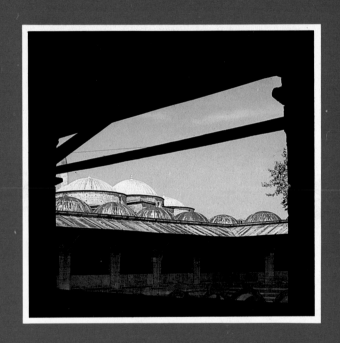

The public facade contrasts with the
serenity of the inner courtyards.

The main courtyard has been transformed
into a garden for the new hotel.

RUSTEM PASHA CARAVANSERAI. Client: Department of Pious Foundations, Turkey, Fikret Cuhadaroğlu, Director; Mehmet Ozturk, Regional Director; Architect for Restoration: Ertan Cakirlar.[1]

Among the largest owners of urban properties in the Islamic world are ministries or departments of pious foundations. Individual buildings with social and religious functions—such as mosques, schools, and hospitals—or ones that produced incomes, were part of private pious foundations. In many countries, they have been assigned to government agencies for administration and maintenance. Thus, these bureaus control much of the older urban fabric and have the potential to change or preserve it through programmes of restoration and rehabilitation.

Caravanserai, whether located along old trading routes or in urban centres, are typical pious foundation properties which have fallen into disuse and ruin. Such was the state of the Rustem Pasha Caravanserai when, in 1966, the Turkish Department of Pious Foundations sought first to restore the monument, and subsequently to revitalise its function as a lodging for travellers.

The Rustem Pasha Caravanserai is located in the historic centre of Edirne. Sited on the main land route between Europe and Asia, Edirne had been capital of the Ottoman Empire for a short time in the fifteenth century and continued to be the key military and commercial centre of the European provinces. In the 1560s, one of the Grand Vezirs, Rustem Pasha, commissioned the eminent court architect Mimar Koca Sinan to design the caravanserai at Edirne. Sinan designed the building surrounding the great rectangular courtyard with

1. Edirne was an early capital of the Ottoman Empire, retaining its importance as a military and trading centre throughout the empire's history. The caravanserai was part of a pious foundation complex funded by Rustem Pasha.

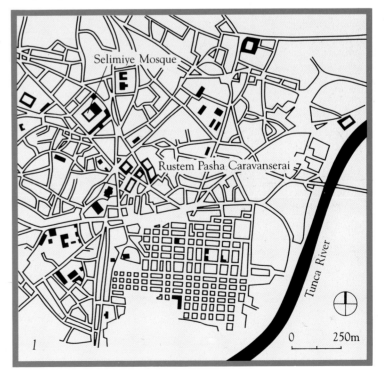

its marble basin in the centre. (The secondary court was added later; its architect is unknown.) The spaciousness of Sinan's quadrangle reflects the ample dimensions of the whole, as do the galleries which offered vistas to the traveller seeking the seclusion of his cell. Walls were built in alternating courses of stone and brick. Sinan's circular arches in the lower range facing the vaulted structure are broad in span, as are the pointed arches of the second level's domical structure. Between each arch was placed a sandstone balustrade carved with bold traditional motifs. From the street, the main facade turns back slightly where the two quadrangles join, and this gives an added sense of size. Seen from the back, the caravanserai's massing is monumental, for the land drops and there is an expanse of bare wall rising from the valley below before the tiers of windows and the crowning batteries of domes and chimneys are reached.

Before reconstruction began, many of the building's walls, vaults, and domes had collapsed. Using measurements taken from the ruins as a guide, walls and vaults at the ground level were consolidated with concrete used as infill. Vaults were further strengthened with concrete beams. The domes of the upper level were reconstructed with concrete and supported by concrete beams. Rubber sheets, far less expensive than the original lead coating, were used to cover the roofs. The stone, ceramic tile, and marble used in reconstruction were local and were worked by local craftsmen. Three years after reconstruction began, the Department of Pious Foundations decided to complete the project by adapting the building to serve as a hotel capable of catering to the area's tourist trade. Thus the

2. *Plan and section of the Rustem Pasha Caravanserai.*
3. *Domes prior to restoration. Built as an income-producing facility for the pious foundation, the caravanserai had fallen into disuse and disrepair over the past century.*
4. *Restored domes. Restoration entailed the repair and rebuilding of all major roof structures. After structural restoration, work began to adapt the facility to a tourist hotel in an effort to reactivate its economic functions.*
5. *Typical guest room. Features of domestic architecture traditional to the Edirne area, the fireplace form, wood furnishings, and tiled floors were incorporated into the restored caravanserai.*
6. *Caravanserai shop front. Further economic support for the hotel complex was foreseen by the Department of Pious Foundations through the renovation and rental of the original shop stalls.*

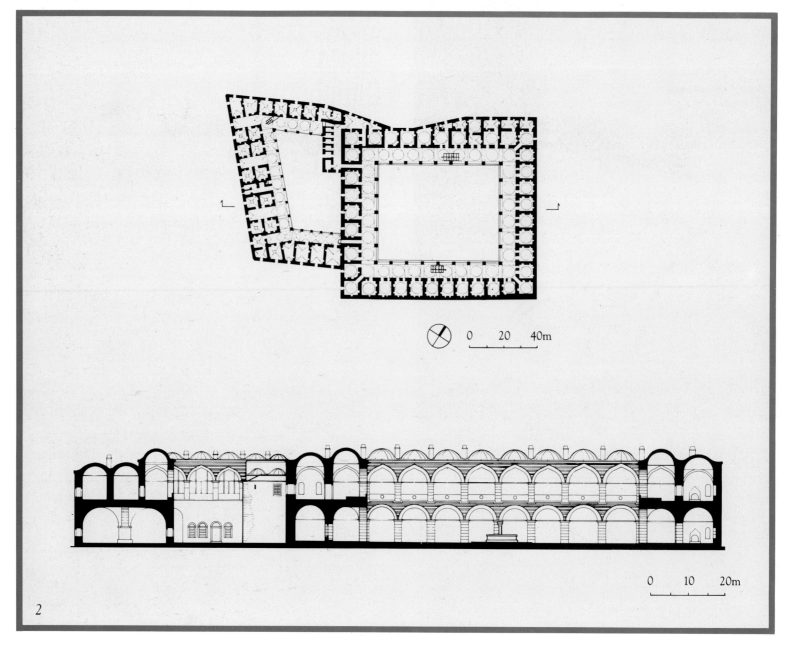

2

rooms on the second floor of the small court and both floors of the large court were redesigned and half the rooms on the upper level were serviced with connecting baths. A restaurant, cafeteria, and bar, with separate entrances from the street, were designed for the ground level in the small court (these rooms occupying the space formerly used as camel stables and an imaret). Wood finishes and furniture inspired by traditional Turkish styles were manufactured in Ankara for the hotel. Shops fronting the caravanserai were restored and once again leased to merchants.

The Department of Pious Foundations' undertaking at the Rustem Pasha Caravanserai was ambitious. Looking beyond the preservation of a major architectural monument in converting the structure into a hotel, the Department sought to reactivate the facility and, in so doing, generate an income sufficient to maintain the building. The caravanserai's tourist trade has not as yet reached projected levels, thus preventing the facility from achieving economic self-sufficiency. However, the reconstruction and programmatic concept of the project are sound and worthy of consideration as an approach to national programmes of preservation.

ERTEGÜN HOUSE
BODRUM, TURKEY
COMPLETED OCTOBER, 1973

Patio with the newly added living room beyond.

Living room. The old *selamlik* with its
fireplace, stylistically typical to the region, has
been integrated into the new living room.

Harbour elevation. The street facades of the
nineteenth century Salih Efendi Konak
were retained in the 1973 restoration.

ERTEGÜN HOUSE. Clients: Ahmet and Mica Ertegün; Architect: Turgut Cansever; Carpenter: Cemil Ormanlar.[1]

The approach to Bodrum should be by sea. The town wraps itself around the sheltered crescent-shaped harbour of this Aegean port located on the southwestern coast of Turkey, opposite the Greek island of Kos. The hills of the Belen and Tirmar ranges encircle the town, rising to a height of over 600 metres, and the area is green with lemon, tangerine, and olive trees that thrive in the lime-rich soil and mild climate.

Bodrum is an ancient port, Halicarnassus, and the site of the fourth-century B.C.E. mausoleum, one of the wonders of the ancient world. There can still be found many remains of Bodrum's Hellenistic prominence, among them the ruins of the amphitheatre, carved into the hill above the harbour. Bodrum continued to flourish in medieval times, as is evidenced by the spectacular fifteenth-century crusader fortress of St. Peter, built by the Knights of St. John, which today still dominates the harbour entrance. During the first centuries of Ottoman rule, Bodrum became a backwater and seems to have lost most of its population. The famous Turkish traveller Evliya Celebi, visiting Bodrum in the early eighteenth century, noted that it was mostly fields and vineyards, overlooked by the castle. The Ottoman development began with the establishment of an arsenal in the 1720s. What is today called traditional Bodrum is in fact a nineteenth-century town, with separate Turkish and Greek neighbourhoods and with the konaks (mansions) of the elite lining the shore.[2]

The economic base of Bodrum in the last century has been fishing and citrus fruit growing, with the navy arsenal activities a new addition. Today the traditional farming and fishing are giving way to a burgeoning tourism industry. The permanent population of 7000 swells with the seasonal influx

1. Bodrum, Turkey. The Ertegün house sits on the north shore of the circular bay and faces the crusader fortress of St. Peter.
The Ertegün house is an imaginative conservation of two seaside houses demonstrating that new structures can indeed be sympathetically added to the old, without resorting to direct imitation.

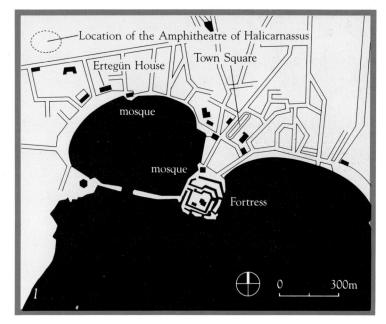

of visitors, and it is yachts, not fishing boats, that fill the harbour.

The Salih Efendi Konak.   In 1971 Ahmet and Mica Ertegün purchased a konak with the idea of using it as a seasonal residence, primarily in the summer and early autumn. The house sits on the north shore of the circular bay and faces south to the harbour. The original house consisted of two double-storey wings joined by a single-storey entrance, and is thought to date from the early nineteenth century.[3] It was a white-washed masonry structure built of the typical uncut, heavily mortared stone, with a private walled garden behind it. The house was known as the Salih Efendi konak and had once been the home of the local Aga.[4] The two-part division of the house is characteristic of Turkish domestic architecture: to one side would have been the men's quarters, used for recep-

tions (*selamlik*); to the other side, the women's quarters (*haremlik*). There is speculation that the house was initially built by two brothers, a separate house for each brother and his family, with a shared entrance between. The separation of male and female would have been made within each house. While the house is similar in type to others in the area, it is larger and seems to have been built according to a higher standard than its neighbours'.

At the time the Ertegüns purchased the konak it was in a general state of ruin. Because of the need for additional space, the Ertegüns also purchased a small adjoining two-storey house. In the autumn of 1971 Turgut Cansever was selected as

2. Roof terrace. The resort house's roof terrace commands an impressive view of the hills, town, and harbour. Restoration of the house has spurred other conservation efforts in Bodrum where many traditional houses are in danger of being lost.
3. Partial garden elevation. The restoration retained the existing structure (the old portal shown here) and extended it with an addition designed in a contemporary idiom.
4. Plan of house and garden, garden elevation. The large private garden, surrounded by a high masonry wall, was once an orchard. It is dense with orange, lemon, and pine trees, flowering oleander and potted geraniums.

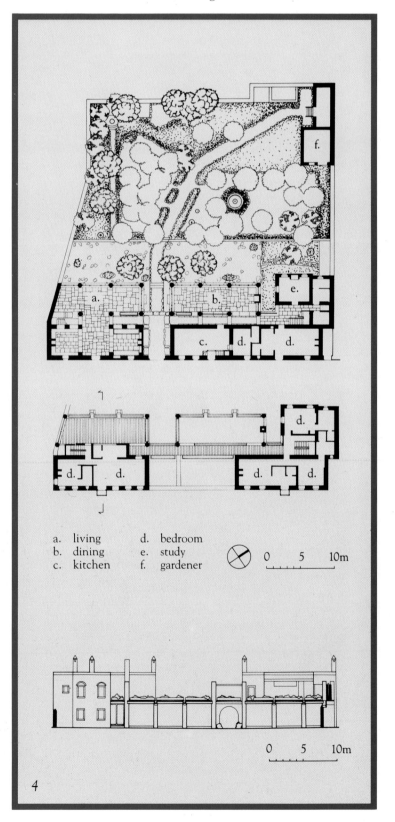

a. living   d. bedroom
b. dining   e. study
c. kitchen   f. gardener

0   5   10m

0   5   10m

the architect. From the outset, the architect and clients hoped that the restoration of the Salih Efendi konak would become a model for conservation efforts in Bodrum, where many of the traditional houses were in danger of being lost.

The Programme. The project entailed reconstructing and renovating the original house and expanding the living space with the addition of two rooms along the garden side.

The plan is organised into three linear bands: the two wings of the existing house stretching along the street; the single-storey addition, which joins the two wings along the garden side; and the large garden with its surrounding masonry wall. The addition is clearly distinguished from the existing house by its structure. The reconstructed portions are of thick masonry bearing walls with small openings; the new structure is a concrete frame, with round columns and wood infill. While shunning mere imitation, the new structure parallels the old, and there is a consistent simplicity of spatial organisation and a concern for craft.

The entrance to the house through a central gate leads from the bright street into a shaded entryway and through a covered passage north to the garden beyond. From either side of the covered entry, a shallow ramp rises into each wing of the house, slipping between the separate structures of the old and new sections of the house. To the right, in the older portion along the street, lie the kitchen (with basement area below), service areas, and a guest room. At the far end, facing the garden, is a library in what was once a separate house. Opening onto the garden is the new large dining area.

To the left of the entry is the large living room. The north wall of the existing house was opened by creating masonry

5. The new structure parallels the old, and there is a consistent simplicity of spatial organisation and concern for craft.

piers out of the bearing wall, unifying into a single large space the old reception room and the new room added at the garden side. The oak shutters of both the living and dining areas can be completely raised, further opening those spaces onto the garden, and expanding the house to the rear garden wall.

At the upper level, the east wing functions as a guest wing, with three bedrooms, each with a bath. The west wing contains the master bedroom, dressing room, and two baths. The roofs of the living and dining areas serve as terraces overlooking the garden. The four columns that project above the terraces at the entryway are intended to support the beams of an as yet to be completed pergola. The pergola, often found in traditional Turkish houses, is to be covered with native bougainvillaea. The roof of the original west wing of the house has also become a terrace, with views of the harbour, mosque, citadel, and surrounding hills.

The large private garden, surrounded by a high masonry wall, was once an orchard. It is dense with orange, lemon, and pine trees, flowering oleander, and potted geraniums. The living and dining areas open onto a large terrace, shaded by pine trees, paved with small pebbles set in concrete, and enclosed by a low wall. The stone walkway, which begins at the entrance, crosses the terrace and leads to the orchard beyond. The walk beneath the lemon and orange trees is also paved, here with rubble cobblestones. The walkway continues on a diagonal to the gardener's cottage, built into the garden wall in the far northeast corner of the garden. This masonry cottage, also designed by Cansever, has three rooms, plus a laundry that serves the main house.

A number of antique remains are found throughout the garden, informal reminders of the property's past. A small round fountain beneath the fruit trees and opposite the dining area is a recent addition. The construction of a *hamam* (Turkish bath) is being considered.

Tradition of Craft. Rich finishes, all Turkish in origin and all finely crafted, are used throughout the house.[5] The architect has consciously juxtaposed materials: precisely crafted wood-work contrasts with simple whitewashed stucco, and the crisp surfaces of the marble floors are in deliberate contrast to the rough pebble paving.

High-quality Turkish oak was used for the window frames, doors, cupboards, and shutters. The shutters, modelled on traditional forms, were designed by the architect and, like all the

wood cabinetry, were crafted in Istanbul. Most of the walls and ceilings in the older portions of the house are whitewashed stucco. However, black pine, readily available in the Bodrum area, covers the ceilings in the bedrooms. Walls in the baths are finished with Turkish marble and ceramic tile. The tiles, patterned after traditional Turkish tiles, were produced in the Kutahya ceramics factory, which once manufactured ceramic ware for the Ottoman sultans. Floors of the upper-level bedrooms are finished with oak. Cobblestones and pebbles set in concrete are used in the entryway, in the circulation areas, and throughout the garden. Young teenagers from Bodrum designed and installed the pebble paving.

In selecting furnishings for the house, the client also emphasised the richness of Turkish crafts: Mica Ertegün chose handwoven Turkish cottons, kilims, straw mats, and eighteenth-century Edirne trays, all acquired in the bazaars of Bodrum or Istanbul.

6. *East elevation and transverse section. The original bearing-wall structure was extended with a room defined by concrete piers.*
7. *Dining area. The high standard of available craftsmanship was appreciated by the architect in designing "sail-like" oak shutters, crafted by carpenter Cemil Ormanlar. The shutters open and close to adjust the light and movement of air. When open, they visually extend the interior into the garden.*
8. *Master bedroom. Textiles and furnishings throughout the house were produced in the region, and selected and arranged by Mica Ertegün.*
9. *Ground floor. The three zones of the ground floor—old enclosure, circulation, and recent addition—are clearly distinguished by the load-bearing structure.*

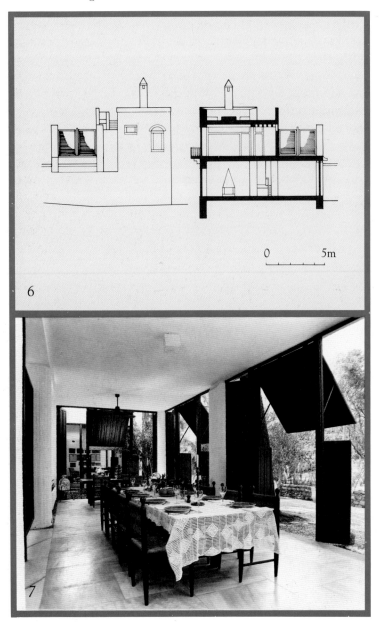

0   5m

Rebuilding and New Building.   Construction on the project began in April of 1972. However, the existing houses were in serious disrepair: the facades of the east wing had been severely altered, the walls of the west block were in ruins, and the roofs of both were in poor condition. It proved necessary first to rase substantial portions of the existing structures, then to strengthen the foundations, and to rebuild the masonry walls, reusing the old stones. Work began with the complete reconstruction of the floors, roofs, and oak balconies of the existing house. The new reinforced-concrete structure was then poured under careful supervision in order to assure quality.

The construction progressed slowly. Many of the workers were farmers from the Bodrum area or from Anatolian villages. They were able to work only when their farming activities permitted. (Around Bodrum, September is the month of the main harvest, while olives are harvested from October to January, and oranges and tangerines in the early spring.) As the building schedule had to be adjusted to these seasonal fluctuations, construction was not completed until October 1973.

10. Garden detail. Antique fragments, original to the site, have been incorporated into the garden. Here, an Ottoman fountain is set within the wall.
11. Exterior wall. Characteristic Bodrum masonry, heavily mortared and whitewashed, has been restored on the street facade.

10

Climate Control.   Winter in Bodrum is mild and wet; frosts are rare, and the temperature in January reaches an average high of 12.8° C. The rainy season extends from October through March, accounting for almost all the 65 centimetres of annual rainfall. Summer, however, when the house is in use, is dry. Temperatures in July range on average from a low of 20.6° C. to a high of 33.3° C., becoming more moderate by September. During these summer months the prevailing wind is the *lodos,* from the southeast, off the Aegean.[6]

The house is designed, according to the architect, "to open or close according to the time of day, or the season of year." All openings are provided with adjustable shutters which filter light and air. The thick south-facing masonry wall with its small openings minimises the heat gain during the warm summer days, and cooling is provided by cross ventilation. (Only the guest bedrooms have been provided with backup electrical air-conditioning units.) During the day, the living and dining areas can be completely opened, and activity shifted to the cool, shaded garden to the north. In the evening, the activity moves to the roof terrace overlooking the harbour. Heating, when required, is provided by Ottoman conical-shaped fireplaces in the living and dining areas and in three of the bedrooms.

Conservation Effort.   The reconstruction of the Salih Efendi konak is credited with spurring an interest in conservation in old Bodrum. In 1979, with financial support from the Ministry of Cultural Affairs, a study of restoration needs in the area was undertaken.[7] A restoration cooperative was formed. The restoration effort began in earnest in 1982 and will be financed jointly by the individual owners and the Bank of Tourism of Turkey. Further financial assistance to fund the infrastructure is being sought. The restoration effort will also include new infill construction, the rehabilitation of urban spaces, and the development of the tourism capacity, all to be undertaken with the hope of bringing new activity to old Bodrum. The Ertegün house sets an example for both Bodrum and other cities of a way in which old can accommodate change, and new respect the existing.

TURKISH HISTORICAL SOCIETY
ANKARA, TURKEY
COMPLETED OCTOBER, 1966

Entrance view. The overall impression is one of
texture, precision, and craft achieved by
drawing on local materials and construction skills.

Oak window screens on entrance facade.

Atrium. Light fills the central court, constantly changing its
spatial character with the time of day and season.

TURKISH HISTORICAL SOCIETY. Client: Türk Tarih Kürümü, Uluğ Iğdemir, Director; Architect: Turgut Cansever; Ertur Yener, Assistant.[1]

Ankara is a capital of the twentieth century. Although communal life there dates from prehistoric times and although it was a sizable town in the classical and medieval periods, it remained a small provincial center until the founding of the new Turkish Republic by Kemal Atatürk. He wanted to start anew, away from Istanbul, the centre of the Ottoman Empire. Named the capital in 1923, Ankara, in the heart of Anatolia, became the focus of the new Turkish national identity. The compact old city clustered around the citadel began a south-easterly expansion. The narrow winding streets and mud-brick homes which had characterised the old town gave way to the broad avenues and flat-roofed concrete apartment blocks, government offices, and embassies of the Yenişehir area to the south. Other residential and business areas now extend farther south, culminating in the Çankaya district that houses the presidential palace.

A central area of Ankara designated the cultural zone, contains the various faculties of Ankara University, several museums, and other cultural institutions. The Turkish Historical Society is sited in this zone, on a corner plot adjacent to the Faculty of Letters, from which it draws most of its membership.

Background. The Turkish Historical Society (Türk Tarih Kürümü) is a research organisation founded in the 1930s by Kemal Atatürk for the purpose of promoting research on the history of Turkey and the Turkish people. Although limited in

1. The Turkish Historical Society is located within the administrative and academic district of Ankara.

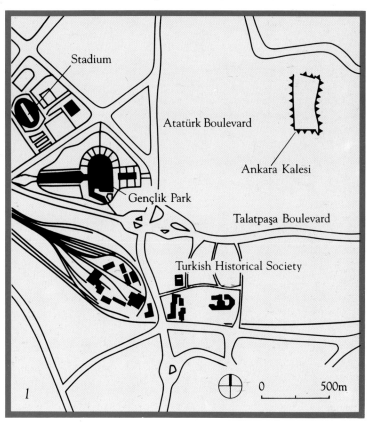

membership, it serves not only members of the society, but also faculty members of the neighbouring universities, researchers and doctoral candidates, and the interested public. From its founding until 1966, the society was housed in two large halls and three rooms in the Faculty of Letters of the University. In 1951 an annex was built near the Faculty of Letters to be used for the society's library and for printing facilities for the society's scholarly publication, *Belleten*. That same year, 1951, the society selected the architect Turgut Cansever to conduct preliminary studies on a proposed new structure to serve as the home of the society. Acting upon these studies, the society in 1960 commissioned Cansever to design the building. He was joined by the young architect Ertur Yener during design development and the subsequent implementation. Construction began in 1962 upon completion of the design, and was realised in 1966.[2]

A Contemporary Madrasa. Cansever was concerned with the prevalence of Western architecture that accompanied postwar development in Ankara. While he did not wish to reject every element of this international architecture and its associated technology, he sought to adapt the architecture and technology to the culture of the region in which he built. For Cansever it meant translating the Islamic ideals of interiority and unity into a contemporary idiom. He incorporated features of plan and layout of earlier Turkish architecture and through a modern technology adapted these features to a new use. The madrasa served as a model in the planning of the Turkish Historical Society building. The madrasa, a residen-

2. Section through entrance, ground-level and first-level floor plans. The central atrium maintains axiality and geometry in the layout and unites public and private spaces.

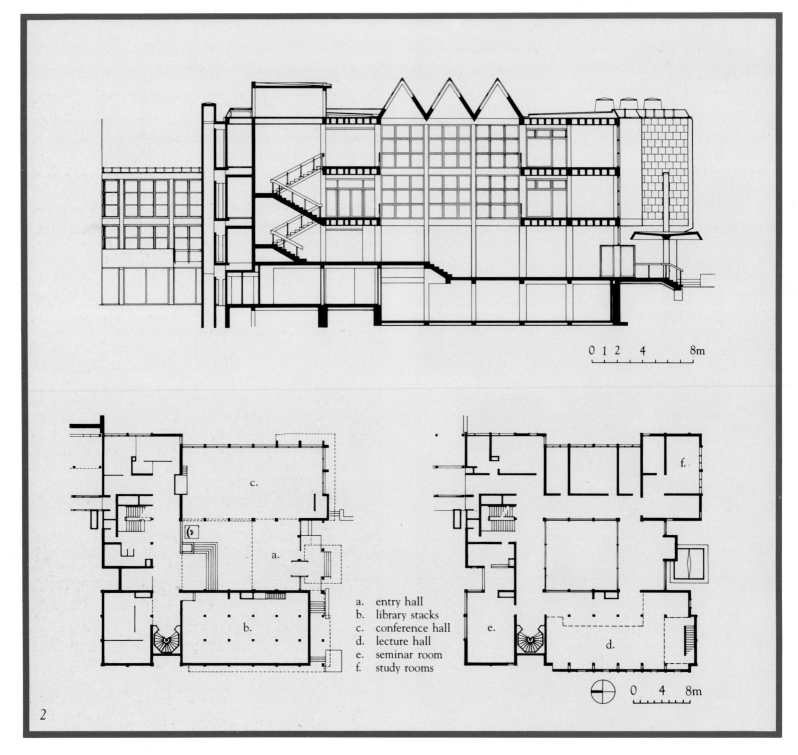

0 1 2 4 8m

a. entry hall
b. library stacks
c. conference hall
d. lecture hall
e. seminar room
f. study rooms

0 4 8m

2

tial college for the study of Islamic law, was typically at two-storey structure surrounding an inner court which was open or was lit from above. Medieval Seljuk examples, which are numerous in Anatolia, seem to have provided ample inspiration. The design for the Turkish Historical Society adapted the inward character of the madrasa, arranging the building spaces around a skylit central court which serves as the focus of all activity.

Programme. The massing of the building suggests the organisation of functions inside: separate volumes for the meeting rooms, library, and administration space.

The building is set back from the street, and entrance is through a central portico into the main hall. There the central atrium rises the full three levels of the building and is covered with a skylight. To the right, opening off the court, there is a large meeting room and to the left are the library stacks. A series of wide steps leads to the administrative of-

fices and service areas along the rear of the building.

The organisation of functions remains the same on the upper levels, although the activities are increasingly less public. Circulation is always around the open atrium. At the first level, above the meeting room, are small conference rooms and offices, and above the stacks, the double-storey library reading room with balcony. Above the entrance, and overlooking the atrium space, is an informal sitting area. The area repeats at the second-level, separating the main conference room and the entrance to the reading room balcony. The remainder of the space serves as offices.

Connected to the building by a hall is the previously existing annex, now a printing and storage facility, which defines the rear of the site. It is separated from the new building by a U-shaped courtyard.

3. Wall section and elevation. Reinforced concrete, red Ankara stone, and aluminium frame windows are juxtaposed to emphasise the quality of each.
4. Detail of west facade. The roofline and deeply set windows stress the bastion-like image of the building.

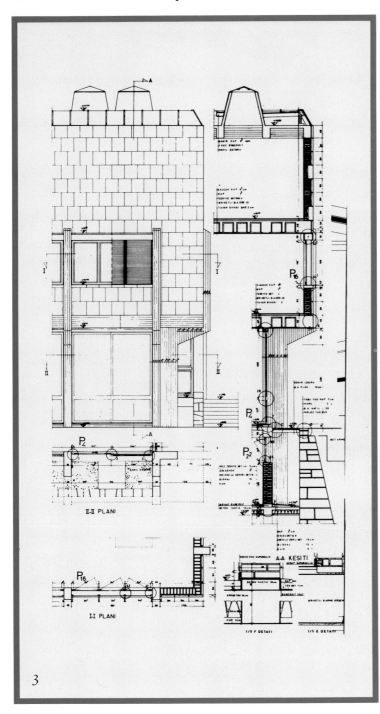
3

4

Light and Air. Natural light is brought into the building in varying ways, and is carefully controlled to emphasise the public character of the central space and the more intimate qualities of the adjoining spaces. Light fills the central court, with shafts of sunlight entering through three large skylights, changing in character with the time of day and season. Oak screens *(kafess)* filter light in the more private spaces outside offices and in the sitting areas. In the library reading room, reflected north light enters from above through six skylight monitors, and at table level through a few small deeply set windows. In the second-level conference room, light enters through eight skylights set in the concrete waffle ceiling and dramatically illuminates the interior.

All exterior windows are provided with adjustable awning screens except at the ground level, where they are protected by overhangs. Where appropriate, artificial light is used, such as at desk level in the reading room. Natural light in the book stacks is kept to a minimum in order to protect the volumes from damage. The cylindrical hanging light fixtures which are used throughout the building were designed by the architects.

The entire building is heated and cooled mechanically.

5. *Balcony overlooking atrium.*
6. *Council room. Located on the second level above all public functions, the room is skylit through a waffle slab ceiling.*
7. *Reading room of the library. At night the room is lit by fixtures designed by the architect. During the day reflected north light enters through six skylight monitors above, and at table level through small, deeply set windows.*

149

This provides the control of temperature and humidity levels necessary to assure the preservation of the valuable library materials. At the same time, it permits the introduction of generous amounts of natural light through the skylights and windows.

Structure and Materials. The structure is a reinforced-concrete frame, with columns supporting waffle slabs. The high quality of the poured-in-place concrete work can be readily seen. Of equally high quality are the infill materials, all clearly distinguished from the structural frame. Brick, faced with hand-cut red Ankara stone (tracyandesite) is used on the facade and in the central court. Elsewhere, aluminium frame windows, oak shutters, and oak doors fill the frame. The three groups of skylights, each set within the frame structure, enliven the roofscape.

In keeping with the architect's intention to combine the traditional with the modern, both handcrafted and industrial materials were used. These were then juxtaposed, emphasising

8. The Turkish Historical Society. Three groups of skylights, each set within the frame structure, enliven the roofscape.

the contrasting qualities of each. Thus the rough surface of the stone appears against the sharp, brilliant aluminium. However, the architect did not feel constrained to use the materials only in their natural forms as long as the basic characteristics of each were emphasised. While the reinforced-concrete frame was painted to harmonise with the red Ankara stone, the marks of the formwork are still clearly visible.

Overall, the impression is one of precision and craft. And this is achieved drawing solely on materials and skills available in Turkey.[3]

The Building's Success. The Turkish Historical Society building is highly praised by its users, most of whom are associated with the university. The library drew 18,000 researchers in 1980, and society conferences attract an average of 10,000 people a year. Faculty, staff, librarians, and researchers who use the building find it a very peaceful place in which to work. Uluğ Iğdemir, the Director of the Historical Society, has described the building as a virtuoso contemporary monument. The success of the project is in large part the result of extraordinary cooperation between the architect and the client and of the continued appreciation of the building by the users.

INTER-CONTINENTAL HOTEL AND CONFERENCE CENTRE
MECCA, SAUDI ARABIA
COMPLETED AUGUST, 1974

Roofline of auditorium with Sirat hills beyond.

The centre is organised around two courtyards,
partially shaded by wood screens.

Detail of the tensile structure of the auditorium.

INTER-CONTINENTAL HOTEL AND CONFERENCE CENTRE.
Client: Kingdom of Saudi Arabia, Ministry of Finance and National Economy; Architects: Rolf Gutbrod, Frei Otto.[1]

In 1966 the Saudi Arabian Ministry of Finance sponsored an international competition for the design of a conference centre with hotel and mosque.[2] The German team of Rolf Gutbrod and Frei Otto won the competition. Their design, inspired by bedouin tents, proposed an enormous tent structure which would shelter beneath it an artificial oasis surrounded by the conference facilities and hotel rooms. The tent structure, marked at the centre by a 60-metre-high mast carrying a water tank, would have been open at the sides and top, permitting air to flow in and vent upward. After the competition the architects were asked by the ministry to develop their scheme for a different site, one located four miles west of Mecca, along a dry wadi bed, surrounded by the rugged Sirat hills. The winning design which had been suitable for the flat desert site near Riyadh was no longer appropriate. The new site's proximity to the holy city and the surrounding rugged terrain suggested a different solution, one less obtrusive and more in harmony with the landscape.

Spatial Organisation. The new design preserved the relationship between the auditorium and seminar rooms and the loose polygonal arrangement of the terraced hotel rooms. However, the single tent structure was eliminated. Instead, the architecture focussed around two partially shaded gardens—places of quiet refreshment and a welcome respite from the arid desert surroundings. The informal distribution of spaces around the open areas recalls traditional community layout.

Approaching the complex along the Mecca-Jiddah road, one can see the expressive gleaming forms of the auditorium and seminar structures, outlined against the craggy hills behind. The rest of the hotel complex is low, barely visible, spreading along the valley floor. The visitor approaches the complex along a drive that leads to a central, partially shaded arrival area shared by the hotel and conference facilities. The

1. Regional map. The Inter-Continental Hotel and Conference Centre lies in a rocky wadi on the north side of the road that connects Jiddah to Mecca.

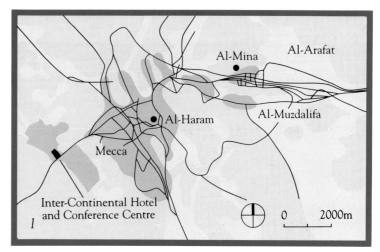

hotel complex is to the left. Each of the 170 rooms has a balcony which overlooks either the central garden or the gardens and hills surrounding the complex. Five large private suites extend into the garden at the ground level.

The conference centre, to the right of the central arrival area, is served by a second entrance which leads directly to the lobby area off which are all the meeting rooms. In addition to the main space, a 1400-seat auditorium, there is a variety of meeting areas which accommodate conferences of almost any size or nature;[3] three seminar rooms, each seating 200 people; six smaller meeting rooms; a royal suite; and reception areas. A separate entrance used by women attending receptions is provided from the enclosed parking area. Between the two major parts of the complex are the kitchen and several dining areas shared by both sections of the centre.

A landscaped path leads from the main arrival area to a

2. Site plan of the centre.
3. Design sketch. Fascinated by tent structures in Saudi Arabia, the engineer/architect, Frei Otto, utilised a spanning system using high-stress steel cables.
4. Constructing seminar facilities. The spanning structure was covered with sun-reflecting aluminium ribbed sheeting.
5. Interior of auditorium. The tension cables supporting the roof are revealed in the ceiling of the hall.

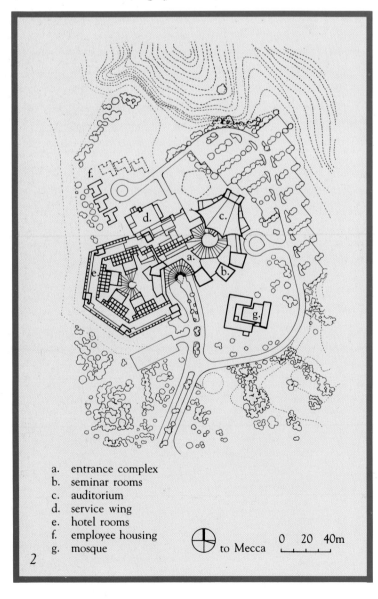

a. entrance complex
b. seminar rooms
c. auditorium
d. service wing
e. hotel rooms
f. employee housing
g. mosque

0   20   40m
to Mecca

2

3

4

5

small mosque. Offices are located on the first level; at its ground level are the ablution area, reception, and the main court (an open shaded space). The qibla wall incorporates the minaret. Reached by stone steps, the minaret recalls those in older mosques of the region. There is a small enclosed garden to the side of the building.

Three on-site residences for the management are provided at the rear of the site, accessible through the service yard. There is also provision for a future banquet hall which would be built adjacent to the auditorium.

6. *Plan of the auditorium with shaded forecourt and auditorium section. The hanging roof structure relying on the weight of the roof itself is a first in high-technology construction. Such innovations are beginning to appear in the Middle East, now a key locus for large-scale construction.*

Architectural Expression. The architecture of the hotel and conference centre incorporates traditional elements and functional design to preserve Saudi custom. At the same time, innovative responses were made to the demands of contemporary life, taking full advantage of modern technology.

The designers drew their initial inspiration from the contrasting forms of heavy Saudi mud houses and lightweight bedouin tents. From this came the low concrete frame structures of the hotel complex and the lightweight steel suspension roofs of the conference spaces. The auditorium and three seminar rooms are treated as separate volumes, each volume clearly expressing the functional space within. All are covered with sun-reflecting aluminium ribbed sheeting. (The auditorium is the first hanging roof structure in the Middle East and it is the first of its kind anywhere to rely on the weight of the roof itself—which includes three layers of mineral rock plank

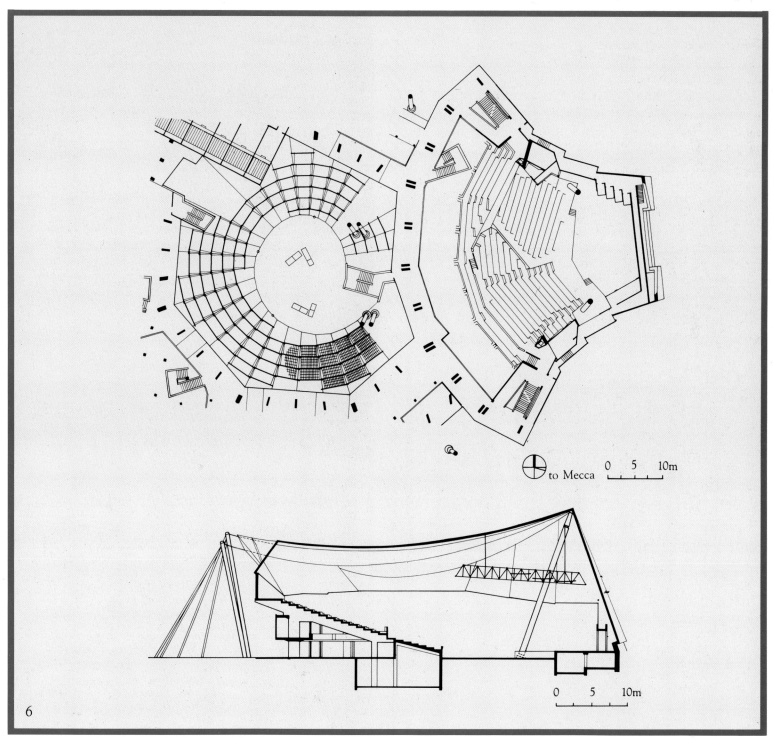

6

insulation—to balance uplift forces.) The dynamic interior space of the auditorium cascades down to the stage area. In contrast to the light, tensile roof structure which envelops the room are the poured-in-place concrete seating structure and stair towers. The wood acoustic-absorption panels suspended from the roof structure give the room a warm tone. Lighting above the stage is carried on a suspended space frame.

Wooden lattice screens, seen in old Mecca and Jiddah, were another source of inspiration for the designers. Terming the wooden screens *kafess*, the designers adapted them in a variety of ways as shading devices. In the two interior garden areas and at the main entrance, wooden slats supported on webs of wire cables form a canopy which sweeps around each open space, filtering the bright sun and casting patterned shadows on the paving beneath. A fixed wooden lattice, supported by a grid of steel columns, covers the courtyard of the

mosque. The hotel room balconies are shaded by *kafess* on pivots, making it possible to adjust the angle of shading. Vertically, *kafess* are used to protect the large glazed areas of the reception spaces and mosque offices. Throughout, the slats vary, combining horizontal, vertical, and diagonal patterns, adding texture and scale to the surface and a richness through the play of light and shadow. The *kafess* provide protection from the direct sun—badly needed in the arid climate where temperatures in the summer can reach 45° C.—reducing the heat loads carried by the central air conditioning.[4]

The concern for detail led to the inclusion of a rich variety of materials, both native and imported.[5] Basaltic stone, the

7. Section and roof plan of shaded mosque court and first level plan of offices.
8. Mosque courtyard. To provide greater comfort during prayer, the courtyard of the mosque is shaded by a system of wood screens similar to those used throughout the complex.
9. The orienting qibla wall of the mosque showing the extruding mihrab niche and pulpit.

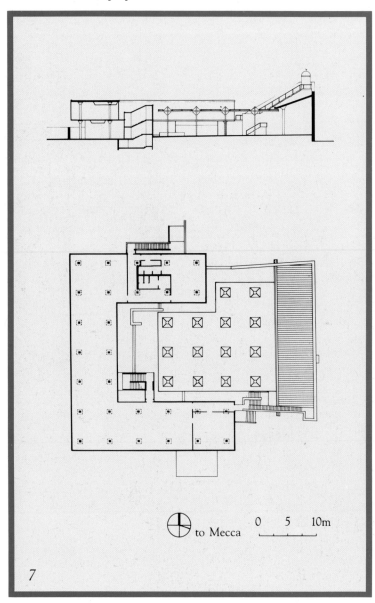

0   5   10m
to Mecca

7

8

9

material of the surrounding hills, was used extensively for exterior wall facing, low garden walls, and paving. Redwood from Scandinavia was used for all the *kafess* and window frames. Floors were finished with various tiles and stone juxtaposed in rich patterns, and these at times are covered with carpets. Paving in the outside garden areas combines pebbles, rough and finished stone, concrete, and tile. Plant materials, restricted to those that survive in the saline soil and arid climate where less than 13 centimetres of rain falls annually, include tamarisks and acasias. Decorative patterns and Koranic texts, hand-carved by Saudi craftsmen, were integrated into various elements of the conference centre.

10. Hotel facade. The hotel room balconies are shaded by wooden lattice screens (kafess) on pivots, making it possible to adjust the angle of shading.
11. Construction detail. Wood, aluminium, glass, and concrete constitute a rich palette of materials for this contemporary complex.
12. Paving details. A variety of finely wrought stone paving covers all the terraces, floors, and paths of the centre.
13. Detail of the minbar exterior.

NATIONAL MUSEUM
DOHA, QATAR
PHASE I COMPLETED JUNE 1975

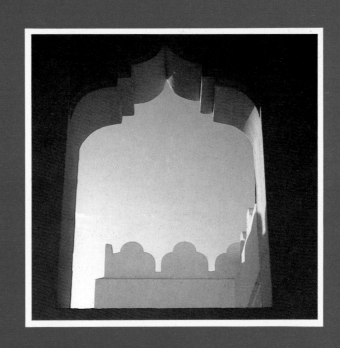

The museum grounds after four years of use. The nucleus
of the reception hall is surrounded by exhibition pavilions.

View from the second-storey portico
of the main reception hall to the sea.

NATIONAL MUSEUM. Client: H.H. Sheikh Khalifa bin Hamed Al-Thani; H.E. Mr. Isa Ghanim Al-Kawari, Minister of Information; Department of Antiquities and Tourism; Planners/Designers: Michael Rice and Company; Design Construction Group, Anthony Irving; Restoration: Qatar Department of Public Works, Ahmad Assad Al-Ansari.[1]

The advent of oil prosperity has greatly affected the society and culture of Qatar, as it has all the oil-producing states of North Africa and the Middle East. Among the results of prosperity has come the inevitable alteration in traditional life styles, values, and sense of heritage. In the face of rapid economic, social, and cultural change, the Qatar National Museum was founded to preserve for posterity essential physical artifacts, mental images, and historical facts and ideas. Qataris (and foreign visitors) of all ages can use the museum to learn about the past, gaining insights into their own history and identity. As one of the first such museums in the Gulf region it is particularly important as an example for other institutions and as a resource for scholars both in the region and around the world.

Preparations for the museum began soon after Sheikh Khalifa assumed power in February 1972. A team of specialists

1. The grounds of the museum, built to include the old Amiri Palace, lies on the seaboard and includes a series of old and new constructions: the rebuilt structure of the old palace, a new museum wing, marina, parking facilities, and a new aquarium.

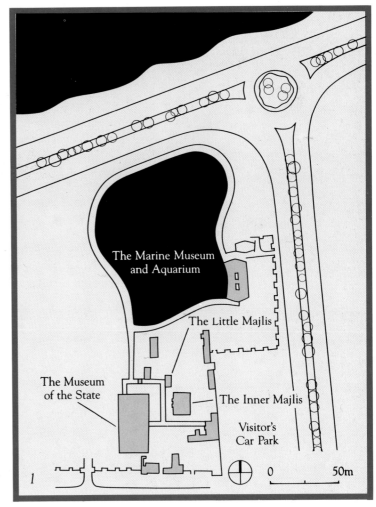

was brought together in order to develop a comprehensive plan. Included among the specialists were the museum consultants, Michael Rice and Company; the Design Construction Group (architects for the grounds and the Museum of the State); the restoration supervisor, Ahmad Assad Al-Ansari, head of the Maintenance Section, Engineering Services Department of the Ministry of Public Works, State of Qatar; a committee of distinguished Qataris was also established by Sheikh Khalifa to advise on the collections of the museum. Many scholars assisted in the research needed to produce the body of information from which the exhibits were drawn. (This research in many instances unearthed significant new information on the ethnology, archaeology, ecology, and history of the country and region.) By December 1972 the initial museum planning and building design were completed. The exhibits were assembled and designed simultaneously with construction, from 1973 through June 1975. A second phase of work included the Marine Museum and Aquarium which was completed and opened by October 1977.

The Qatar National Museum is housed in a distinctive group of structures centred around the prominently situated Amiri Palace, former ruling seat of the Al-Thani family. Adding modern structures to the palace, including extensive landscaping, required sensitive architectural solutions to ensure compatibility with the old buildings.

The Old Amiri Palace—a History. During the period of Ottoman influence in the nineteenth century, Sheikh Abdullah bin Qasim Al-Thani, head of Doha's ruling family, felt the need to establish a seat of power removed from the Turkish garrison in the central part of Doha. He therefore ordered the construction of a government complex on the seashore. There, at a discreet distance from the seat of foreign authority, Sheikh Abdullah carried out his duties as governor of Doha, overseer of waterfront activity, and liasion officer with the Turks. By the end of the nineteenth century construction of his own family residence at the complex began. After the forced withdrawal of the Turks in 1916 the increased responsibilities of the sheikh required that he enlarge the facilities. By 1923, however, the seat of government had moved back to the central part of Doha, and the family of the sheikh moved with it. Although the palace complex remained inhabited for some fifteen years it was later abandoned altogether, and by the 1970s was in ruinous condition.

The layout of the palace complex was the result of the

2. The museum grounds immediately after completion. The basin for the marina exhibit was developed to re-create the original coastline which has now been moved out to allow for a corniche road. 3, 4. The site of the Amiri Palace became a ruin after the seat of government left in 1923. The grounds proved adequate for a new use: a museum of the environment, history, and culture of Qatar.

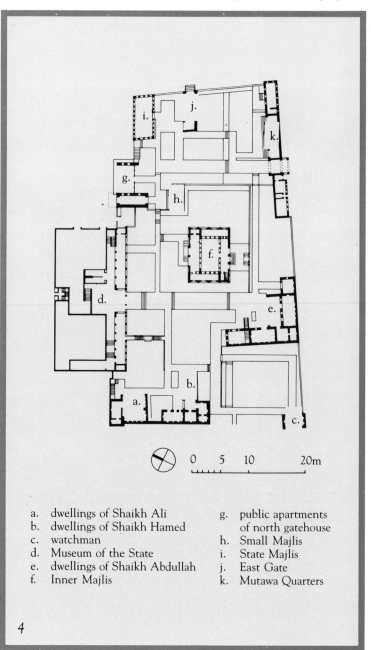

a.	dwellings of Shaikh Ali	g.	public apartments
b.	dwellings of Shaikh Hamed		of north gatehouse
c.	watchman	h.	Small Majlis
d.	Museum of the State	i.	State Majlis
e.	dwellings of Shaikh Abdullah	j.	East Gate
f.	Inner Majlis	k.	Mutawa Quarters

4

series of building campaigns that culminated in the construction of the Inner Majlis in 1918.[2] The original complex was formed around five walled courtyards. The four western courtyards made up the domestic half of the complex, comprising a communal private entrance court and then the three residential courts of Sheikh Abdullah and his two sons. The eastern courtyard functioned as the reception area where public activities took place. To the north, in the area now occupied by the Museum of the State, were extensive kitchens and storage areas.

The three residential areas of the compound were similar in design to other surviving traditional houses in Qatar. The plan basic to all consisted of two rooms opening off an arcaded porch, with one of the rooms divided by a partition that stopped below the ceiling. When expanded, these houses often took an L-shaped form. The Inner Majlis was built for public functions and as the principal residence of the Sheikh. The plan of this structure was dominated by a central room on each floor, a strictly organised design considerably removed from the traditional planning of the other buildings of the complex. The Inner Majlis was, in fact, constructed by an outsider, the famous Bahraini builder Abdullah bin Ali al-Ma'il. He is said to have based the form of the building on a type then used for important buildings in Bahrain.[3] Of special interest was the fully arcaded gallery around the central room on the upper level of the building.

At the corner of Sheikh Abdullah's enclosure was the guest reception room, also called the coffee hall or Little Majlis. It opened onto the eastern courtyard and was directly opposite the north entrance gate. The north gatehouse also had public reception areas, as did the east gatehouse. Situated between the two gatehouses, in the northeast corner of the courtyard, was the assembly room, a distinctive arcaded struc-

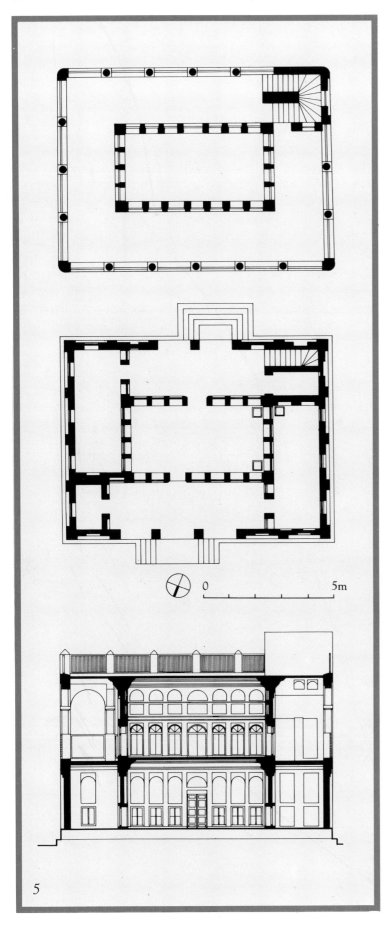

5. *Upper and lower-storey plans and elevation of palace's main reception hall.*
6. *Restoration of the old Amiri Palace required extensive reconstruction.*

ture which was the most formal of the public apartments. The eastern courtyard was completed by residential quarters for the *khadim* (custodian) of the now destroyed mosque which stood immediately to the south.

The construction methods and decoration of these original buildings form a fascinating field for study.[4] While many arches were used in a decorative manner on the buildings, the actual structure was of post-and-lintel type. The posts were rubble-stone piers, which supported beams of mangrove poles supporting a bed of small rubble stones, all cemented together with the local gypsum plaster, known as *juss*. The stones were in large part coral rock taken from the seabed. The whole structure was neatly finished in *juss* and then the openings left were filled with ornamental plaster work, with solid panels forming storage recesses, or with casement windows. Generally these infill types were arranged with the ornamental screens at top, followed by the solid panels in the middle, and with the windows on the bottom level. In some instances the ornamental screens were fitted with slots at the bottom of the panel, to direct the wind inside, providing natural ventilation to the space. The infill panels often had arched heads giving a lively rhythm and grace to the building's appearance. As noted, the arches did not act structurally, but were used purely as a decorative device. The roofs of the buildings were built of wood poles, generally tamarisk or mangrove, covered by a lattice of palm fronds supporting matting. On top of this structure was laid the finish coat of mud and pebbles. The buildings were all finished with relatively simple decorative plaster-work, including the screens mentioned above, cornices, door surrounds, and minor surface embellishments. A final touch was added by the fine carved woodwork found

primarily in the doors and door frames. The buildings were white, a result of the gypsum plaster coating, and the only color used was found on some exposed woodwork, particularly the pole-and-lattice ceilings. The construction techniques and basic forms of the buildings were typical of the building style to be found along the entire east Arabian coast, from Kuwait south to Muscat.

With the conversion of the complex to museum use a number of changes in the original arrangement had to be made, including relandscaping the courtyards to integrate the complex into one readily accessible and understandable group of display buildings. Certain original features could not be retained, for example the courtyard walls, because of new circulation and access requirements. The restoration of the buildings themselves has diverged in some instances from their original appearance. Because buildings were in a ruinous condition they had to be dismantled and rebuilt on their original foundations. Some of the reconstruction work was carried out

7. *Restored, the main reception hall, the Majlis, is arranged as it was when used by the amir.*
8. *A side pavilion is used for historic display.*
9. *Lower floor of main hall, now a numismatic display.*

using the traditional materials coral block and *juss*, but some modern materials, such as reinforced concrete, were also used. The use of concrete has necessitated a regular program of painting to keep all the structures uniformly white, a surface treatment previously achieved with a gypsum-plaster finish. Some decorative features were simplified while others were elaborated. The intent has been to preserve the ambience of the traditional setting and to present the space and the spirit embodied in the old buildings as ones worthy of preservation

10. Attempts to restore and include examples of traditional plaster work are illustrated on the wall of a small service pavilion.
11. Museum grounds after four years of use.

10

11

and of consideration for contemporary applications.

The museum collection and planned exhibits could not be accommodated in the buildings of the palace alone, and therefore two additional structures were constructed—the Museum of the State and the Marine Museum and Aquarium. The Museum of the State required a three-storey structure, thus presenting the problem of integrating a building of that scale into the context of the existing complex. This problem was met with a sensitive solution. The height of the building was reduced by sinking one floor below ground. This device allows the Inner Majlis, directly across from the new building, to dominate the complex as before, since it remains the tallest and most architecturally expressive structure. Reflecting traditional forms, the arcaded front facade of the Museum of the State harmonises with the arcades of the inner majlis. The other facades of the new structure are simply treated so as not to overpower their surroundings. The building is of reinforced concrete construction with exterior walls finished with a white gypsum-cement rendering.

A second major new building, the Marine Museum and Aquarium, is located on the edge of a new lagoon, outside the walls of the palace complex. The position of the lagoon repeats the former relationship of the palace to the seafront (the shoreline has recently been moved out to allow construction of a corniche road). The building itself is lower in height than the complex walls so as not to compete with the palace buildings. Although the structure is modern in style, the same white rendering on its exterior contributes to the continuity of the entire complex.

The Museum. The museum's objective is to inform visitors of the history and traditions of Qatari life. In addition to static displays, extensive use has been made of modern communications techniques, including films. The exhibits' subject matter begins with the earth—the physical reality of the Qatari peninsula. Geological, geographical, and ecological aspects are presented in the museum's entrance area, creating the background for the study of man's presence on the peninsula. The history and traditions of Qataris from the Stone Age to the recent past are then explored in depth, always keeping in mind the duality of desert and sea, and the great influence of Islam on the people. Archaeological, historical, and ethnographical materials are exhibited and interpreted, including major displays concerning all aspects of bedouin life. The other side of Qatari life, the sea, is well represented by the displays of the Marine Museum exhibiting traditional fishing and pearling craft, and by the collection of Gulf sailing craft moored in the lagoon. It is believed that the materials held by the Qatar National Museum represent the most complete extant collection of information and artifacts concerning life in eastern Arabia.[5]

The buildings of the old palace complex serve as ideal environments in which the recent history of Qatar, the traditions of town life, and the characteristics of traditional Qatari architecture are interpreted. These buildings have a special meaning within the museum complex. By their preservation they stand as artifacts of the past. But they also provide an appropriate milieu in which to display and explain the objects associated with traditional life.

WATER TOWERS
KUWAIT CITY, KUWAIT
COMPLETED DECEMBER, 1976

One of five mushroom tower groups; each group is
distinguished by number, height, and ornamentation.

On the city's bay, the Kuwait Tower group
is regarded as a national landmark.

WATER TOWERS. Client: H.H. Sheikh Jabar Al-Ahmed; Ministry of Electricity and Water; Designers: VBB, Prof. Sune Lindström, Joe Lindström, Stig Egnell; Björn & Björn Design, Malene Björn.[1]

Water in the Arabian Peninsula and Gulf area has always been a precious commodity. Earlier in this century a single perennial water-course supplemented by a number of wells was sufficient to support Kuwait City's population.[2] However, in times of water shortage and later when the sources within the city could not supply the expanding population, water had to be shipped from Iraq and Iran to reservoirs at the harbour. From these reservoirs water was transferred to goatskin bags to be sold individually to consumers at the suq. This method of supply was adequate for household use through the first half of the twentieth century, but was inadequate by the middle of the century when prosperity through oil production led to an increased population desiring a higher standard of living. In response, the city provided itself with two seawater desalination plants built between 1950 and 1953; distribution at that time was handled by tank trucks. Further population increases resulted in the need for a more efficient distribution system. So in 1965 the Ministry of Electricity and Water commissioned the Swedish architectural and engineering firm, VBB (Vallenbyynadsbryan), to develop and implement a plan for a

1. Kuwait City, Kuwait. Kuwait City's new water distribution system was fully implemented in 1976.

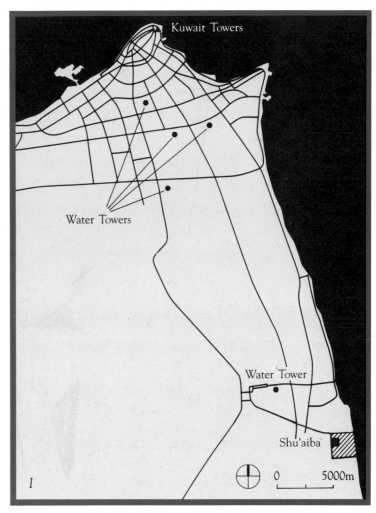

1

modern water-supply system for Kuwait City.

VBB first determined the existing demands. Their plan then divided the city into six service zones, five of which were currently occupied; one was a zone designated for future expansion. The service zones were arranged according to altitude as well as to the location and density of population. The number of ground-level reservoirs, pumping stations, and storage towers serving each zone would necessarily differ according to quantity of demand and distance from the desalination plants. Furthermore, the height of the towers would vary as needed to ensure adequate pressure. VBB's computer-controlled dual distribution system provides fresh and brackish water through separate piping.[3] The fresh water supplies residential as well as other needs requiring potable water. The brackish water is used for a number of purposes including firefighting, washing, street cleaning, and irrigation. Kuwait City can thus be enhanced by greenery with public parks and private gardens offering welcome relief from the desert environment.[4]

In December 1976 the new water distribution and storage system was completed. The most visible aspect of the system is the thirty-three storage towers. With a combined storage capacity of 102,000 cubic metres, thirty-one of the thirty-three structures are concrete mushroom towers. Erected within five zones, the number of mushroom towers in any one zone varies between six and nine. The two towers for the sixth zone, know collectively as the Kuwait Tower, were specially designed for the Kuwait Bay promontory.

Mushroom Towers.   The mushroom tower groups are distinguished from each other by variation in height, arrangement, and colour. The grounds around the towers are treated as public open spaces with paving and planting. Each group serves as

a landmark, conveying a sense of identity for its district while contributing to the unity of the complete system and of the city as a whole.

Two types of concrete structural systems are used in the mushroom towers—and in the Kuwait Tower group: standard reinforced concrete and prestressed concrete. The concrete was mixed at each site using cement and local sand and gravel collected in the desert.[5] The concrete work had to be of high quality in order to make waterproofing unnecessary.

Tower shafts were constructed of standard reinforced concrete, cast in place. (Construction of the mushroom towers utilised a sliding wooden formwork; that of the Kuwait Tower, a climbing formwork of plywood panels to achieve its tapering profile.) The mushroom reservoir formwork was designed as prefabricated elements which were assembled at ground level and hoisted into place for the actual pouring. After casting and prestressing of the shell, the formwork was removed, lowered, and prepared for reuse. This cycle took fifteen weeks. With the five sets of prefabricated reservoir forms available, a shell casting was performed every three weeks at maximum

2. *Tower group, one of five.*
3, 4. *The process of assembling the mushroom towers. Shafts were poured in place. Storage containers were cast on site and then hoisted onto shafts with cranes.*

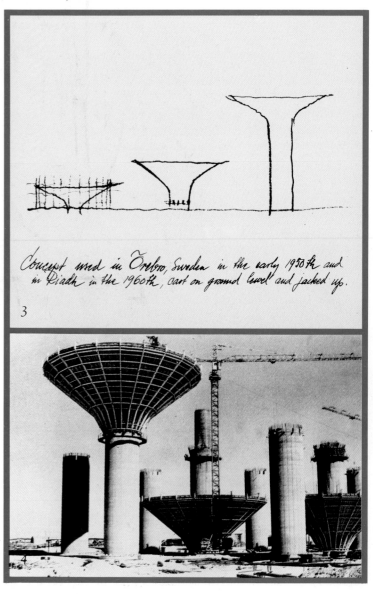

3

4

capacity. With this standardised system all thirty-one towers were constructed rapidly and accurately, easily allowing for the difference in height and number of towers in each group.

The conical shape of the mushroom reservoirs was a structurally economical design as well as being functionally appropriate and aesthetically pleasing. The slope of the shell walls was calculated to direct the forces downward from the shell to the shaft continuously and uniformly. This constant and uniform force thus generated low stresses, enabling a minimum of concrete and reinforcing to be used. The relatively small size of the reservoirs (each 3000 cubic metres) was economical, since it facilitated the rapid, easily controllable pouring of the shells, especially important in the hot Kuwait climate. The

inverted conical shape ensures delivery at a constant pressure, even at lower water levels.

The Kuwait Tower.   The sixth tower group was to be sited on the tip of a small promontory jutting into Kuwait Bay.[6] Due to their special location Amir H.H. Sheikh Jaber Al-Ahmed requested that the towers designated for this site be treated differently from the standard mushroom towers. VBB generated ten design studies of which three were presented to the Amir. Of these three one had been created by architect Malene Björn. It was her striking design which was chosen.

The programme for the design called for a water storage capacity of 9000 cubic metres. In addition, certain public facilities were envisaged on this site, which was close to the city centre. Reception and banqueting facilities, restaurants and observation areas were all considered appropriate. The final design has combined all these features in a magnificent sculptural grouping.

5. Section through two mushroom towers, elevation of one mushroom group. The specific shape of the water tower assures a constant water pressure, and can be considered a major improvement in water delivery technique.

5

The general exterior appearance of the Kuwait Tower group is enhanced by the careful composition of the three towers. Two of the towers contain 4500-cubic-metre water reservoirs; one of these also contains all the public facilities. The composition is completed visually by a third needle-like tower which houses lighting equipment to illuminate the group at night—the illumination of the towers creates a spectacular nighttime scene.

According to the architect, the Kuwait Tower group refers to ideals of humanity and technology, symbolised by the globe and the rocket, respectively.[7] Reference to the Islamic past through the minaret-like quality of the shafts and through the multicoloured mosaic-like facing of the globes, recalling the tiled domes of historic mosques and shrines, was a welcome result of the completed design. Approximately 41,000 enamelled steel discs cover the three spheres in shades of blue, green, and gray. The discs are arranged in spiral patterns around the spheres. On the larger tower the public spaces are faced with special radiant-heat-reflective glass. The upper globe is glazed across most of its surface with triangular pieces of glass held in a spherical space frame of aluminium members. The tip of each tower is covered with stainless steel and acts as a lightning arrestor connected to the ground through the steel reinforcing of the shafts as well as through the water piping and copper wires.

The main tower is entered at the base through a reception hall. Elevators transport diners and visitors to the first sphere. A separate entrance and elevator are provided for the observa-

6. *The Kuwait Tower lies at the tip of the Kuwait City waterfront.*
7. *Interior of observation/restaurant bubble.*
8. *The Kuwait Tower during construction.*
9. *Distribution network for fresh and brackish water.*
10. *Architect's concept sketch, plan of restaurant floor, and section of the Kuwait Tower group.*

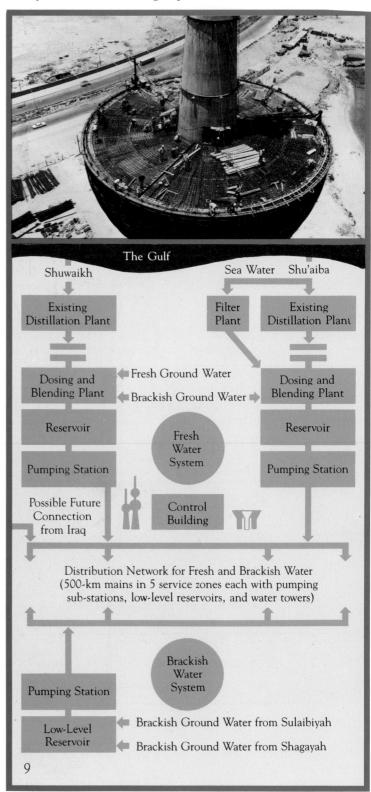

tion deck and café in the top sphere. Arriving at the first sphere the visitor walks out from the central shaft into a brilliantly lit lobby featuring a curved marble stair. The lobby is nonetheless dominated by the views through the encircling wall of glass. Descending the stair, one reaches the restaurant floor, which contains a restaurant seating ninety, a banquet hall for sixty, a small room for private parties, and parts of the kitchen and support services (the remainder of which are a level below). Above the restaurant floor is the open indoor garden area, reached by ascending stairs from the elevator landing. This floor, the space of which is enhanced by its high domed ceiling, is capable of accommodating receptions for up to 400 people. The upper sphere also has two levels, containing below an observation terrace and above a revolving café with seating for seventy. From this level the other two towers may be seen in their entirety.

The largest tower is one of the tallest structures in the Middle East, rising 185 metres above ground level. From the observation deck and rotating café, approximately 120 metres above ground, there are magnificent views over the city and Kuwait Bay. The second tower stands 140 metres tall and the third approximately 100 metres. It is easy when visiting the Kuwait Tower to forget that below the restaurant floor of the largest tower is a 4500-cubic-metre reservoir and that the second tower also contains a reservoir of the same capacity. The group works as a landmark and symbol of the city and as a public facility, while fulfilling its initial reason for being, to supply water to the central city.

The Water Towers. The water towers of Kuwait have become an accepted, important part of the urban fabric of the city. Dominating the skyline, they are recognised and welcomed for their functional importance and for their aesthetic enrichment; indeed, the Kuwait Tower has become a national landmark. The water towers are as impressive technologically as they are visually and symbolically. They represent progressive structural and architectural design and create a unique, appropriate monument for Kuwait.

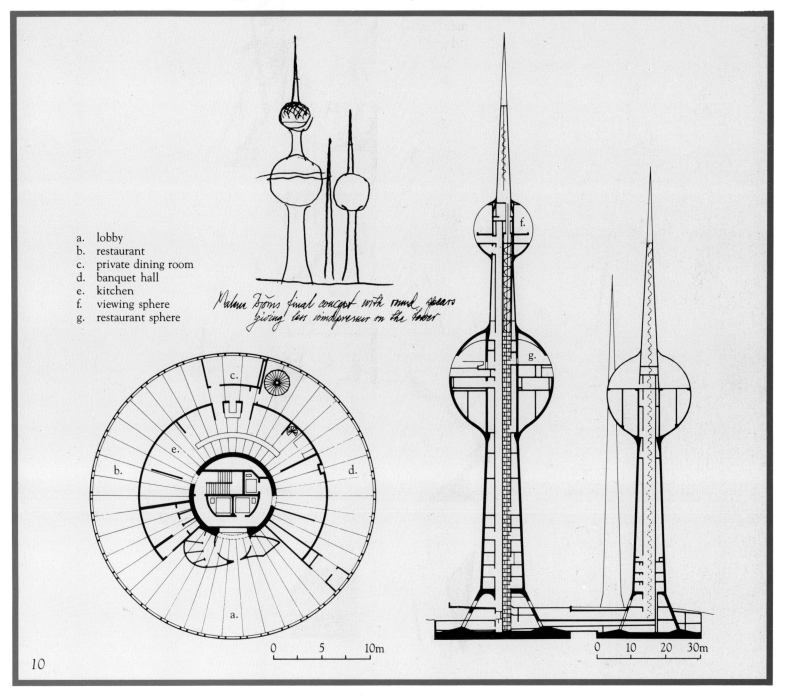

a. lobby
b. restaurant
c. private dining room
d. banquet hall
e. kitchen
f. viewing sphere
g. restaurant sphere

Malcolm Björns final concept with round spears giving less windpressure on the tower

0 5 10m

0 10 20 30m

10

RESTORATION OF THE ALI QAPU, CHEHEL SUTUN AND HASHT BEHESHT
ISFAHAN, IRAN
MAJOR RESTORATION COMPLETED 1977

View from the *talar* of the Ali Qapu.

View of the *talar* and the adjacent north facade of Chehel Sutun.

Ceiling of upper story in the Ali Qapu.

View of restored inner hall of Hasht Behesht.

RESTORATION OF THE ALI QAPU, CHEHEL SUTUN, AND HASHT BEHESHT.

Client: National Organisation for Conservation of Historic Monuments of Iran (NOCHMI), Dr. Bagher Shirazi; Restoration: Istituto Italiano per il Medio ed Estremo Oriente (ISMEO), Eugenio Galdieri.[1]

The contemporary city of Isfahan has surrounded the historic core and has gradually eaten into it with new roads, increased traffic, electric wires, neon signs, and new construction. Nevertheless, much of the dramatic, world-famous layout of the sixteenth- and seventeenth-century capital can still be discerned. The great maidan, the Maidan-i-Shah, and its monuments, the Masjid-i-Shah, the mosque of Lutfullah, the Ali Qapu and the monumental entrance to the Qaisariyya Bazaar, form one major ensemble of the capital. The second is the great garden avenue of the Chahar Bagh and its flanking palace gardens, but these remain in their most general aspects only. The two areas are contiguous and have been proposed as a great city park with cultural and commerical activities, religious monuments, greenery, and open spaces. Though the fi-

1. Historic Isfahan. The Safavid city was built adjacent to the earlier medieval town.

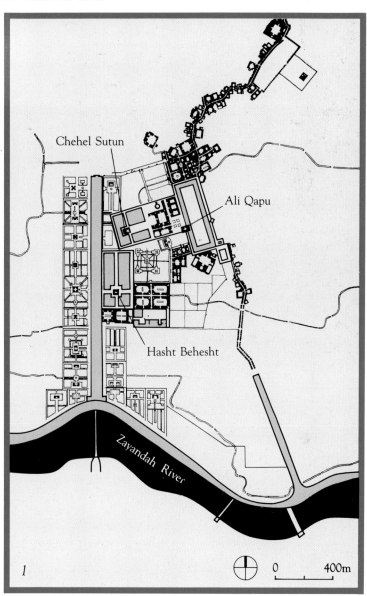

Chehel Sutun

Ali Qapu

Hasht Behesht

Zayandah River

1

0   400m

nal implementation of such a scheme is still in the future, the key elements are already in place.

In 1964, Iranian authorities in charge of the conservation of historical monuments were concerned with the dangerous state of deterioration of Ali Qapu. A decision was made to call in Italian experts associated with the Istituto per Studii Medio e Estremo Oriente (ISMEO). Out of this initial meeting, there developed a fifteen-year programme of collaboration that resulted in the restoration of Ali Qapu, Chehel Sutun, and Hasht Behesht, three palace pavilions of the seventeenth century, in the partial rehabilitation and restoration of the peripheries of the great maidan, in the designation of a protected historical zone, in the publication of major new studies on Safavid architecture, and most importantly in the training of Iranian restoration experts.[2]

At the instigation of ISMEO, the National Organization for the Conservation of Historical Monuments of Iran (NOCHMI) established its own construction department to ensure a stable and increasingly well-trained work force and to avoid difficulties with individual contractors. The restoration program thus developed its own specialists in masonry, plastering, carpentry and woodworking, mirrorwork and the like. At the same time, the students of the School of Fine Arts were assigned restoration work, particularly that of the painted decoration, as part of their curriculum. More than one hundred certificates of collaboration were given out by ISMEO and nineteen young specialists received advanced training in restoration in Italy. The young specialists (architects and archaeologists) employed by NOCHMI had the unparalleled opportunity to collaborate on and then take charge of various apsects of this restoration program.

Ali Qapu. Standing 30 metres high on the west side of the maidan, the gate pavilion consists of a square, three-storey core and a series of additions, the most notable of which is the second-storey portico or *talar.* Built in several stages between 1597 and 1668, the building served as monumental gatehouse

2. *A master plan for the conservation and rehabilitation of the historic core of the Safavid city of Isfahan.*

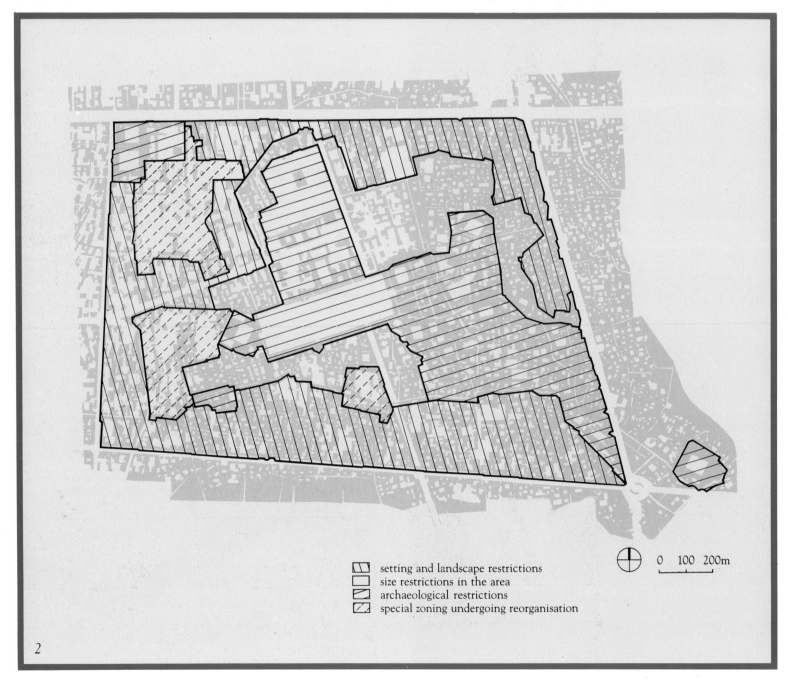

setting and landscape restrictions
size restrictions in the area
archaeological restrictions
special zoning undergoing reorganisation

0   100   200m

2

to the palace precinct and as a reception pavilion and reviewing stand. Its splendid painted and punctured *muqarnas* ceilings of the upper levels totally cover a very light and elastic structural system of thin vaults cross-braced with vertical diaphragms and with wooden beams and pillars.

Extensive analysis completed in 1966 indicated that the building had suffered a seismic shock some years before. The damage produced two major cracks along a north-south line and was threatening to split the building apart. The rotation and lowering of the pillars of the *talar* caused the more serious of the secondary mechanical damages. The wooden skeleton of the building was in very poor condition. Its structural capacities were greatly diminished through rot or infestation by parasites. The foundations of the building, particularly those below the *talar,* had settled because the latter's original horizontal roof had been replaced by a low-pitched one, too heavy for the light skeleton of the building.

Restoration work proceeded with a clearly enunciated plan, according to the 1964 Charter of Venice of the II Con-

3. *A segment of the restored peripheral bazaar of the maidan.*
4. *Ali Qapu. Main facade on the maidan.*
5. *Ali Qapu. Transverse section showing main areas of structural restoration work.*
6. *Ali Qapu. South facade under restoration.*

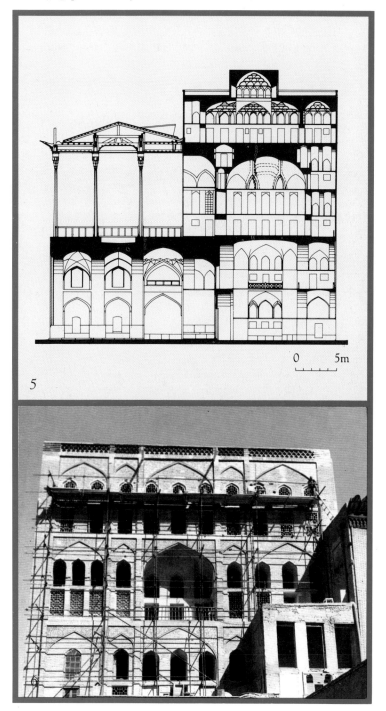

0   5m

gress of Architects and Technicians of Historic Monuments. Structural damages were repaired first, and with as many of the original materials as possible, before proceeding to the restoration of the surface. The footings of the building were increased twenty-seven percent. The large ground-floor vault was consolidated by a stiffening diaphragm of arches. Vaults, pillars, and masonry on the upper levels were strengthened. Vertical loads over vaults were transferred to horizontal wood or steel beams and tie rods. Cracks were repaired with a special resistant cement. The painted surfaces were cleaned and reinforced and retouching was kept to a minimum to make clear to the visitor where there had been any restoration. The restoration of the Ali Qapu entailed research into the materials of the building, a detailed survey of its structure and the further collection of data from old photographs and written

sources. During the process of this programme, clear evidence was produced on the several phases of the construction of the building and their relative dates.

Three years after the beginning of work on Ali Qapu a proposal was made for the restoration and rehabilitation of the peripheral bazaar, for the restoration of the spatial and functional qualities of the maidan and for the improvement of the urban and historical character of the immediate area. By 1978, part of the work, the restoration of the peripheral bazaar and the cleaning of the monumental entrance to the Qaisariyya, were partially completed.

7. Restoration detail of steel structure to support talar.
8. Axonometric showing masonry diaphragms which were added to stabilise vaults.
9. The vaulted structures of Ali Qapu were extensively damaged by earthquakes and the wood tie rods were infested by termites. The first step in restoration was structural reinforcement of the building—here, rebuilt vaults.
10. Ali Qapu. Restoring painted surfaces, 1973.

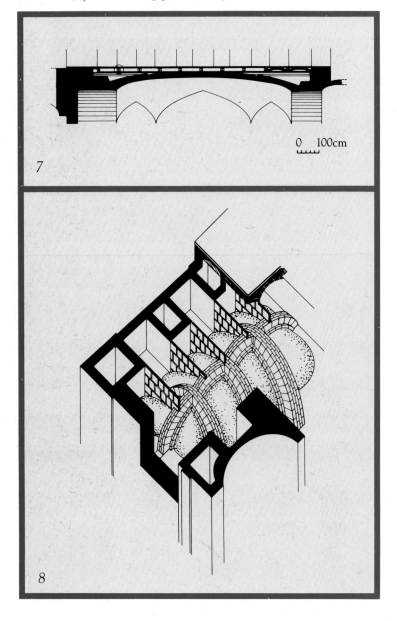

0   100cm

7

8

9

10

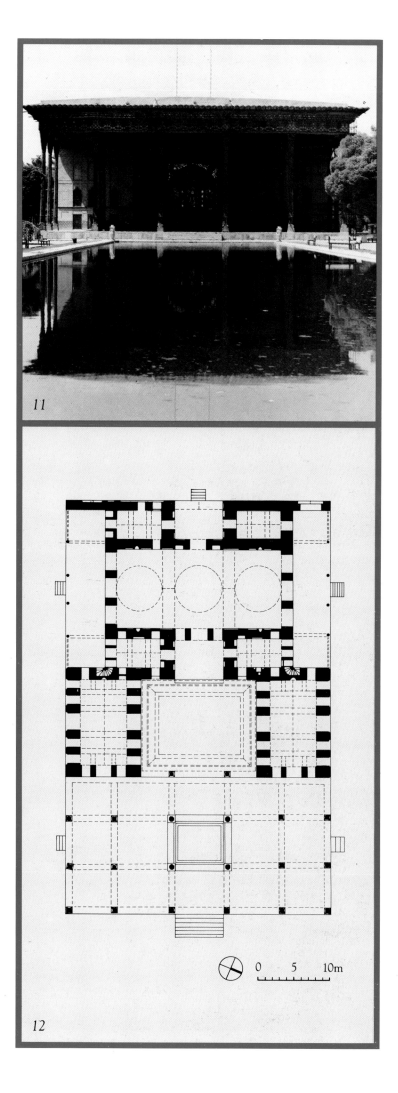

11

12

Chehel Sutun. The Chehel Sutun was part of the restoration programme begun simultaneously with the Ali Qapu. Built during the seventeenth century in three phases, the pavilion consists of a great reception hall flanked by east and west *eyvans*, a south *eyvan* with accompanying rooms and the later great *talar* with its twenty pillars. The hundreds of metres of painted decoration required major restoration because of over-

11. *Chehel Sutun. West facade reflected in its rectangular pool.*
12. *Chehel Sutun. Plan of pavilion without its reflecting pool.*
13. *Chehel Sutun. Restored south facade and eyvan with the re-built upper balcony and newly replaced porch.*
14. *The program of restoring the painted surfaces of the Chehel Sutun started with the decorative program of the side rooms and the lower panels of the main hall.*

14

painting, water infiltration, smoke damage, and architectural modification. Initially, the Iranian authorities were most interested in restoring these surfaces, but soon it became clear that the structure had to be stabilised first. The tall and slender (13 metres high and 40 to 60 centimetres in diameter) wooden columns of the *talar* were treated for parasites and reinforced by the insertion of steel beams. Metal tie rods and concrete supports further consolidated the structure of the building. New wooden frames and grating, built on carefully researched original patterns, were installed in the openings. The restoration of the paintings in the pavilion has brought to light the richness and monumentality of the seventeenth-century Isfahan school of painting best known through the master Riza-i ʿAbbasi.

15. *Structural reconstruction drawing for Chehel Sutun's wooden columns. All columns had to be reinforced with steel beams.*
16. *Chehel Sutun. The eves and ceiling of the main and side porches required considerable surface restoration.*

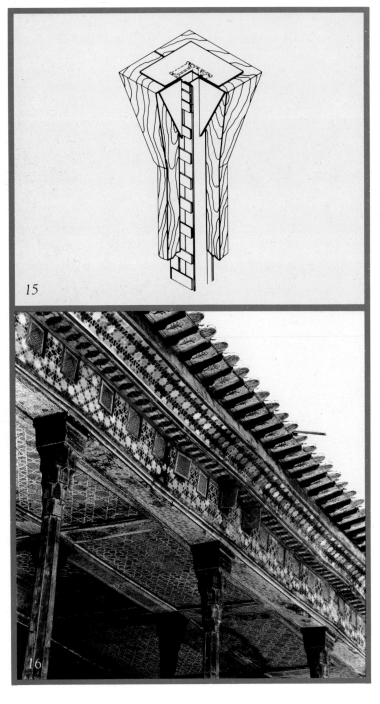

Hasht Behesht. The Hasht Behesht became government property only in the late 1960's so work was slow in beginning there. It had been a private residence up to that time and had been substantially altered in the nineteenth century. It was consolidated structurally, and the nineteenth-century accretions were for the most part removed. The full beauty of the

17. *Plan of Hasht Behesht, ground level and section.*
18. *Hasht Behest under restoration. View of southeast corner.*
19. *Hasht Behest. Room on the second floor facing south, the muqarnas ceiling fully restored.*

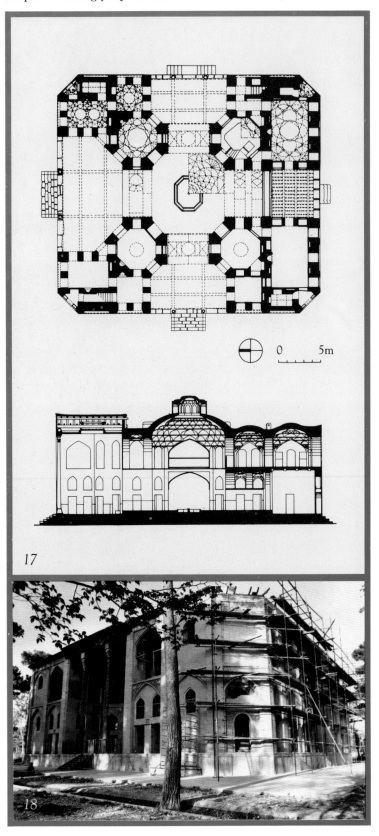

pavilion was then revealed, with its Safavid ceilings, chimneys, and wall decoration. These were cleaned and restored; wood railings and gratings were installed. In this last building, the newly trained Iranian experts assumed much of the responsibility for restoration.

Finally a concerted attempt was made to incorporate both pavilions into an archaeological park. The Chehel Sutun became the nucleus of restoration for neighbouring historical buildings such as the Talar Ashraf, the Qajar Tower and an important Safavid bath. The area around the Hasht Behesht was prepared for a park. And four years later, a comprehensive urban planning and design project was commissioned.

Replicability. From the Isfahan restoration programme, the newly trained work force and the ISMEO experts moved to other buildings in Isfahan, Linjan, and Barsian. NOCHMI moved its technicians to other regions in Iran, and there they began to work with the methods learned during the programme in Isfahan. Departments of Restoration were established in the National University of Iran and the Farabi University of Isfahan.

The programme could be used as a guide for restoration programmes in neighbouring countries where national services for the restoration of monuments have been founded quite recently and where skills are rare or inadequately developed.

19

MUGHAL SHERATON HOTEL
AGRA, INDIA
COMPLETED OCTOBER, 1976

Northwest corner of hotel complex. Openings in the west
wall are recessed for protection from the long afternoon sun.

Cypresses, fruit trees, lantern niches
and waterfalls recall a Mughal garden.

Planters at the base of the walls are a screen for
the rooms and a transition to the landscape.

The gardens are the places of greatest activity, in much the same manner as were the garden courts at Fatehpur Sikri. The three landscaped courtyards are enclosed by the guest wings. The walls of these wings form wide planters at their bases, providing a privacy screen for the rooms and a transition from building to landscape. From the room level the courtyards gradually step down, through a series of terraces, planters, pools, and fountains, to a level 3.65 metres below grade. The cooling presence of large water tanks, well understood by the Mughals, has been introduced here also. Pools are used extensively with tanks of varying size, the largest designed as a swimming pool. A network of walkways weaves among the planters and pools, forming small terraces and seating areas, and linking the various courts.

In the centre, on an axis with the Taj Mahal, is a formal garden similar to the gardens of the Mughal period. Cyprus trees line the terraced water tank, which is enclosed at the far end by a sandstone wall carved with lantern niches, characteristic of Mughal design. The water spills over low walls, also with lantern niches, into small pools and fountains.

Surrounding the guest wings are two hectares of informal gardens which offer further recreation, including putting greens and archery and croquet facilities. The entire site is bounded, not by a wall, but by thick bougainvillaea.[3]

Response to Climate. Agra is hot, with temperatures in midsummer typically reaching 40° C. Although the temperature moderates in winter, the season of heaviest tourism, it is still warm and dry. Even in winter months temperatures are known to reach 36° C.

The Mughal Hotel serves as a cool haven from the hot, dusty Agra plain. All the rooms are oriented to take advantage of the cooling effects of the gardens and pools. The thick masonry walls of the guest wings aid in cooling, and window

5. Reception lobby. Agra is noted for its marble and has a continuing tradition of workers skilled in its cutting. White marble is used extensively as a finish; in the floor of the lobby area it is set in distinctive circular patterns. The large chandelier was brought from Firozabad, 30 kilometres from Agra.

6. Restaurant interior. The four restaurants, each with its own distinctive character, are at the garden level, as are conference rooms and a ballroom.

7. Interior of a guest room. Both the guest rooms and restaurants have brightly panelled walls and wood furnishings from Rajasthan and other regions. Many of the guest rooms have canopies above the beds. Some include a typically Indian low sitting and resting platform (taq) in the bay window.

openings are limited to thirty percent of the wall area to minimise the heat gain. Openings to the east (subject to rapid increase in temperature in the mornings) and those to the west (exposed to the long afternoon sun) are recessed for further protection. Trees and thick planting around the entire building perimeter also help to screen the sun's rays.

In the central block of public spaces there are large areas of glass to take advantage of the views. However, these openings are only in the north and east facades. They are sheltered from the direct sun by a double-wall system consisting of a masonry screen wall wrapped around the primary concrete frame structure.

All the public areas and guest rooms are centrally air-conditioned. The mechanical distribution system consists of a network of underground service tunnels which loop around the complex, paralleling the circulation routes. Services are also grouped in shafts which form vertical massing elements. This separation of services facilitates access and simplifies maintenance. An on-site auxiliary diesel generating plant assures the continued functioning of the mechanical system should the municipal electricity supply fail.

Structure and Construction.   The hotel was designed to avoid all unnecessary dependence upon foreign technology, basing the structures and construction technology on the materials and skills readily available in the region at the time of construction. This meant the use of reinforced concrete and, above all, brick, a material used in the region for centuries.

All the guest wings are made of brick bearing walls, 34.3 centimetres thick on average, supporting concrete slabs. The

8. *North/south and east/west sections.*
9. *Detail of formal garden. The terraced water tank is enclosed at the far end by a sandstone wall carved with lantern niches.*
10. *Formal gardens. On axis with the Taj Mahal, this garden is similar to those of the Mughal period.*
11. *The Mughal Hotel with the Taj Mahal beyond.*

central block of public spaces, the pedestrian bridges, and the service block, all of which require longer spans, are concrete frame structures with concrete waffle slabs. There brick has been used as infill and as facing on the concrete.

The construction documents were completed in May of 1975, but the start of construction was delayed until September, at the end of the rainy season.[4] The construction process was labour intensive, drawing on the ample available labour force. The only machinery used on site was a small hand-fed concrete mixer. All other work, including the installation of large air-handling units, was done manually. In addition, donkeys were used for heavy hauling. At its peak, there were about 2000 men, mostly from the surrounding villages, working in three shifts on the site.

During the fifteen months of construction the site was transformed into a construction camp, with most work done on the site. A plant nursery was established on the property to produce the landscape materials and a workshop set up for the manufacture of wood furnishings and finishes and for fabrication of metal ductwork. To manage this vast project, the client established an in-house construction management team to purchase materials and coordinate the subcontractors. The work was closely supervised on site by two representatives of the architects.

To ensure that the designers' intentions were realised, before beginning construction each detail was drawn on the mud floors, mocked up, and modified if needed. This included the preliminary construction of a complete guest room module. In this way workers and craftsmen were able to suggest improvements in technique and detailing.

Construction was completed in October of 1976 and the Mughal Sheraton opened in November. It is now maintained by a staff of 400 employees.

Materials and Finishes.   All materials for construction were obtained locally, or at least from within a truck haul distance from Agra. Bricks were supplied by local kilns, which were

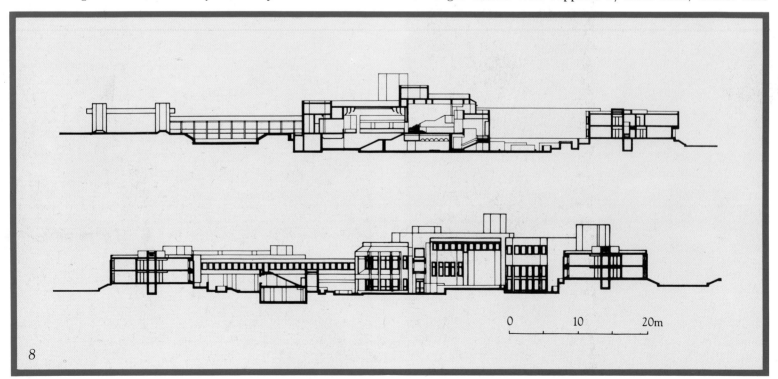

0   10   20m

8

able to increase their production from 1.5 million to the three million required for the project. Cement was brought from Delhi, 200 kilometres to the north. Local stone, crushed manually on site, constituted the aggregate, and sand came from the local river bed and was washed on site. The steel for reinforcing, obtained in Delhi, was manufactured outside of Calcutta; it was rolled and cut on site.

Agra is noted for its marble and has a continuing tradition of workers skilled in its cutting. White marble, finely cut and polished, was used extensively as finishing in the pedestrian bridges and the lobby areas where it is set in distinctive circular patterns. The marble came from a quarry in Makrana, 110 kilometres from Agra, the source of the marble used for the Taj Mahal. Other craftsmen skilled in cabinetry and woodworking fabricated the teak doors, window frames, and some of the furniture, working on site in a special workshop. The decorative plaster ceilings hung in the restaurants were also manufactured in the workshop by local skilled craftsmen.

Throughout, much use is made of local fabrics, regional carpets, and traditional crafts, emphasising the Indian character of the hotel. The large chandelier which hangs in the lobby was brought from Firozabad, thirty kilometres from Agra. The restaurants and guest rooms have brightly panelled walls and wood furnishings from Rajasthan and other regions. Many of the guest rooms have fabric canopies above the beds, and some include typically Indian low sitting and resting platforms (*taq*) in the bay windows. Eighty of the rooms are in Indian style with exposed floors and raised platforms with mattresses in place of the standard movable beds.

In the gardens, paving is of brick and slate. The formal garden is set with sandstone tiles in geometric patterns. Structural ceramic tiles were used for the planters, curbing, and pools. All of these materials were acquired locally.

Continually drawn into the gardens while moving from pavilion to pavilion, visitors to the hotel are offered recreation as well as rest, in surroundings which evoke and develop the spirit of Mughal design. In both building layout and landscape design, in the choice of materials and furnishings, and in construction technology, the hotel complex is rooted in the culture of the region.

9

10

11

KAMPUNG IMPROVEMENT PROGRAMME
JAKARTA, INDONESIA
ONGOING SINCE 1969

Aerial view. The Kampung Improvement
Programme has created healthier urban
environments by providing municipal services.

Secondary drainage channel. In Jakarta, building
drainage systems are essential in turning squatter
encampments into the formal urban fabric.

KAMPUNG IMPROVEMENT PROGRAMME.

Client: Jakarta City Government, Ali Sadikin, Former Governor; Planners: K.I.P. Technical Unit, Mr. Darrundono, Chief; Pik Mulyadi, Vice Governor of Jakarta, former Head of Regional Planning Office; People of the Kampungs.[1]

In 1969, under political pressure from the large and diverse kampung populace, the Jakarta city government initiated the Kampung Improvement Programme (K.I.P.). Stated simply, the programme's objective was to alleviate the extremely low standard of living endemic to all the city's kampung areas. Given the magnitude of the problem (approximately three million people were then living in unimproved kampungs covering 7200 hectares) and the limited financial resources available to address it (a development budget of about ten million U.S. dollars for 1969–70), a comprehensive yet inexpensive approach was imperative.

Jakarta's Kampungs. The history and development of Jakarta's kampungs are closely tied to the city's chronic shortage of low-cost housing. Like many primate cities in the developing world, Jakarta has long served as a magnet for rural migrants attracted to the city by the promise, whether real or imagined, of employment and an improved standard of living. The first large wave of unskilled and uneducated migrants swept the city during the 1950s and '60s in response to a booming construction industry—an industry supported heavily by a newly independent government anxious for its capital city to affect the appearance of a modern, progressive, twentieth-century metropolis with highways, public monuments, administrative offices, multistorey hotels, and a large sports complex.[2] Between 1961 and 1971 the city's population swelled from not quite three million to five million inhabitants.[3] Though in part the result of natural increase, the larger portion of this population surge was directly attributable to migration, which accrued at an estimated rate of 89,200 people per year.[4] Un-

1. Jakarta, Indonesia. Indonesia is the most populous Islamic country, with approximately eighty million Muslims. Jakarta is sited on a low-lying coastal plain, subject to regular flooding. Proper engineering can control health hazards and property damage associated with flooding.

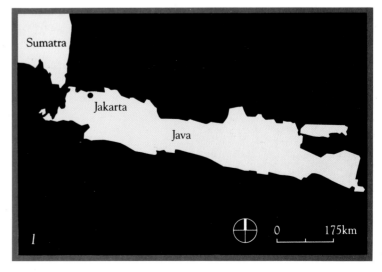

able to find, much less afford, conventional housing in the private market, poor newcomers settled in unplanned, unserviced, and overcrowded urban villages known as kampungs. By 1969 approximately seventy-five percent of Jakarta's total population lived in these settlements, which then covered sixty percent of the city's urbanised land area.[5]

The early migrants to the city would occupy land—abandoned rice paddies, marshes, or vacant lots—usually available for the taking, along the city's periphery and there build their own shelter. Semirural in nature, these kampungs were, nevertheless, located as close as possible to jobs in commercial, industrial, or residential sectors of Jakarta. Their desirable locations continued to attract new migrants, and over time the village-like, spontaneous settlements became congested urban slums. In the meantime, the planned city spread in leapfrog fashion southward from the low-lying areas along the coast to higher elevations and cooler temperatures and left many kampungs undisturbed, permanent enclaves within the expanding urban fabric. For these enclaves, planning controls did not exist. Open space was haphazardly subdivided into minute plots so that in some centre-city kampungs ninety percent and more of the available land was taken up by residential plots. Such practices, coupled with the prevailing low-rise character of building, created population densities as high as 700 to 1200 persons per hectare. The physical sum of this growth was a near-solid massing of one- and two-storey structures broken only by mazelike footpaths and waterways.

Housing Conditions. Housing conditions within Jakarta's kampungs are generally overcrowded, averaging two families of five members each per single dwelling, which consists of bamboo matted walls, tempered clay floors, and thatched roofs. Amenities such as electricity and indoor plumbing for water and sewage are virtually nonexistent. Yet kampungs are

dynamic communities, continuously in transition. This state is perhaps best exemplified by the use of and variation in construction materials from kampung to kampung. Such differences depend in large measure on settlement age and location, and on individual household income.

Older, more centrally located kampungs are often the densest (average plot size, 40–50 square metres), but exhibit a more varied, permanent housing stock than newer kampungs. Households earning above subsistence incomes typically invest in home improvements. Traditional rural building materials like bamboo and native woods are being replaced with urban ones such as masonry walls, cement or brick floors, glazed doors, and tile or corrugated iron roofs. By comparison, housing within the city's newer kampungs, those emerging along rail lines, roadways, and outlying areas, while less dense (average plot size, 160 square metres) is less varied. Very low household incomes prohibit expenditures for housing beyond the self-constructed, traditional mode. Temporary structures of bamboo and thatched grasses prevail. Also prevalent in these

2. Detailed plan of an improved kampung.
3, 4. Before and after. The success of the K.I.P. is immediately evident. Improved public streets and municipal services were the incentive for private property owners to improve their homes.

a. school
b. health center
c. mosque

0   50m

2

4

areas are more transient shelters constructed of cast-off building materials and found objects. Despite such overcrowded and substandard housing conditions, the need for shelter pales before the need for basic infrastructure to alleviate the intolerable environmental conditions of most kampungs.

Environmental Conditions. One important factor that contributed to keeping housing costs low in Jakarta's kampungs was the complete absence of water, sewer, and electrical infrastructure. Indeed, the very reason kampungs developed at all was their initial appeal as reservoirs of raw, vacant land, meaning roadways were unpaved and plots were unserviced by the municipality. Under rural village densities, the lack of such infrastructure, in particular the lack of human- and solid-waste disposal facilities, posed few environmental or public-health hazards. Sufficient open space surrounded these early kampungs to absorb and dissipate the waste load generated.

However, under heavily congested urban conditions with little or no open space, the lack of adequate sanitation facilities creates serious short- and long-term environmental degradation and health hazards.

Residents without access to private or communal lavatories or to pit privies frequently resort to nearby rivers and canals for defecation. These same waterways are also used for bathing and laundering, and in some instances as sources of drinking water. Since the city has no central, water-borne sewer system, those sanitary facilities that do exist empty their raw sewage directly into either roadside ditches or septic tanks. Improperly sized, sited, or maintained septic systems encourage seepages that often contaminate shallow groundwater wells and threaten underlying fresh-water aquifers. Since more than fifty percent of the city's population relies on groundwater wells for potable water, the longterm adverse consequences of aquifer pollution are considerable.

In tandem with the problem of sewage disposal is that of solid-waste collection and disposal. Like raw sewage, uncollected garbage makes its way to roadside drainage channels, canals, and rivers, where it accumulates and decays during the dry season (June through August) and exacerbates flooding during the rainy season.[6] Unless cleared before the monsoon season (December through February), this debris clogs drainage ways and together with raw sewage is redeposited in adjacent low-lying areas. As a result of such sanitation deficiencies and subsequent flooding conditions, Indonesia claims one of the highest incidences of cholera in the world.[7]

The provision of potable water has been equally inadequate. Before the Kampung Improvement Programme was instituted, a 1969 survey of households revealed that sixty percent were without access to city-distributed, piped water. In

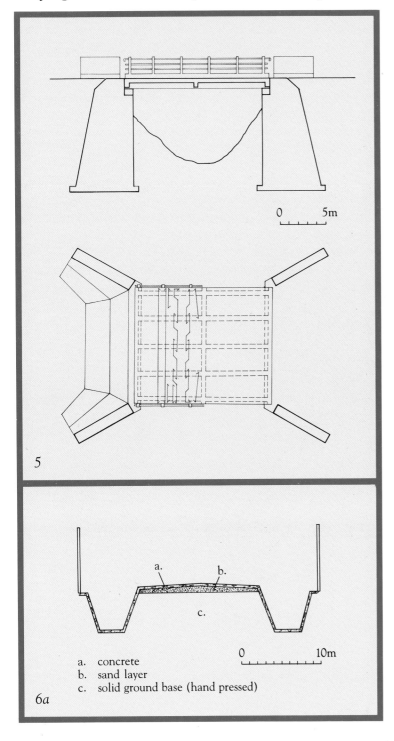

5

a. concrete
b. sand layer
c. solid ground base (hand pressed)

6a

5. Pedestrian bridge with construction details below. Vehicular as well as pedestrian bridges were erected in designated communities. 6a. Section through typical footpath. Footpaths 1.5 metres wide were made of a sand base covered by a concrete surface. 6b. The paths, like the streets, are raised to the level of the houses, with drainage channels on either side that flow into open primary channels.

6b

lieu of this service, residents are forced to obtain water from shallow, oftentimes contaminated wells; from street vendors at prices five times greater than that of piped water; or from area rivers and canals.[8]

Community Cohesion.   In spite of basic infrastructure deficiencies and the resultant environmental degradation, kampungs remain socially stable communities, harbouring a diverse mix of income groups. Many kampung residents are middle-income government or trade and service sector workers who command modest though steady incomes. Even so, the scarcity and cost of available housing and the lack of any type of mortgage system precludes these households from relocating in more affluent areas.[9] Instead they remain within the kampung community, and in doing so provide secondary employment for other, lower-income workers. Typically these workers serve their middle-income neighbours as building labourers, craftsmen, market vendors, hawkers, or transport carriers. This symbiotic relationship between middle- and lower-income households promotes social tolerance and community stability. Whether by choice or because of financial constraints, kampung residents are more likely to remain within their community and upgrade their present dwellings than move, thus accounting for the frequent juxtaposition of houses constructed of permanent materials immediately adjacent to haphazardly constructed shacks.

The Kampung Improvement Programme.   Initially the city government entertained three alternative approaches to improvement. The first called for building new, single-family houses on relatively inexpensive land in the outlying areas of the city, an ambitious but fiscally irresponsible proposition. In light of the limited budget and the costs of providing complete housing units, this approach would produce only 4000 units annu-

ally, thus providing a mere thirteen percent of the projected number of units needed per year. To offset costs and increase volume this approach was to be modified through the institution of rent and mortgage collections. This latter notion was soon abandoned, however, when it was discovered that with average household incomes between ten and fifty dollars (U.S.) per month, the target population's ability to pay for such housing was limited at best. Also, it was reasoned that while this approach might lure some inner-city kampung residents to outlying areas, their numbers would be insufficient to make any appreciable difference in the congested conditions of existing kampungs. In effect this approach required all monies to be channeled into developing new residential areas in outlying regions at the expense of existing kampungs.

A second approach considered was modelled after the "urban renewal" concept of redevelopment. Under this suggestion the city government would acquire and rase existing kampungs and in their place construct new, multistorey residential buildings. In theory, the use of full-service, high-rise buildings allowed for high densities of population without the congestion and environmental degradation that so often accompany overcrowded, tightly packed, low-rise structures. In practice, the cost of providing such buildings on expensive urban land in the quantities needed far exceeded the expenditures anticipated for single-family units on less-expensive suburban land. This cost factor aside, urban-renewal schemes required the mass removal and interim relocation of kampung residents during rasing and construction activities, thus introducing complex logistical and social problems generally associated with large-scale displacement. Although this approach ad-

7. *Greater Jakarta and its kampung areas.*
8. *The Kampung Improvement Programme. An organisation chart, showing agencies necessary for successful implementation.*

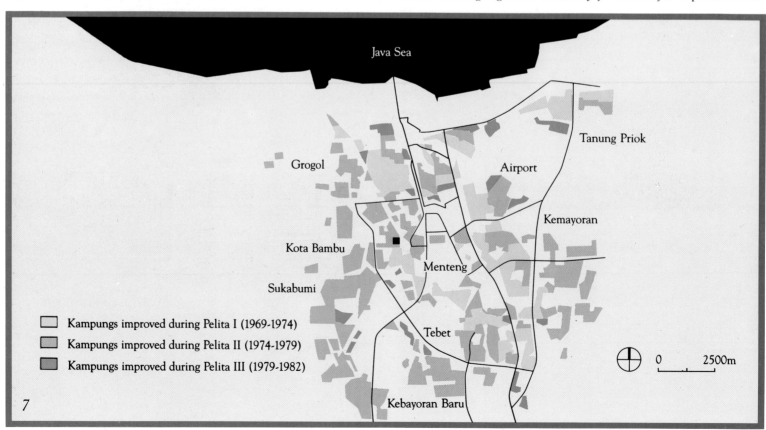

Java Sea

Tanung Priok

Grogol

Airport

Kemayoran

Kota Bambu

Menteng

Sukabumi

☐ Kampungs improved during Pelita I (1969-1974)
☐ Kampungs improved during Pelita II (1974-1979)
☐ Kampungs improved during Pelita III (1979-1982)

Tebet

0   2500m

7

Kebayoran Baru

dressed the problem of dealing with existing kampungs, its economic and social costs proved prohibitive.

A less ambitious yet more fiscally and socially responsible solution evolved from the idea of "site and service." As the name implies, site and service schemes deal only with the provision of land and a minimum level of services; no attempt is made to provide complete houses. Instead government funds are used to acquire vacant land and develop it by the installation of basic infrastructure such as paved roadways, sanitary facilities, and public water taps. The provision of housing is then left solely to the imagination and financial resources of individual households. By eliminating construction costs, the government estimated it would be able to provide serviced plots to twice as many households as it could under the single-family approach.[10] The genius of the K.I.P. was to adapt this approach to existing urban kampungs.

Because of the high cost and scarcity of raw urban land, site and service schemes, as described above, are typically restricted to outlying areas of the city where raw land is cheaper and more abundant. One serious, and sometimes overlooked, drawback to these schemes concerns locational considerations. The popularity of Jakarta's urban kampungs as preferred living areas is attributed as much to their proximity to employment centres as to their tolerance of low-income housing. Without access to private or reliable public transportation, kampung workers in the city's vast trade and service sectors must reside within walking distance of their jobs. This need is illustrated by the very high densities found in the city's more centrally located kampungs near established job markets. The programme began by developing solutions for infra-

structural needs of existing, centrally located kampungs.

The Kampung Improvement Programme came to recognise that, like housing conditions, existing infrastructure conditions vary from kampung to kampung. Thus the level and type of assistance provided was to be adjusted accordingly. Initially, however, design standards were uniform, determined on an areawide basis that assumed all kampungs are similar physically and therefore required the same level of upgrading. Thus, during the programme's first five years (1969–74), roadways, footpaths, sanitary facilities, and public water taps were provided according to a prescribed formula: 75 metres of paved roads and 132 metres of paved footpaths per hectare, one public toilet per 11 hectares, and one public water tap per four hectares. Difficulties with this approach were that it did not take into account pre-existing levels of infrastructure or user behaviour. As a result, certain facilities were duplicated while others were underutilised. A third problem involved the uneven distribution of improvements throughout the kampung. Given a fixed level of service per hectare, residences located along improved roadways or in close proximity to public water taps and sanitary facilities benefited more than those located farther away.

To counter this unevenness as well as account for infrastructure variations among kampungs and user behaviour, functional design standards were adopted, replacing predetermined and less flexible areawide standards. Functional design standards set minimum levels of infrastructure per household rather than per hectare. For example, roads are planned so that all dwellings are within 100 metres of a roadway capable of carrying emergency service vehicles. Similarly, all dwell-

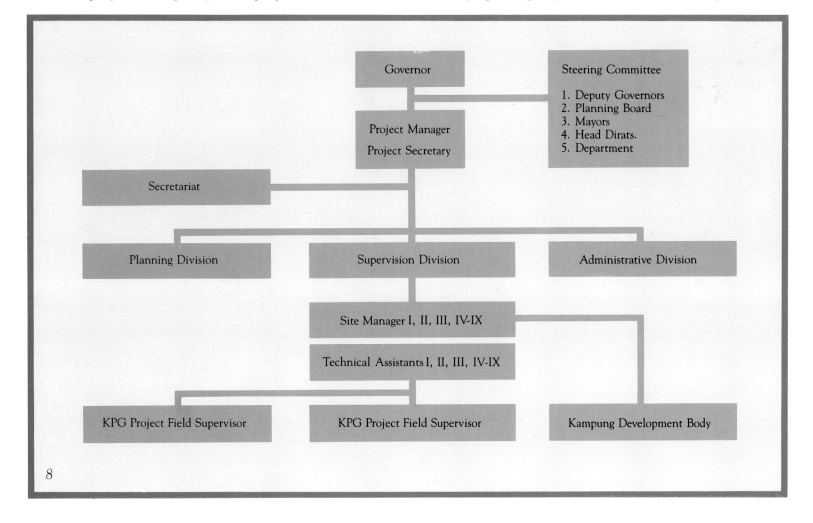

8

ings must be within 20 metres of a paved footpath. Roadway size varies from 4 to 6 metres in width (depending on the anticipated traffic levels) and roads are constructed of sand and crushed stone with a binder course surface. Footpaths are 1.5 metres wide and made of a sand base covered by a concrete surface. All roadways and footpaths are flanked by secondary drainage channels which flow into open primary channels. When appropriate, fill material is used to raise all access routes above the prevailing flood level.

Functional standards for public water taps and sanitary facilities vary depending largely on local environmental conditions (i.e., proximity to and availability of potable shallow ground water, topography, soil characteristics, etc.). At a minimum all dwellings are to be within 125 metres of a public standpipe. Where feasible this level of service is increased to one tap per twenty to fifty families. Minimum public sanitary facilities are provided on the basis of one seat per twelve families. However, because of problems with land acquisition, maintenance, and social acceptance of communal toilet and bathing facilities, individual or multiple family pit privies are installed whenever possible. These are single bamboo enclosures positioned over soil pits where wastes are treated via anaerobic and aerobic bacterial decomposition.

Community facilities such as health centres and primary schools are provided according to population clusters. Health posts, two-room structures offering first-aid treatment and education in hygiene, nutrition, and family planning, are allocated at one per 3000 persons. Health clinics, larger structures that provide more comprehensive medical treatment, are distributed one per 30,000 persons. Primary schools, capable of accommodating at least 500 students on a double shift basis, are built one per 6000 persons. These buildings are generally one or two storeys high and are sited to be within walking distance of the children they serve.

Programme Administration. The K.I.P. is administered by the Muhammad Husin Thamrin Proyek (MHT), an independent technical unit of Jakarta's city government. Under Repelita I, the First Five-Year Development Plan, the programme was administered piecemeal by various departments. Poor interdepartmental coordination, resulting in contractor and scheduling conflicts, precipitated a fundamental change in the programme's implementation. In 1974, under Repelita II, the Second Five-Year Development Plan, the MHT was created as an umbrella organisation to consolidate and expedite programme administration. Although some elements of the K.I.P. such as the payment of contractors and acquisition of private property remained under individual department jurisdiction, the overall responsibility of programme execution became the charge of the MHT. In terms of management the approach is modelled after conventional public works programmes.[11]

The functions and operations of the MHT are distributed among four divisions: administration, finance, planning, and supervision. These divisions coordinate, document, and monitor the progress of each improvement scheme as well as providing detailed physical planning assistance. All activities of the MHT are subject to approval by the Steering Committee. This committee, consisting of district mayors and various DKI

department heads, also oversees the selection and recommendation of kampungs for improvement. Final approval, however, rests with the governor.

Kampung Selection. Although occasionally selected in response to political pressure, kampungs are typically chosen for improvement under the K.I.P. according to their existing social, economic, and physical conditions as compared with established criteria. These criteria consider kampung age, density, household income, and prevailing environmental conditions, giving preference and priority to the oldest, densest, and poorest kampungs, which exhibit the worst environmental conditions. Nevertheless, some kampungs, by virtue of their location, are precluded from consideration. Kampungs located in areas considered unsuitable for permanent settlements because of unavoidable health and safety hazards (e.g., along canal and riverbanks, under high-voltage cables, or along railway lines) are classified as Never-To-Be-Improved. Also in this category are kampungs located in areas zoned for other use (industrial or green-belt areas) or on land belonging to private developers. Thus the K.I.P. is integrated into the city's larger and more comprehensive development plan.

9. In unimproved settlements, water is expensive.
10. Public washstand. Pure water for drinking and washing makes a major difference in the quality of life.

9

Implementation Procedures. Kampung selection is followed by programme implementation. The K.I.P. planning staff prepares a plan that outlines the type and location of proposed improvements based on specific infrastructural and social deficiencies. This plan is modified during discussion with the *camat* (subdistrict head) and *lurah* (urban village head), who represent the kampung community. The plan is then transformed into engineering drawings and tender documents and contracted out to local contractors. All planning and design work up to the tender documents stage is the responsibility of the K.I.P. planning division. All coordination with kampung residents is the responsibility of the *camat* and *lurah.*

Community Participation. When a kampung is selected for improvement, the *camat* within whose district the kampung is located is appointed site manager. In this capacity the *camat*'s chief responsibility is to act as a liaison between the K.I.P. technical staff and the residents of the host kampung. This responsibility is frequently shared with the *lurah,* and all negotiations regarding the selection of access routes and alternative sites for schools or health clinics are conducted through them. Although these representatives are not obligated to consult with anyone, they usually seek advice from unpaid community leaders who represent 400 households and unpaid neighbourhood leaders representing forty households prior to final plan approval. In turn these leaders may hold open meetings of the official village forum, where the proposal improvement plan and work schedule are discussed. Since the level of community involvement is a function of the *camat*'s discretion, it is highly variable. Community participation is essentially limited to removing or setting back buildings that obstruct proposed access routes; to maintaining the infrastructure, once provided; and to organising the collection of refuse from households.[12]

Programme Funding. Under Repelita I, the K.I.P. was funded by the city government at a cost of 15.6 million dollars (U.S.), or thirteen dollars per capita. Eighty-seven kampungs were improved under this programme, covering an area of 2400 hectares and affecting 1.2 million people.[13] For Repelita II, the city acquired a World Bank Loan to cover approximately fifty percent of the K.I.P. budget, thus doubling the rate of kampung improvements from 500 hectares to almost 1000 hectares per year. Funding for this second phase totalled approximately $125.3 million, or sixty dollars per capita.

No funds are collected in the form of a tax on improved kampungs. Instead residents are required to contribute, without compensation,[14] those portions of their properties required for road widening and access routes. In addition, the village forum is expected to assume the maintenance costs of cleaning and repairing footpaths, drainage channels, lavatory facilities, and garbage-disposal facilities. These costs are paid out of voluntary community funds.

The K.I.P. as a Model. Cities in the contemporary Islamic world, like most cities in the Third World, are faced with providing suitable living environments for a burgeoning population. Housing built by government agencies has not been the most effective answer. It is too slow and too expensive and has never quite reached the lowest income groups. The K.I.P. is an alternate approach. It accepts squatter settlements rather than removing them. It emphasises urban amenities, not bricks and mortar. It is a concept which began within the city government of Jakarta; it has mobilised grass-roots organisations; it has provided an urban environment quickly and cheaply; and, what is more, it has developed management skills and administrative networks to continue the process. The result is the transformation over time of squatter settlements into prospering urban communities.

PONDOK PESANTREN PABELAN
CENTRAL JAVA, INDONESIA
ONGOING SINCE 1965

The students of the *pesantren* are schooled
in the building trades, and have built many
of the school's and village's structures.

Food preparation and storage for the village and school.

The library together with the plaza in
front are the centre of the pesantren.

PONDOK PESANTREN PABELAN. Client: Hamam Djaᶜfar, Kyai; Habib Chirzin, Deputy; Planners/Designers: Amin Arraihana, Fanani; LP3ES, Abdurrahman Wahid; Builders: People of the Pesantren.[1]

For more than five centuries traditional religious boarding schools have played a major role in the Islamic system of education in Indonesia.[2] Independent of the government, today's *pesantrens* educate an estimated four million students or eighteen percent of school enrollment.[3] Concentrated in rural areas, *pesantrens* exert an influence far stronger than their numbers would suggest, not only in religious education but in teaching practical skills for community development. The Pondok Pesantren has distinguished itself in the teaching of contemporary building skills to its students and the surrounding community.

Development of the Pesantrens. Pesantrens are individualistic, each headed by a *kyai,* who is a charismatic leader and a learned teacher. His training varies; typically he is a graduate of another *pesantren,* often having had further religious study. A *kyai* begins by gathering in his own home a number of students (*santris*), to whom he provides religious instruction. Most *pesantrens* today have expanded from this individual instruction to include a broader general curriculum. Since *pesantrens* do not have to comply with government prescribed curricula, the amount of religious instruction and the nature of the secular education, including the sciences, vocational training, and instruction in agriculture, vary widely.

The background of students educated at the *pesantrens* falls into three groups. There are the children of the religious elite, and since these may go on to become *pesantren* leaders or religious scholars, their study emphasises religion. Then there are the children of the local village farmers and small traders, who attend the *pesantren* free of charge. The third group are children of village families of moderate means, children of urban traders, or children of civil servants. Members of these groups are likely to follow their parents' professions after acquiring basic skills at a *pesantren.* But individual education is not the main goal. The *pesantren*'s aim is to train a cadre to serve the

1. Located in Central Java, the Pondok Pesantren Pabelan, is one in a chain of educational institutions throughout Java.

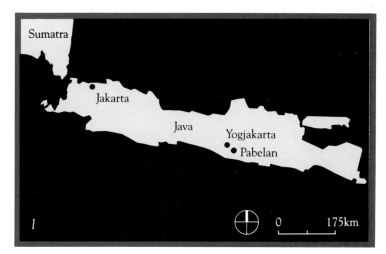

1

rural development needs of the Islamic community. And just as the strength of the *kyai* comes in the community recognition of his role as model, so too the strength of the *pesantren* lies in the degree to which it embodies the values of the community around it. For the *pesantren* is part of the community. Its primary function is community service, and as such it has actually become an informal institution for rural community development.

The Pondok Pesantren Pabelan[4] is just such an institution. Its success as a community development institution is evident in the level of community involvement in its activities. The *pesantren* has concentrated on training programmes that develop needed skills in agriculture and health care, and a particularly notable programme in building. All this is carried out in a spirit of cooperation and directly benefits the villagers as well as the *pesantren* members.

2. Site plan of pesantren and village.

Pabelan and the Pesantren. The village of Pabelan is in Central Java, a region densely populated and heavily cultivated; an area of volcanic mountains, numerous streams, and dense jungle growth nurtured by the heavy rains and nearly constant warm temperatures. Pabelan is about 40 kilometres inland to the east of Yogjakarta, near the town of Muntilan and along a branch of the Kali Progo River. Most villagers are small-scale farmers. Their houses, simple rectangular wood-frame structures, cluster along the village streets. The *pesantren* structures are concentrated in the midst of the village within a five hectare area, and village houses sit alongside *pesantren* buildings. The bond between the two is strong because their aspirations, social, economic, and cultural, are linked.

Pondok Pesantren Pabelan was begun in 1965 by Kyai Hamam Dja'far, a skilled farmer and a graduate of Gontor, a *pesantren* noted for its training of teachers. Dja'far's first students were from the village, all transfers from the formal government schooling. His facilities were limited to a traditional

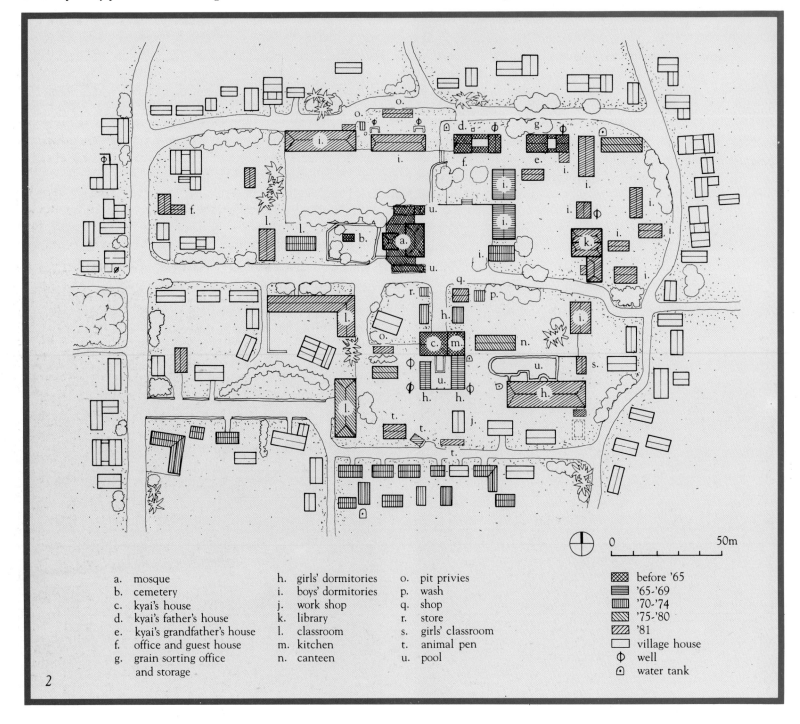

a.	mosque	h.	girls' dormitories
b.	cemetery	i.	boys' dormitories
c.	kyai's house	j.	work shop
d.	kyai's father's house	k.	library
e.	kyai's grandfather's house	l.	classroom
f.	office and guest house	m.	kitchen
g.	grain sorting office and storage	n.	canteen

o.	pit privies
p.	wash
q.	shop
r.	store
s.	girls' classroom
t.	animal pen
u.	pool

before '65
'65-'69
'70-'74
'75-'80
'81
village house
Φ well
water tank

0   50m

2

mosque, two houses belonging to Dja'far's family, and a third small structure, plus 0.25 hectare of house yard. Most of the thirty-five students continued to live in the village houses, but would gather daily with their teacher for instruction which combined Koranic studies with training in agriculture. Financing for the *pesantren* came from the proceeds of Dja'far's family farm and the sale of volcanic sand and stone as building materials.

Students from outside Pabelan began to join the *pesantren* in 1970, living in the *kyai's* home. By 1978 the *pesantren* had grown to 971 students (668 males and 303 females) taught by sixty teachers (forty-eight males and twelve females), overseen by the *kyai's* deputy Habib Chirzin. The students come from throughout the Indonesian archipelago, seventy-five of them from the village of Pabelan. The teachers tend to be graduates of the *pesantren* at either Pabelan or Gontor. The curriculum is divided into six levels and includes instruction in Arabic and English, reflecting the influence of Gontor, which is also noted for its language programme.

With the help of community resources, the *pesantren* facilities have gradually expanded. The facilities developed without an actual plan, but according to need. There are today more than forty structures (several public buildings, twenty-two classrooms, sixteen dormitories, and various service buildings and economic enterprises) built by members of the *pesantren* with the assistance of builders from the village.[5]

The old mosque marks the centre of the village and the *pesantren*. The mosque and the large sandy square it faces serve as the major meeting place for the villagers and *pesantren* members. To the north of the square are the *pesantren* office

and guest house. To the south is the *kyai's* house. These were the original *pesantren* structures. The mosque is over sixty years old, considered particularly old in a region where timber structures have a short life, continually worn by the heavy rains and high humidity. The mosque consists of the traditional three ascending spaces, indicated in the roof heights, and reflecting increasing sacredness as they rise. The outer porch (*serambie*) is used as a classroom and a place for debates and public meetings. The inner chamber (*ruang dalam*) is used for prayer. The highest innermost area (*mustoko*) is the storage place for the *pesantren* valuables and holy books.

The first buildings added in the late 1960s were dormitories to the east of the square. When enrollment grew in 1970, some additional dormitories, classrooms, and storage facilities, were built, all located along the central village road which passes through the *pesantren*.

Construction activity increased considerably in 1974 with the addition of more classrooms, dormitories, canteens, and a cooperative shop. The boys' dormitories are clustered in two groups, one to the northeast and a second to the north of the mosque and cemetery. The girls' dormitories are to the southeast, close to the *kyai's* home, and grouped around a pool. The classrooms are concentrated along the western portion of the site. The workshop and animal pens are found at the southern edge of the *pesantren*. Canteens, kitchens, washstands, and lavatories are scattered throughout the site. A library and meeting hall built in 1976, used by both the villagers and the *pesantren*, stands alongside the village road, just to the east of the main square.

The *pesantren* buildings are grouped together defining open spaces, in clusters similar to those of the village houses. Throughout the site, low walls of rough volcanic stone form terraces and further delineate these outside open spaces. The

3. Morning exercises in the pesantren square are part of the carefully balanced but tightly packed daily schedule.

3

areas are communal, and function as playgrounds for Girl Guide and Boy Scout activities and for sports, particularly badminton and table tennis.

Outside the five-hectare area are ten fishponds, built by the *pesantren,* and a small piece of agricultural land.

The *kyai* has long since ceased providing the main financing for the *pesantren.* Today the major source of income is student fees. Each student able to do so pays a monthly fee for food, lodging, and tuition.[6] Added to this are income from the sale of rice and tobacco produced on the student farm,[7] income generated from the fishponds, and income from the sale of volcanic stone and sand. Village donations, difficult to quantify, are collected every Thursday and come in the form of cash or rice.

Daily Activities. The goal of all *pesantren* members is to learn to live the Muslim way of life, based on Muslim teachings and Muslim law, looking to the *kyai* as a model.

The *pesantren* students keep a rigourous schedule centred around the five daily prayers. They rise at 4:00 A.M. for morning prayer. By 5:00 A.M. the *pesantren* is a flurry of activity with students sweeping the grounds and clearing away refuse. Until breakfast at 7:00 there is time for sports or, for the younger students, reading the Koran. Formal classes begin promptly at 7:30 and continue until 1:00 when they break for noon prayer and lunch. Afternoon classes in Arabic and English meet from 2:00 until afternoon prayer at 3:30. At 4:00 an hour and a half of sports begins, followed by Maghrib prayer. Dinner and evening prayer begin at 7:00. There is one last hour of guided study in the evening before retiring at 9:30. Sunday and Thursday evenings are set aside for public speaking (in Bahasa, Arabic, and English). On Thursdays, two hours of lesson time are devoted to vocational training[8] and

social work; the afternoon is set aside for Boy Scout and Girl Guide training. Time is found for theatrical performances, music, folk singing, poetry reading, and painting. Adherence to such a strict schedule is intended to produce a disciplined student. At the same time, a spirit of mutual aid pervades all the *pesantren* activities.

The *pesantren* is self-governing and financially self-reliant. The daily administration of the *pesantren* is carried out by a two-level system: the Pesantren Association, which includes the villagers, the teachers, and the students; and the student organisation (also including the teachers). The student government is open to students from the second year onwards. It consists of a five-member Executive Committee, elected annually, and subcommittees which oversee the various *pesantren* activities. The student government decides the day-to-day affairs, calculates project expenses, and plans fund raising. Both the daily routine tasks and special activities are carried out by the student organisation without requiring the involvement of the *kyai* or his deputy.

Training in Building. The *pesantren* offers students and villagers training in carpentry, masonry, and tile laying—skills put directly to use as the *pesantren* expands and builds needed structures with readily available materials. For example, in 1975 the decision was made to build a library and meeting hall and

4. *Classroom built by the pesantren students.*
5. *The mosque at prayer time. The mosque is the oldest building within the pesantren.*

to use the actual construction process as a training programme in building to benefit both the *pesantren* members and villagers. A Jakarta-based research organisation, LP3ES, assisted in setting up the programme. Two young architects, one still a student, were responsible for the design of the building. To oversee the construction and the associated training programme, two representatives from the Ministry of Industry were invited to the *pesantren.*

Beginning in early 1975, twenty students and twenty villagers took part in the nine-month instruction programme. The programme was divided into three-month phases: the initial selection and treatment of timber and the construction of the foundation and plinth, the erection of the timber frame and truss, and the construction of the brick walls and tile roofs. At the end of nine months the two instructors left and the trainees continued to work. The building was completed in October of 1976 and opened in November. Buildings constructed after this date reflect the high standard of skills developed during the training programme.

Community Development Projects. In keeping with the spirit of mutual aid and dedication to community service, a number of community development efforts were undertaken by the *pesantren* to benefit the village as a whole. In 1978, using funds from a government grant from the Department of People's Welfare, the *pesantren* began a village home-improvement programme. During the period forty houses were improved, involving three sections of the village. Members of the *pesantren* helped to organise the villagers into construction teams, each consisting of five households. The working groups were directed by councils which decided which houses to repair. The decisions were not necessarily made on the basis of need, but on the desire of the owner and his ability to supply matching funds. Any expenses beyond the 10,000 rupiahs contributed by the *pesantren* were borne by the owner. Construction was in stages, work being done on five houses at a time. Dirt floors were replaced with

6. *The village and school have cooperated in the management of water systems. A washing area is shown here.*

stone foundations and cement floors, walls were reconstructed to sill level, windows were installed, roofs were replaced, and areas around houses were paved and stone retaining walls constructed to prevent flooding.

The same working groups took part in a road-building and retaining wall/flood control project. Working groups would carry stones in chainlike fashion up from the river. Masons assisted, charging only half their normal rate. The *pesantren* contributed the needed cement. Families contributed, based on their distance from the road and size of their garden plot. The *pesantren* also built a hydraulic pump for water supply.

The *pesantren* is involved in a number of nonbuilding development projects, among them a health service staffed by a cadre of forty students and forty villagers, and a credit scheme which allows villagers to buy goats and chickens from the *pesantren,* repaying the loan from the income. A number of demonstration plots were cultivated to show villagers what can and cannot be grown in the region. Using the meeting hall as a training centre, the *pesantren* provides the village with counselling on housing, architecture, and settlement of land; agriculture and cattle breeding; and community health care. The *pesantren* continues to try to improve the quality of service and to extend the area it serves.

Shortly after its completion, the library/meeting hall was used to house a six-month-long community-development training project, held under the auspices of the Food and Agriculture Organisation of the United Nations. The twenty-four participants came from eight different *pesantrens* located throughout Indonesia. The *pesantren* has since hosted several training programmes, workshops, and seminars attended by members of other *pesantrens* and rural development groups.

As a self-financed and self-governing institution, the *pesantren* is itself a model for the community. It relies on economic use of materials, use of existing resources, materials, and technologies, and extending those skills through training. The training, involving the villagers as well as *pesantren* members, becomes a key part in the process of community development, aiding both the village of Pabelan and the villages to which the graduates return.

HASSAN FATHY
CHAIRMAN'S AWARD

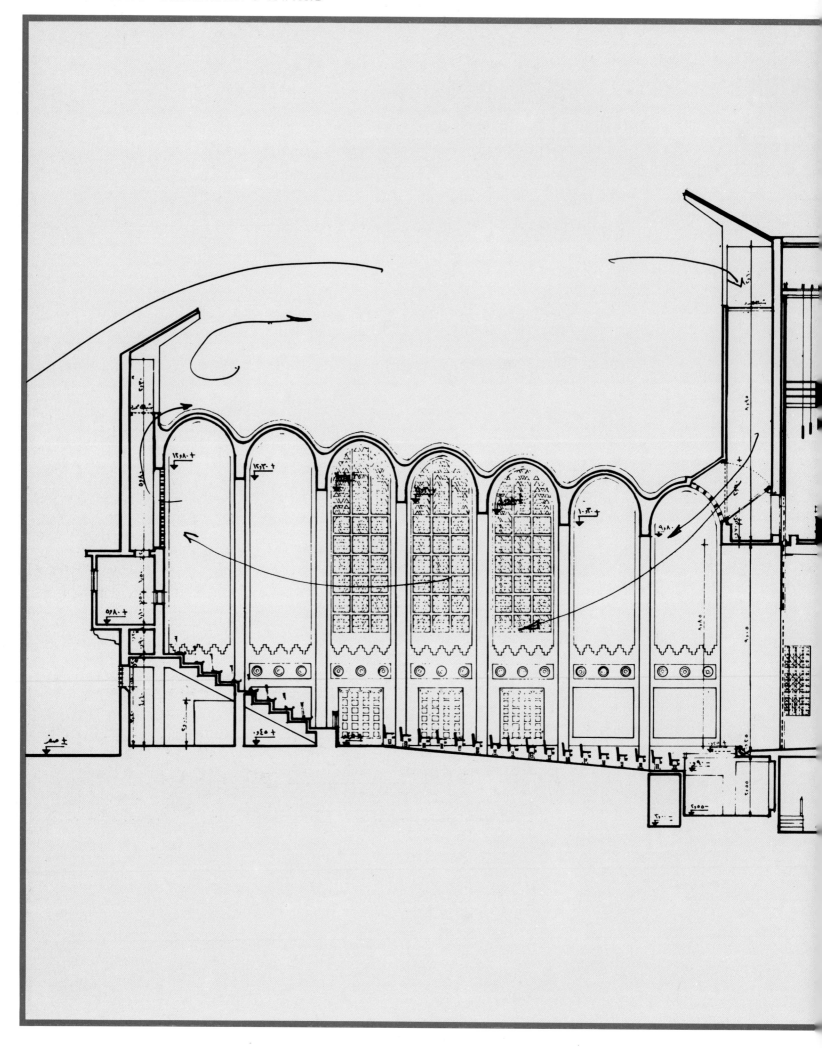

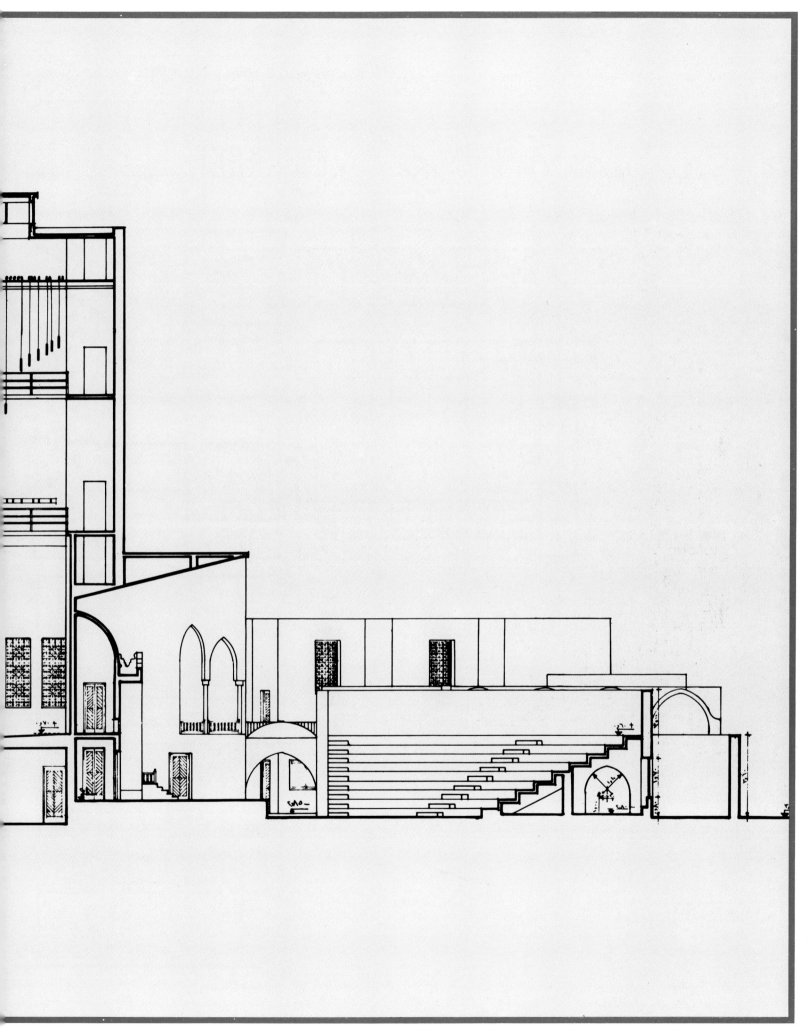

The Nile Festival Village Project, Tarh el-Bahr Island,
Luxor. Project for the Luxor cultural center.

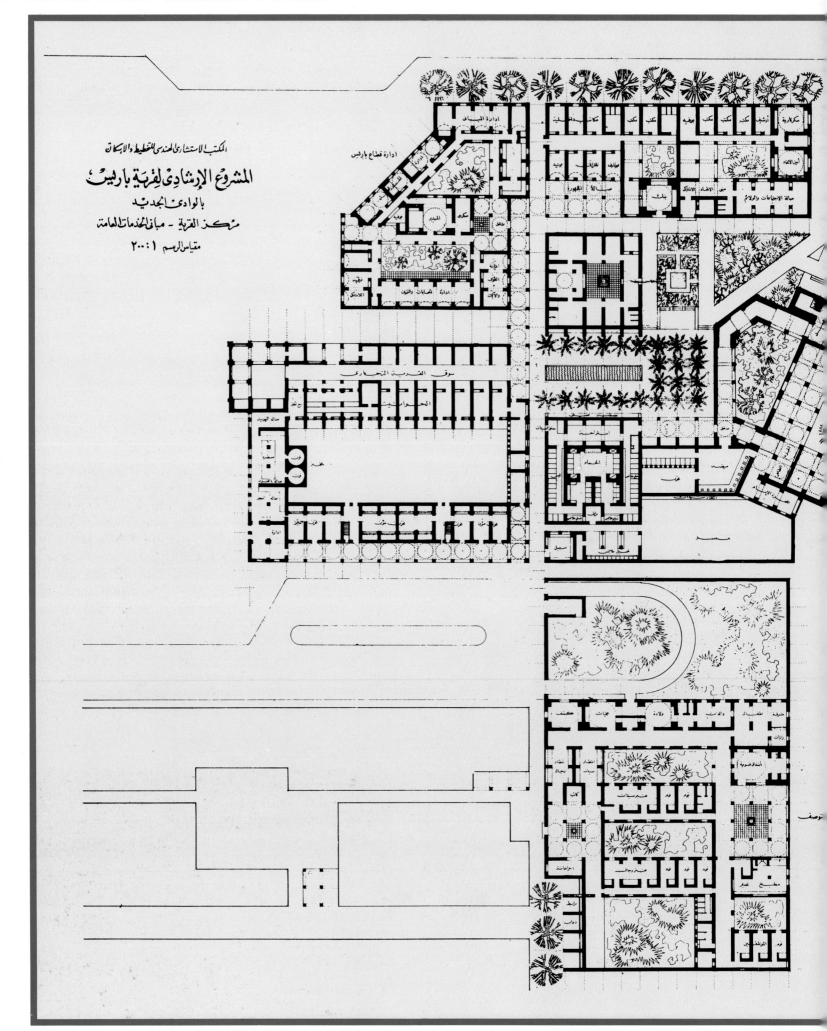

A partial plan of the village of Bariz.

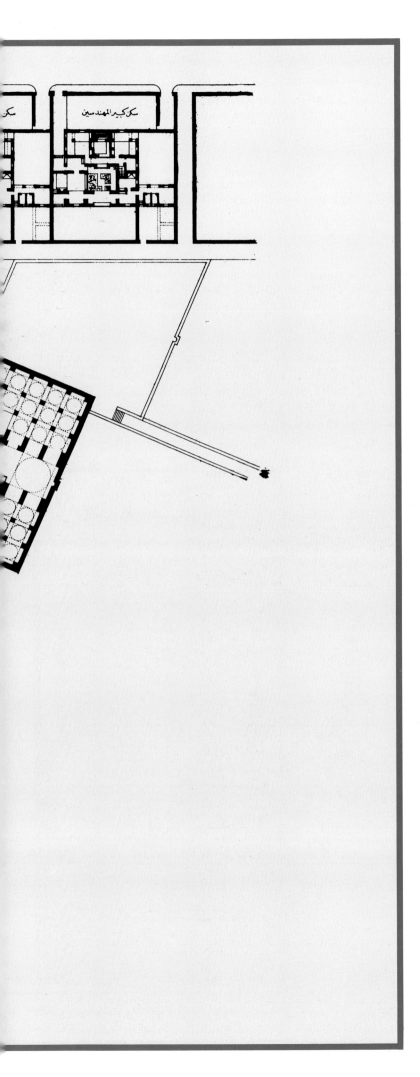

HASSAN FATHY.
Chairman's Award

During the process of the development of basic guidelines for the Award, the Steering Committee came to realise that special cases may present themselves which fall outside the bounds of the general criteria. As Chairman of the Steering Committee, I have established the Chairman's Award to honour such special achievements.

I have the pleasure of naming as the first recipient of the Chairman's Award Hassan Fathy, an Egyptian architect, artist, and poet, in acknowledgement of his lifelong contribution and commitment to architecture in the Muslim world. The Master Jury has supported this decision.

Hassan Fathy's early works and teachings revealed the kernels from which later works would flourish: his commitment to the poor and his extraordinary aesthetic sense. They led him from youthful attempts to improve the conditions of worker housing on his father's estates to the mature expression of his ideas, fully developed in the village of New Gourna, Egypt. As champion of indigenous building, he has proved the graceful mud brick structures to be both economical to build and admirably suited to the climate.

Hassan Fathy has taught us the value of the vernacular environment. And he has shown us that the lessons to be learned are modern lessons. His impact has been worldwide. —Aga Khan

It was as early as 1947 that the architectural press recorded the bold experiment in design, construction, and community planning which Hassan Fathy had undertaken in the building of the village of New Gourna. At a time when the Modern Movement was captivating more and more architectural imaginations and was beginning to gain ground internationally, this Egyptian architect was advocating an alternate aesthetic and a different constructional ethos. The idea was as simple and as complex as the nature of traditional society in Egypt. It identified the best preindustrial building systems of Egypt and strove to understand their climatic efficiency, to appreciate their aesthetic, and to extend their performance limits. One such system was that of the residential architecture of Mamluk and Ottoman Cairo, with its ventilated two-storey halls (qa'ah), screens (mashrabiyya) and courtyards. The other was

The plan of Gourna.

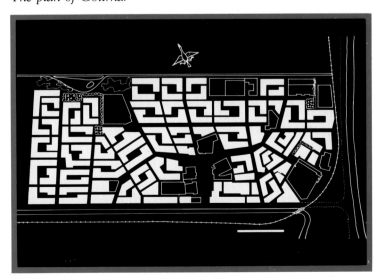

one of mud brick construction first observed by the architect in Nubia: leaned vaults, built without scaffolding; domes on squinches which were built over square rooms and laid in a continuing spiral.

These universes of forms did not exist in isolation. While the urban forms were no longer accessible to the architect because the building tradition which had created them had disappeared in Cairo, the rural forms were still a direct product of rural Nubian society. There the masonry skills, particularly those for building in mud brick, had continued unchanged into this century. Fathy discovered them on a trip to Upper Egypt. The architect accepted not only the forms of this building tradition but the entire constructional system and its constraints. By working within it, he elaborated its spatial and structural aspects. What evolved from a close observation, filtered through the architect's superb aesthetic sense, was a distinct, clearly ordered universe of architectural hierarchies based on the juxtaposition and arrangement of the following elements: the square domed unit, the rectangular vaulted unit, the semidomed alcove, the breezeway/loggia, the courtyard. The urban forms of Cairo, which he so lovingly collected and to which he referred in his sketches and studies, served to enrich this architectural universe and provided models for later larger-scale projects.

Yet the moving force behind his acceptance of this constructional system was not the innate beauty and restraint of its forms alone. It was a much more keenly felt need, the need to provide shelter and the possibility of building shelter for the poor. It might seem obvious today that the most efficient way to provide shelter for this burgeoning population is to provide access to tools and skills, so that they can build themselves. At that time, the idea was almost revolutionary among professional circles, architects and planners, not only in Egypt but world-wide. What Fathy proposed was a collaborative effort between architect, craftsmen, and the eventual users of the building, where skills and lessons in layout and building could be immediately returned to the community. Turning to local materials and traditional techniques allowed for the making of a house, a street, an entire environment without much outlay of cash. In Egypt, this meant turning to the use of earth as building material.

The need for answers to the problem of shelter, which Fathy felt already in the late 1940s, much before anyone else, created the powerful idea of reliance on one's own resources or *self-help*. It also turned attention to the most readily available materials, such as earth. It raised the status of traditional rural constructional systems and presented them as a viable alternative, indeed the only alternative for building sanely and beautifully in areas of Egypt and by extension in similar areas throughout the world.

Hassan Fathy was born in 1900, at the time when Egypt was under the economic and political control of Western Europe. He reached adulthood in the period of struggle for national sovereignty against the British and for popular sovereignty against the Egyptian Crown. His formative years as architect and thinker were also the very fruitful years of Egyptian literary and intellectual modernism, with its twin trends of Romanticism and Enlightenment. Poetry, novels, drama, biographies, literary and political criticism dealt with issues of identity and modernity, secularism and Islam, elitism and populism. This avalanche of writings greatly enriched the Arabic language, and even the forms and the concepts which had been taken from other literatures and philosophies had been transformed and naturalised. Almost none of these writings addressed the questions of architectural criticism or of the built environment. Moreover, the visual language of architecture as taught and built remained wholly an import.

The architectural education which Hassan Fathy received in the Architecture Section of the School of Engineering at Giza was the model curriculum established and promoted by the Ecole des Beaux Arts of Paris. Its visual vocabulary, its major formal and professional concerns did not include any recognition of particular local needs, desires, or historical references. While surrounded by intense literary and intellectual activity in other spheres, a young architect had to find his own architectural equivalent to the new Arabic language.

For Hassan Fathy, the years immediately after the completion of his professional education were ones of intense activity and discovery. The vast array of residential architecture of the Mamluk and Ottoman periods provided him with the basic spatial and formal units of the new vocabulary which he was assembling. It was a period during which he internalised the prevailing concepts of Egyptian architecture, urban as well as rural. It was also a period of his first experiments of building with mud brick. From these beginnings came also the perseverance, in spite of all odds, to call for and build a *natural* architecture, closely allied with a place and a culture.

Throughout his life he designed more than thirty projects, more than two-thirds of which have been realised in part or in full. But for him all are called studies, because they develop in one aspect or another the elemental units of the new or renewed architecture. His writings and thoughts serve to underline his main concerns for cultural integrity.[1]

HASSAN FATHY SPEAKS.

Musicality in Building. If the building, the room, the space I surround myself with is proportioned harmoniously, it is musical. That is why we have to introduce musicality into our town planning and into our architecture by respecting proportion, as in musical harmony. In a room the eye will discern the main line, the main chord, and will perceive at the same time, just as it perceives them in music, any other elements

Gouaches in this chapter by Hassan Fathy.

that contribute to either a sense of harmony or a sense of discord. The harmonic form should radiate, and create in colour, texture, and shape, a congruence with your inner feelings, as harmonic music does. The modern architecture that is pure engineering creates discord because it does not harmonise with the natural and the human. This discord affects us internally; psychologically, ugliness is refused. If only the eye could suffer like the ear, and if only the eye, when it sees bad proportions or ugly things, could become red or have tears. Unfortunately, this doesn't take place. But we have the tears within us.

Technical architecture must be subordinated to the natural principles of harmony and reaction to forces, as well as to the human principles of tradition, human scale, and spirituality. Technique, which can be taught in the schools, is not the same as art, which is a gift of God. Technique is like musical scales. Scales are not music by themselves. If we used technique mechanically, it would be like going to a concert and

hearing someone playing the scales. There must be more—and when there is, we hear music, we see harmony, we create culture. And when technique is given to different people, just as when the scales are used by different people, the results will differ, because the cultural background of each individual or group will differ.

There is a monastery in the desert in Egypt, and I met one of the monks. The monk had made his own cell with his hands—very simple—it was modelled and it radiated spirituality. Later I visited the same monastery and I found they had built ten rooms, ten cells of concrete. I was horrified. I went to the bishop and asked, "Father, what have you done to your monks? These rooms are the rooms for servants in a third-class hotel in Cairo. You have taken away their spirituality."

Building as a Spiritual Act. When man is handling raw material, natural material like stone, what is he doing? When he is dressing stone he is removing what is superficial and preserving what is essential. So he is spiritualising himself and spiritualising the stone. There is a story of a man passing three men who are dressing stone. He asked them, "What are you doing?" The first said, "I am making a living." The second said, "I am dressing stone." And the third said, "I am building a cathedral." Only the last had a sense of his task in the context of man's desires and the material's capabilities together, and saw beyond merely his own purposes or the technical problem of working with the stone.

The Mechanical is Death. We might look to the classical architecture that has been preserved from antiquity and imitated to find an architecture that represents an ideal combination of nature and culture, that answers local needs, and that incorporates the human scale and tradition. If you visit Venice or any part of the Old World where there is man-made architecture from natural materials, normal materials, you will find culture. Venice is human. Walking through its narrow streets, more beautiful than the big squares and fashionable piazzas, you meet surprises in human scale and reference. When you consider the work necessary for a handmade structure; the placing of every brick was the decision to put it here as an arch, there as a wall, and so on, and in the effort of every decision was the basic nature of man. There is an aesthetic

value in this method of working by hand. If you take the opposite method of prefabrication and you just have bulks which you carry with a crane and set with a crane, you see that man contributes nothing. Too often now we build in this way. We build one house and put six zeroes next to it, making it a million. But the mechanical takes away from human harmony with nature, materials, and tradition; the mechanical, like symmetry, is death.

The Shell of a Snail. In the ideal architecture, modelled by craftsmen, by artisans, man would be putting something of himself into the material and radiating something, giving it something that, along with the essence of the material, would be reradiated to man, and would be doing him good. The principle of accretion allows for the constant interaction of man and material and environment. To my mind, architecture is like the shell of the snail, the soft part secreting calcium carbonates, and by natural forces making the form by movement and surface tension. The grains would arrange themselves in a village, returning on the soft, living part that created it and gave it form. For man, the universe, the sky, the sun, the moon, the wind, his own body, his brain, his heart, and all his reactions are transferred to his fingers, shaping the brick, shaping the mud, sculpting; he is radiating from his body into the material as the environment has radiated into him. When he creates a form, it becomes a part of his environment, and will reradiate the feelings he invested in it, which in their turn are derived from the universe around him; so man works in harmony with his world.

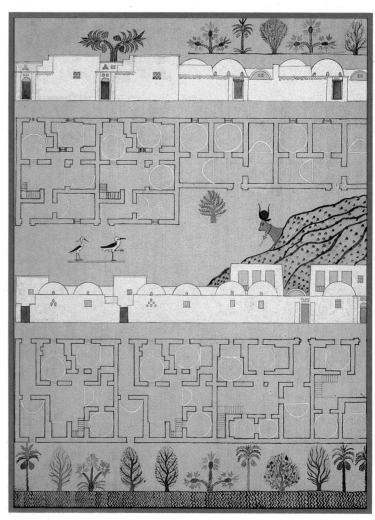

Civility in Building. Architecture is a communal art, because we put the building into the city to be seen by everyone; architecture, in fact, forces itself on everyone. If a bad painting is made, it will end up on the painter's studio wall, and bad music will never have the chance to be played in the concert hall. But the architect can, to my mind, be like a dictator, because people are forced to pass through the door he designs, and when he puts anything that is ugly in his building, it is a pity, because it is forced upon the community. An ugly or senseless building is an insult to every gentlemen passing in front of it; it says: "This is your worth, Mister."

But beautiful architecture is an act of civility towards the man who comes to the building. It is as if the building were bowing to you at every corner, as in a minuet. Every building should add to the culture of man. But how can it do this when it does not respect human reference and human scale? We should reintroduce man into our architecture; we must reintroduce human scale, human needs, and human tradition.

Culture is more than what goes into construction, and this is why we cannot simply import methods and materials that may seem, scientifically, to be efficient. Culture is the unique response of man to his environment in his attempt to answer both physical and spiritual needs. Because both needs and environments vary in different parts of the world, culture, necessarily, is variable, too.

Forces of Climate. For example, in architecture, the element of heat would, as a force, create a different form than would the element of cold. We would not expect an Arab in the desert to have a Swiss chalet with a gabled roof to run off rain and snow, because he has no rain or snow; he sleeps on the roof.

When you have a 30° C. difference between day and night, you have to live in coolness. So here is the importance in the forms which the different people produced reacting with the environment—building for heat, for warming or for cooling. And all my work has been in the hot, arid zones in which I have been designing for cooling. I have seen that what serves the form for heating cannot serve the form for cooling. (From remarks recorded at Aiglemont, April 1978)

Whenever we build a human settlement, whether a village of fifty families or a city of a million, the inescapable and basic unit is the individual family dwelling, and in town just as in village it has the same function. The house, more than sheltering us from rain, sun, dust, and other elemental afflictions, shelters us from the world. A house is not a machine for living in; it is a private world, dependable, unchanging, a constant kindly refuge in the cultural avalanche that we are pleased to call civilisation. If the family is the fundamental social group—the interpreter and buffer between the individual and society—then the house has an analogous function as be-

tween the individual and the world of things. It is the objective and tangible projection of the family, and the most important thing in a family's or an individual's life.

Even in a village it is desirable that the houses should be restful, private, human in size, and related simply to their environment; how much more does a townsman, whose daily labour is not with the elemental realities of ploughing and harvest, but rather with the artificial business of office and factory—how much more does he need some structurally comprehensive refuge to protect his individuality and to calm his spirit.

Let us not be too frightened by the size of the problem to make our solutions human. (From *The City of the Future, the Dwelling within the Urban Settlement*, 1960)

Human groups are like individuals—each has its own personality and its speciality in the different branches of science and the arts in which it excels. This collective personality is the outcome of the contribution of the mass of individuals that make the group. It depends upon the genius of the race, the accumulated experience relegated to the memory of the group in the shape of tradition, as well as on many other factors. In consequence, it is the duty of the planner to consider the interaction between the configuration of the city in space and its cultural movement. In other words, to recognise the cultural vitality of the group. (From *Inaugural Address*, The International Round Table Conference for the Architecture and Planning of Cairo, sponsored by the Ministry of Culture, September 1969, Cairo, Egypt)

In the policy of rural housing and village rehabilitation we should merge the technology of building with the aims of philosophy in the planning of new settlements and old, where men will be able to realise their true potentials. Just as each village in Nubia, when the people were given the chance in 1934, has developed its own personality and flavor, and made its distinctive contribution to the understanding of the nature of culture, so we may expect each one of the modern villages to develop its own flavor of cultural life, starting with the very buildings that make it, and thus enrich the lives of its inhabitants and of the country. And, just as we have brought down the physical planning to the level of the brick, we have to bring down our socioeconomic planning to the level of the family and the individual man.

Above all, we have to avoid the attitude taken by some planners, who take the easy way out and try to transplant the town into village, succeeding only in creating a suburban environment instead of creating a superrural one.

In using earth and vaulted roofs resides the only probable solution to the problem of peasant housing in the hot arid zones. In this way we shall have subjected the technology to the economy of the people, and not the other way round. To do this we have to secure the collaboration of three technicians, the soil mechanic, the structural engineer specialised in shell structures and the architect acquainted with the exigencies imposed by these techniques on the design.

As a matter of fact, these structural impositions save the architect from the pitfalls of futile superficiality. In a way, they play a role similar to the classical orders in the architectural design, as a safeguard from the aesthetic point of view. (From *Rural Settlements in Developing Countries*, Habitat Conference, Vancouver, B.C., 1976)

From the point of view of thermal comfort the use of cement blocks for peasant housing is a scientific anachronism. Several experimental rooms were built at the Building Research Centre in Cairo using various building materials including cement block and mud brick. The air temperature within the mud brick room stayed within the thermal comfort zone and the fluctuation did not exceed 2° C. during the twenty-four hours of the day, whereas the air temperature in the cement block room was 20° C. higher at the peak, and in fact it was higher than the air temperature outside. From the point of view of the physical science, the use of cement block

is antiscientific in this case. (From *Technology at the Service of National Culture and Economy in the Field of Architecture and Urban Planning*)

Designing in the Arab style for today presents the architect with various intricate problems. Architectural design becomes some sort of scientific research. For many reasons this style has been abandoned and left stagnant for more than 200 years. So, the architect willing to come back to this style and bring it up to date has to fill the gap and catch up with what should have been done during this lapse of time were it normally developing.

Today, the design, the technique, and tactics of building, etc., have changed completely. In the past most of the work was done almost solely and directly by the craftsman builder; nowadays we find every bit of work has to be designed and drawn by the architect. (From *Memorandum for Maj F. Ashdown, Project Manager, MDDED-M*, Subject: V.I.P. Villa, Tabuk, from Hassan Fathy, 8 October, 1975)

Space in the mosque has to be two-directional; the one vertical tending upwards linking it with the sky, and the other horizontal linking it with Mecca. The horizontal direction is due to the fact that Islam is ecumenical; the idea is expressed by having one sanctuary for all Muslims, the Kaaba in Mecca. This direction is indicated by the mihrab, or niche, but this is not sufficient, and it has to be expressed by the building orienting itself architecturally towards Mecca.

The new techniques of construction and the new building materials such as reinforced concrete, steel, and plastic have freed the architect from the constraints that traditional materials such as granite, marble, stone, wood, and brick imposed on him in the past. This freedom has offered the modern architect great facilities and possibilities that are difficult to resist, but it cut him off from the benefits of the accumulated experience of the generations that have crystalised into traditions.

All that goes into the design, such as the decoration, texture, materials, form, etc., has a symbolic value in tradition. Tradition embraces architecture in its totality with all the elements that together make the religious building; design-concept, space, shape, decorative motifs, colour, light, and even acoustics in the building.

Here, the modern architect has to exercise his creative genius and his artistic sensitivity in creating new forms that suit the new materials without losing touch with the established tradition, preserving the implicit and not overlooking the same spiritual and social virtues or the cultural values as in the past. (From Hassan Fathy, *Mosque Architecture*, undated typescript)

We know that architecture, in all its styles, is one of the most important elements of culture, and that culture may be defined as the results of the interaction between the intelligence of man and his environment in satisfying both his spiritual and physical needs. For the Award, we must define the interchangeable and noninterchangeable elements in, and between, cultures. Anything that belongs to the functional can be interchangeable, since it has no native country and belongs to no specific example. Like mathematics, it is universal; we cannot, however, limit architecture to the functional.

The proportion of the aesthetic to the functional in Islamic architecture differs from that of architecture in Western countries. To show his aspiration toward the Divine, the Arab developed an aesthetic of abstraction, since the barren landscape offered no natural model on which to base his imagery. The natural image, to which he remained sensitive, was joined with the stylised interlacing of geometry and pattern.

The effect of this environment can be seen in architecture, where man decorated his work as a response to what he saw in nature. For example, in the typical courtyard house, open space is closed entirely to nature at the ground level, which is necessary to shelter from the heat and glare. The symbolic idea man added was that the four corners of the courtyard would symbolize the four columns carrying the dome of the sky, the only kindly element of nature the Arab observes. We also know, according to aerodynamics, that wind blowing above the house will not enter the courtyard, but will pass over and create eddies inside. Thus the courtyard will retain the cool air that has settled there, and the air will seep into the rooms and walls, cooling the house. This represents the mercy of God coming from the sky, and explains why in Islam the Deity resides in the sky. Thus the courtyard house did not arise from something spiritual alone, but it added the spiritual to the functional. (From remarks recorded at Aiglemont, April 1978)

NOTES

ISLAMIC PHILOSOPHY AND THE FINE ARTS

Muhsin S. Mahdi

(from *Architecture as Symbol and Self-Identity*), J.G. Katz, ed., Proceedings of Seminar 4 of the Aga Khan Award for Architecture (Philadelphia, 1980), pp. 43–50.

1. Abdul Hamid el-Zein, "Beyond Ideology and Theology: The Search for the Anthropology of Islam," *Annual Review of Anthropology* 6 (1977), pp. 227–254.

2. Al-Ghazali, *Das Elixier der Glückseligkeit, ürbertragen von H. Ritter* (Jena, 1923), p. 148. Cited in Richard Ettinghausen, "Art and Architecture," *The Legacy of Islam*, ed. Joseph Schacht with C. E. Bosworth (Oxford, 1974), pp. 284–285.

3. Meyer Howard Abrams, *The Mirror and the Lamp: Romantic Theory and the Critical Tradition* (New York, 1953), Chapter 1.

SYMBOLS AND SIGNS IN ISLAMIC ARCHITECTURE

Oleg Grabar

(from *Architecture as Symbol and Self-Identity*), pp. 1–11.

CONSERVATION OF THE HISTORIC ENVIRONMENT FOR CULTURAL SURVIVAL

Doğan Kuban

(exerpted from *Conservation as Cultural Survival*, R. Holod, ed., Proceedings of Seminar 2 of the Aga Khan Award for Architecture (Philadelphia, 1980), pp. 1–8.

1. *A Study in Conservation: York* (London, 1968), p. 239.

2. *Ibid.*

3. See Max Weber, "The Spirit of Capitalism," from his "Protestant Ethic and the Spirit of Capitalism," *The Making of Society*, ed. R. Bierstedt (New York, 1959), pp. 400–408.

4. For a short introduction and bibliography to the physical environment, see Terence Lee, *Psychology and the Environment* (London, 1976), p. 35.

5. Kevin Lynch, *What Time Is This Place?* (Cambridge, Mass., 1972), p. 35.

6. *Ibid.*, p. 37.

7. *Ibid.*

ISLAM, URBANISM, AND HUMAN EXISTENCE TODAY

Mohammed Arkoun

(from *Architecture as Symbol and Self-Identity*), pp. 51–54.

1. This text is an English resumé of a presentation made in French by Professor Arkoun.

2. *Toward an Architecture in the Spirit of Islam*, sponsored by the Aga Khan Award for Architecture and held at Aiglemont, Gouvieux, France, April 1978.

3. *L'Étrange et le merveilleux dans la civilization islamique médiévale.* Colloquium held at the Collège de France (Paris, 1978).

ISLAMIC ARCHITECTURE AND THE POOR PEOPLE OF ISLAM

Mahbub ul-Haq

(from *Places of Public Gathering in Islam*, L. Safran, ed., Proceedings of Seminar 5 of the Aga Khan Award for Architecture [Philadelphia, 1980]), pp. 126–130.

URBAN HOUSING IN THE THIRD WORLD: THE ROLE OF THE ARCHITECT

Charles Correa

(from *Housing: Process and Physical Form*, L. Safran, ed., Proceedings of Seminar 3 of the Aga Khan Award for Architecture [Philadelphia, 1980]), pp. 45–49.

ON MOSQUE ARCHITECTURE

Nader Ardalan

(excerpted from *Architecture as Symbol and Self-Identity*, pp. 18–36, charts and illustrations not reproduced.)

CHANGING ROLES AND PROCEDURES IN THE DESIGN OF PUBLIC BUILDINGS

Mona Serageldin and François Vigier

(from *Places of Public Gathering in Islam*, pp. 57–68.)

ON RECREATIONAL AND TOURIST COMPLEXES

Yasmeen and Suhail Lari

(excerpted from *Places of Public Gathering in Islam*, pp. 17–28.)

ON EDUCATIONAL FACILITIES

Ismail Serageldin

(from *Places of Public Gathering in Islam*, pp. 46–47.)

AGRICULTURAL TRAINING CENTRE
Nianing, Senegal

1. Project Documentation. (Credits, Project Timetable, and information on the origin of human and material resources listed in the Project Geography have been provided in the Award documentation by the client and the architects.)

a. Project Personnel. Sponsor: CARITAS, Frère Romuald Picard. Architects: BREDA (a UNESCO Regional Bureau for Education in Africa), Kamal El Jack, Pierre Bussat, Oswald Dellicour, Sjoerd Nienhuys, Paul de Walick, architects; Christophorus Posma, engineer; Professors and third-year architecture students, Dakar Ecole d'Architecture. Construction: D'Iallo, master mason. Site Supervision: BREDA architects.

b. Project Timetable. 1975: prototype construction in Dakar. 1976: brief and design of the Argricultural Training Centre. 1976–77: construction. 1977: occupancy.

c. Project Geography. Nianing: 1) client, 2) masons, 3) labourers. Dakar, Senegal: 1) architects, 2) administrators/managers, 3) master mason, 4) laterite. Mbour, Senegal: 1) cement, 2) wire mesh, 3) plywood. International: 1) UNESCO architects, 2) UNESCO engineer, 3) programmers.

d. Climate Data. Nianing, Senegal: 14.44° N latitude, 17.3° W longitude, 23 m altitude.

Month	Temperature (C°)	Relative Humidity (%)	Precipitation (mm)	Wind Direction	Wind Velocity (km/hr)	Solar Radiation (average Langleys/day)
J	21.1	69	0	N	14	427
F	20.4	75	2	N	16	518
M	20.9	76	0	N	17	590
A	21.7	77	0	N	22	616
M	23.0	78	1	N	15	600
J	26.0	76	15	W	12	554
J	27.3	76	88	W	11	497
A	27.3	78	249	WNW	10	443
S	27.5	79	163	NW	11	447
O	27.5	79	49	N	11	464
N	26.0	73	5	N	13	426
D	23.2	64	6	N	14	424

Source: temperature, relative humidity, and precipitation—World Meteorological Organisation; *Climatological Normals (CLINO) for CLIMATE* and CLIMAT *Ship Stations for the Period 1931–1960.* Geneva: World Meteorological Organization, 1971; Wind direction, wind velocity, and solar radiation—*Climates of Africa,* J. F. Griffiths, ed. Amsterdam: Elsevier Publishing Company, 1972. (World Survey of Climatology, vol. 10).

2. Caritas is the Latin word for charity, and a name taken by independent Catholic social welfare organisations in more than one hundred countries. Caritas Senegal is dedicated to introducing new agricultural methods to the people of Senegal. Their programme seeks to counter what have been identified as key problems in food and crop production: limited productivity of rural labour, lack of access to certain intermediate technologies, insufficient exploitation of available surface and ground water resources, decreasing soil fertility, increasing animal and population pressures on arable land, poor planning and management of agricultural programmes, and ineffective pricing and marketing systems for crops. By establishing a school, Caritas strengthened its grass roots approach to development.

3. For complete climate data, see note 1.

4. Three quarters of Senegal's population are engaged in subsistence farming, so any change in climate has a far-reaching social consequence. A four-year drought beginning in 1968 ravaged the Sahil-Sudan countries (Mali, Mauritania, Upper Volta, Chad, Niger and Senegal). With rainfall in 1972 only 60 percent of normal, the growing season in Senegal shrank from 100 to 55 days. Harvests declined by 40–60 percent and livestock was reduced by half. Rainy-season production, an important source of revenue and export earnings, was non-existent.

5. For Project Geography, see note 1.

6. During the construction of the students' dorm, major changes were made. First, openings in walls were originally designed to be corbelled, but corbelling required two days of mason labour to complete. It was found to be more efficient to make arched openings. Second, the masons attempted to construct an entire length of barrel vault at one time. As interior bearing walls were not buttressed, this nonparallel construction required bracing to counter the vault thrust until the parallel vault was constructed. However, even with bracing, a vault would often fail before the companion was completed. This method was therefore abandoned in favor of staging constructing with short, parallel vaults segments, spaning from end wall to interior wall to end wall.

7. The bricks were made to the following dimensions (in centimeters): 18.5 x 18.5 x 38.5; 18.5 x 18.5 x 18.5; 8.5 x 18.5 x 38.5. A fourth brick size, obtained by cutting the largest brick, measured 18.5 x 18.5 x 28.5. Partway through the school's building an additional mould was introduced to make 18.5 x 18.5 x 28.5 centimeter bricks directly. By eliminating the cutting process, both time and money were saved.

8. UNESCO Regional Office for Education in Africa (Educational Facilities Section), *The Story of a Prototype in Senegal,* Paris, 1978, p. 15.

9. Cost of the student-built chicken coops is included in this average.

10. Comparative costs for 125 m² of foundations, walls, roofs. Note that these figures represent about 60 percent of the cost of construction; the

cost of equipment and labour has not been included. 1) Masonry walls, amiante cement roof, earth insulation: 1,739,305 CFA; 2) Masonry walls, BREDA vaulting: 1,807,798 CFA; 3) Reinforced concrete slab 40 cm. thick; 40 cm. walls: 1,982,284 CFA. Source: D. Heuchenne, ENDA/Dakar Confidential Report, August 1979.

11. The first spin-off was a block of chicken coops built by the staff and students behind the faculty housing at Agricultural Training Centre. Grain silos were built in Ndiarao soon after the completion of the Centre. BREDA provided technical assistance (an architect from Maisons Familiales who prepared plans for the silos) and supervised their construction. Financing came from the American Catholic Relief Service, which also manages the two hundred-ton capacity silos. Other silo projects are underway, as the masonry construction technique substantially reduces waste from spoilage of contents.

A third project was an extension built to a private Catholic school in Nianing. Constructed between November 11 and December 12, 1977, the facilities were built by the master mason of the Agricultural Training Centre with four assistants and eight labourers—no technical supervision was necessary. The project includes a classroom, office, and a sanitary unit, together totaling 124 m². It was financed by Caritas.

The short-span system was also used in 1978 in a chapel at Sandiara; in a nursery school, Dakar; in an intermediate technical school at Nguekohe, financed by the World Bank; and in a centre for Intermediate Practical Education in Koubanao. BREDA was providing technical supervision for this last project when construction was halted, pending increased community involvement in the project.

The widest use of the Nianing Centre prototye to date is the Daara Home, a Koranic school in Melika, Senegal. Only twenty percent of the expenditures at the Daara School was for materials, with eighty percent going for labour.

MEDICAL CENTRE
Mopti, Mali

1. Project Documentation. (Credits, Project Timetable, and information on the origin of human and material resources listed in the Project Geography have been provided in the Award documentation by the client, the architects, and the contractor.)

a. Project Personnel. Client: Mali Ministry of Health; Ministry of Planning and Development. Architects: André Ravereau,* architect; Philippe Lauwers, collaborating architect. Project promotion and funding: European Development Fund, Corrado Cornelli, Director. Construction supervision: Direction Nationale de l'Urbanisme et de la Construction (D.N.U.C.). Construction: Société Anonyme de Travaux Outre Mer (SATOM).

*André Ravereau was educated at the Ecole Nationale Superieure des Beaus-Arts de Paris under Auguste Perret. Since graduating with a D.P.L.G. (Diplôme par le Gouvernement) in 1953, Ravereau has developed a specialised practice in architecture and planning outside France. In the M'Zab, Algeria, he has completed several public buildings, housing projects, and town-planning studies, and from 1965 to 1971 he was the Chief Architect of the Historical Monuments Service of Algeria. Ravereau has published widely on the M'Zab (most recently *Le Mzab une leçon*

d' architecture, Sindbad, 1981), and has participated in the making of films, among them "Le M'Zab—Architecture Inédite en Algerie" and "Pour une vie pour une ville" (Le Courbusier et Alger).

b. Project Timetable. 1968–69: definition of project. 1969–70: selection of architect. 1970–72: design. 1974–77: construction. 1977: occupancy.

c. Project Geography. Mopti, Mali: 1) labourers, 2) clay, 3) sand, 4) gravel, 5) wooden doors. Bamako, Mali: 1) client, 2) construction supervision, 3) contractor, 4) sectional iron and folded sheet metal. France: 1) architect. Belgium: 1) collaborating architect, 2) project promotion and funding.

d. Climate Data. Mopti, Mali: 14.3° N latitude, 4.12° W longitude, 280 m altitude.

Month	Temperature (C°)	Relative Humidity (%)	Precipitation (mm)	Wind Direction	Wind Velocity (km/hr)	Global Radiation* (MJm⁻²)
J	22.6	37	1	NNE	7	559.0
F	25.4	29	0	NNE	8	556.5
M	28.8	24	0	NE	10	675.7
A	32.0	24	3	NE	9	743.5
M	32.9	39	19	NESW	10	775.7
J	31.4	54	55	SW	9	688.8
J	28.1	69	154	SW	10	651.1
A	27.1	77	915	SW	8	647.6
S	27.8	76	104	SW	7	661.9
O	28.5	65	20	SW	7	634.6
N	26.6	49	1	NE	8	602.1
D	23.2	42	0	NE	9	629.8

*Data indicate astronomically possible global radiation; microclimatic effects not taken into account.

Source: temperature, relative humidity, and precipitation—World Meteorological Organisation; *Climatological Normals (CLINO) for CLIMAT and CLIMAT Ship Stations for the Period 1931–1960.* Geneva: World Meteorological Organisation, 1971; (WMO/OMM—No. 117.T.P.52). Wind direction and wind velocity—*Climates of Northern and Eastern Asia,* H. Arakawa, ed. Amsterdam: Elsevier Publishing Company, 1969. (World Survey of Climatology, vol. 8); Global radiation—values adapted from global radiation maps in WMO, *Technical Note No. 172: Meteorological Aspects of the Utilization of Solar Radiation as an Energy Source;* Annex: World Maps of Relative Global Radiation. Geneva: WMO, 1981. (WMO—No. 557).

2. Before independence, a static curative health service of the French colonial administration consisted of regional hospitals and dispensaries, often staffed by nurse-assistants. These facilities acquired the name Assistance Médicale and were designed to combat the area's endemic diseases (malaria, enteritis, pneumonia, cholera, and parasites are the worst health problems). Since independence, emphasis has shifted from a curative to a preventative health programme, though the method of health administration remains unchanged: medical attention dispensed in Assistances Médicales by trained, though inexpensive, paramedical personnel. The Mali Ministry of Health hoped to create, through the building of the Mopti Medical Centre, a regional facility

that would attract both the surrounding rural and the immediate urban population.

3. There were several existing structures on the site at the time the project began. All but one, an administrative building at the eastern end of the site, were demolished.

4. The dry season, from November to June, has low humidity and high temperatures ranging from 32° to 34° C. The *alize* wind blows from the northeast in December through February, making for temperatures around 15° C. From March to June, the harmattan, blowing from the east, brings dust storms and temperatures up to 37° C. For additional climatic data, see note 1.

COURTYARD HOUSES
Agadir, Morocco

1. Project Documentation. (Credits, Project Timetable, and information on the origin of human and material resources listed in the Project Geography have been provided in the Award documentation by the client and the architect.)

a. Project Personnel. Client: Ministry of the Interior. Architect: Jean-François Zevaco.* Consultant: Maghreb Etudes, reinforced concrete. Contractors: Hadj Brahim Arsalane, general contractor; Tanjarat Senauja al Moghrabia, wood and metal joinery; Mohamed Hassoun, sanitary fixtures; Salomon Timsit, electrical; Abdellah Jami, waterproofing; Hadj Ahmed Essafi, floor revetment; Sté Souss Peinture, glass and paint.

*Jean-François Zevaco was educated at the Ecole Nationale Superieure des Beaux-Arts, graduating in 1945. He established a private practice in Morocco, where he has designed educational facilities, government buildings, industrial buildings, and sports facilities.

b. Project Timetable. February 1960: Agadir destroyed by earthquake. 1962–63: brief and design. 1963–64: construction. 1965: full occupancy.

c. Project Geography. Agadir, Morocco: 1) client, 2) contractors, 3) labourers, 4) brick, 5) concrete block, 6) sand. Casablanca, Morocco: 1) architect, 2) contractors. France and Spain: 1) steel. France and Belgium: 1) glass.

d. Climate Data. Agadir, Morocco 30.23° N latitude, 9.34° W longitude, 48 m altitude.

Month	Temperature (C.°)	Relative Humidity (%)	Precipitation (mm)	Wind Direction	Wind Velocity (km/hr)	Global Radiation* (MJm⁻²)
J	14.5	72	48.0	E	2.7	331.9
F	15.5	69	32.0	W	3.3	401.1
M	16.5	70	24.0	W	3.3	592.6
A	17.0	75	16.0	W	3.5	665.0
M	19.5	72	5.0	W	3.5	807.2
J	20.0	78	1.0	W	3.3	741.4
J	22.0	80	0.0	W	2.6	754.1
A	17.5	78	0.5	W	2.9	708.1
S	22.0	76	6.0	W	2.9	557.5
O	20.5	73	22.0	W	2.7	567.4
N	17.5	72	29.0	W	2.3	410.3
D	14.0	73	41.0	E	2.2	372.7

The Agadir, Morocco, Earthquake, prepared by the American Iron and Steel Institute, New York: A151, 1962, p. 13.

*Data indicate astronomically possible global radiation; microclimatic effects not taken into account.

Source: temperature, relative humidity, precipitation, wind direction, and wind velocity—*Climates of Africa*, J. F. Griffiths, ed. Amsterdam: Elsevier Publishing Company, 1972. (World Survey of Climatology, vol. 10). Global radiation—values adapted from global radiation maps in World Meteorological Organisation, *Technical Note No. 172: Meteorological Aspects of the Utilisation of Solar Radiation as an Energy Source;* Annex: World Maps of Relative Global Radiation. Geneva: World Meteorological Organisation, 1981. (WMO—No. 557).

2. *The Agadir, Morocco Earthquake,* prepared by the American Iron and Steel Institute, New York: A151, 1962, p. 13.

3. For complete climate data, see note 1.

4. For Project Geography, see note 1.

5. Materials cost 850,000 DH ($216,750 [U.S.]), and professional fees were 43,700 DH ($11,143) [U.S.]). Land costs are not included in these figures. Comparable construction in 1980 would have cost three times as much as this project cost in 1963–64 (excluding land cost).

SIDI BOU SAID
Tunis, Tunisia

1. Project Documentation. (Credits and Project Timetable have been provided in the Award documentation by the planners.)

a. Project Personnel. Client: Municipality of Sidi Bou Said. Planners: The Technical Bureau of the Municipality, Sanda Popa, chief architect. Conservator: Abd El-Aziz Ben-Achour, historian.

b. Project Timetable. Ongoing since 1973.

d. Climate Data. Tunis, Tunisia: 36.5° N latitude, 10.13° E longitude, 66 m altitude.

Month	Temperature (C.°)	Relative Humidity (%)	Precipitation (mm)	Wind Direction	Global Radiation* (MJm⁻²)
J	11.0	78	70	NW	271.1
F	11.7	77	47	NW	315.8
M	13.4	75	43	NW	544.7
A	15.7	74	42	NE	641.4
M	19.1	68	23	NE	804.6
J	23.4	64	11	NE	787.7
J	25.9	62	1	NE	758.8
A	26.6	65	11	NE	694.0
S	24.6	71	37	NE	476.5
O	20.4	74	56	W	481.5
N	15.9	78	57	W	299.7
D	12.4	78	70	W	236.3

*Data indicate astronomically possible global radiation; microclimatic effects not taken into account.

Source: temperature, relative humidity, and precipitation—World Meteorological Organisation. *Climatological Normals (CLINO) for CLIMAT and CLIMAT Ship Stations for the Period 1931–1960.* Geneva: World Meteorological Organisation, 1971. Global radiation—values adapted from global radiation maps in WMO, *Technical Note No. 172: Meteorological Aspects of the Utilization of Solar Radiation as an Energy Source;* Annex: World Maps of Relative Global Radiation. Geneva: WMO, 1981. (MMO—No. 557); Winds—Besim Hakim. *Sidi Bou Said, Tunisia: A Study of Structure and Form.* Halifax, Nova Scotia: School of Architecture, Nova Scotia Technical College, 1978.

Bibliography.

Besim, Hakim, ed. *Sidi Bou Said, Tunisia: A Study in Structure and Form,* School of Architecture, Nova Scotia Technical College, Halifax, Nova Scotia—Canada, 1978

Ministere de l'Economie Nationale *Plan d' Amenagement de la Commune de Sidi Bou Said,* provisionary document, Tunis, 8 January 1973.

PNUD/Republic of Tunisia project, "Parc National de Carthage et Sidi Bou Said," project No. TUN 77/003/B/01/13, Tunis, March 1979.

Pol Fouchet, Max, *Eloges de Sidi Bou Said,* editions Cères, Tunis, 1975.

Révault, Jacques, *Palais et Residences d'Ete de la Region de Tunis (XVIe–XIXe Siecles),* CNRA, Paris, 1974.

HALAWA HOUSE
Agamy, Egypt

1. Project Documentation. (Credits, Project Timetable, and information on the origin of human and material resources listed in the Project Geography have been provided in the Award documentation by the client and the architect.)

a. Project Personnel. Client: Esmat Ahmed Halawa. Architect: Abdel-Wahed El-Wakil,* Craftsmen: Aladdin Mustafa, master mason, Hassan El-Naggar, carpenter, Muʿallim Attiyah, plasterer.

*Abdel-Wahed El-Wakil graduated from Ain-Shams University in Cairo, where, from 1965 to 1970, he lectured in the Department of Architecture. El-Wakil has acknowledged the importance of Hassan Fathy to his design development. Since 1971, El-Wakil has been in private practice as an architect.

b. Project Timetable. 1972: project definition. 1973: brief and design. 1974–75: construction. 1976: occupancy.

c. Project Geography. Cairo, Egypt: 1) client, 2) architect, 3) carpenter, 4) plasterer. Muqattam, Egypt: 1) sandstone. Agamy, Egypt: 1) labourers, 2) limestone, 3) brick, 4) mud mortar, 5) tiles, 6) terra cotta, 7) cement. Aswan, Egypt: 1) master mason, 2) marble.

d. Climate Data. Agamy, Egypt**: 30° N latitude, 32° E longitude, 1 m altitude.

Month	Temperature (C.°)	Relative Humidity (%)	Precipitation (mm)	Solar Radiation*** (MJm⁻²)
J	14.7	68	41	322.6
F	15.2	66	25	428.7
M	16.8	64	11	585.4
A	19.1	68	3	661.6
M	20.0	70	2	838.0
J	24.5	74	0	746.6
J	26.2	76	0	880.8
A	27.1	74	1	706.2
S	26.2	69	1	632.9
O	24.2	68	7	536.5
N	20.9	68	3	399.9
D	16.6	68	48	325.2

**Data from Alexandria, Egypt.

***Data indicate astronomically possible global radiation; microclimatic effects not taken into account.

Source: temperature, relative humidity, and precipitation—World Meteorological Organisation; *Climatological Normals (CLINO) for CLIMAT and CLIMAT Ship Stations for the Period 1931–1960.* Geneva: World Meteorological Organisation, 1971; Solar radiation—values adapted from global radiation maps in WMO, *Technical Note No. 172: Meteorological Aspects of the Utilization of Solar Radiation as an Energy Source;* Annex: World Maps of Relative Global Radiation. Geneva: WMO, 1981. (WMO—No. 557).

2. For complete climate data, see note 1.

3. Salt air and humidity produce a highly corrosive atmosphere, which leads to flaking paintwork, salt efflorescences, cracked parapets, and leaking roofs.

4. (From Form III, Award documentation).

5. Alexandrine plaster consists in the first layer of a splatterdash coating of cement mortar (450 kg. cement/lm³ sand), in the second of a cement-lime mortar float (1m³ sand and ½m³ lime: 200 kg Portland cement), and in the third of a white cement rendering (1 part stucco: 2 parts lime: 1 part sand; the stucco is 2 parts marble powder and 1 part white cement with sieved white sand locally quarried; proportion of lime reduced for external surfaces).

6. Layers of the following materials were used for insulation in the master bedroom ceiling: bitumen, graded sand, 1 cm mud, and 2 cm mortar over vinyl sheeting.

RUSTEM PASHA CARAVANSERAI
Edirne, Turkey

1. Project Documentation. (Credits, Project Timetable, and information on the origin of human and material resources listed in the Project Geography have been provided in the Award documentation by the client and the architect.)

a. Project Personnel (for restoration). Client: Department of Pious Foundations, Fikret Çuhadaroğlu, Director; Mehmet Ozturk, Regional Director. Restoration Architect: Ertan Cakīrlar, chief architect. Contractors; Kemâl Şen, Ibrâhim Güven, Saban Sahīn, Mustafa Veziroğlu.

b. Project Timetable. 1959–61: definition of

project. 1964: conversion to hotel agreed upon. 1964–65: design. 1964–72: construction. 1972: occupancy.

c. Project Geography. Turkey: 1) client. Edirne, Turkey: 1) craftsmen, 2) labourers, 3) stone, 4) ceramic tile, 5) marble, 6) face brick, 7) brick flooring, 8) concrete, 9) plaster. Istanbul, Turkey: 1) architects, 2) heating apparatus. Ankara, Turkey: 1) woodwork, 2) doors, 3) furniture. Kayseri, Turkey: 1) contractor.

d. Climate Data. Edirne, Turkey: 41.4° N latitude, 26.34° E longitude, 48 m altitude.

Month	Temperature (C.°)	Relative Humidity (%)	Precipitation (mm)	Wind Velocity (m/sec)	Solar Radiation (Langleys)
J	1.9	81	65.1	2.0	100.22
F	3.8	77	50.7	2.3	161.16
M	6.9	73	45.6	2.2	221.98
A	12.6	68	47.8	1.9	323.52
M	17.9	67	47.0	1.6	389.61
J	21.9	63	49.5	1.5	459.80
J	24.6	56	32.3	1.6	458.64
A	24.1	56	22.0	1.6	414.10
S	19.6	63	31.0	1.4	314.18
O	14.3	73	55.3	1.4	226.07
N	9.4	81	72.4	1.5	116.02
D	4.5	83	80.6	1.9	85.43

Source: temperature, relative humidity, and precipitation, wind velocity, and solar radiation—courtesy of Dr. Sahap Aksoy, Director, Building Research Institute, The Scientific and Technical Research Council of Turkey, Ankara. All data, except for solar radiation, from *State Meteorological Service, Mean and Extreme Meteorological Bulletin,* Ankara, 1974.

ERTEGÜN HOUSE
Bodrum, Turkey

1. Project Documentation. (Credits, Project Timetable, and information on the origin of human and material resources listed in the Project Geography have been provided in the Award documentation by the client and the architect.)

a. Project Personnel. Clients: Ahmet and Mica Ertugün. Architect: Turgut Cansever.* Interior design: Mica Ertegün. Consultants: Yalçīn Kaya, static engineer, Salim A. Berkmen, electrical engineer, Turhan Kolak, sanitary engineer. Contractors: Necati Çelik, site foreman and concrete mason; Cemil Ormanlar, chief carpenter; Narettin Gümüş, carpenter; Yusuf Aslan, sanitary installation.

b. Project Timetable. 1971–72: brief and design. 1972–73: construction. 1973: occupancy.

c. Project Geography. Bodrum, Turkey: 1) contractor, 2) masons, 3) labourers, 4) stone, 5) stucco, 6) concrete, 7) botanical material. Istanbul, Turkey: 1) architect, 2) engineers, 3) carpenters, 4) oak, 5) glass. United States of America: 1) interior design.

d. Climate Data. Bodrum, Turkey: 37.02° N latitude, 27.26° E longitude, 27 m altitude.

*For biographical information on Mr. Cansever, see notes to Turkish Historical Society, Project Personnel.

Month	Temperature (C.°)	Relative Humidity (%)	Precipitation (mm)	Wind Velocity (m/sec)	Solar Radiation (Langleys)
J	11.3	72	200.0	3.1	146.15
F	11.6	71	109.0	3.3	197.33
M	12.8	67	66.6	3.0	287.67
A	16.4	66	29.2	2.5	367.09
M	20.8	64	19.8	2.2	443.58
J	25.3	56	4.4	2.4	495.11
J	28.0	51	0.5	2.7	503.30
A	27.8	53	0.2	2.4	473.22
S	24.4	58	8.8	2.2	373.58
O	19.9	66	53.6	2.0	268.10
N	16.4	71	93.9	2.4	173.70
D	13.2	73	186.9	3.0	122.38

Source: temperature, relative humidity, precipitation, wind velocity, and solar radiation—courtesy of Dr. Sahap Aksoy, Director, Building Research Institute, The Scientific and Technical Research Council of Turkey, Ankara. All data, except for solar radiation, from *State Meteorological Service, Mean and Extreme Meteorological Bulletin,* Ankara, 1974.

2. Necva, Akçura, "Bodrum-Alicarnassos, Studio per la difesa e la valorizzazione de una citta," *Palladio,* 1971 (N.S. Vol. 21), pp. 65–122.

3. See C. T. Newton, *A History of Discoveries at Halicarnassus, Cnidus and Branchidae,* London, 1862. He also mentions T. T. Donaldson's visit to Bodrum "several years earlier" when Donaldson referred to a "large konak" that Newton identifies as being the same Salih Bey residence.

4. See note 3.

5. See Project Geography, note 1.

6. For complete climate data, see note 1.

7. See note 2.

TURKISH HISTORICAL SOCIETY
Ankara, Turkey

1. Project Documentation. (Credits, Project Timetable, and information on the origin of human and material resources listed in the Project Geography have been provided in the Award documentation by the client and the architect.)

a. Project Personnel. Client: Türk Tarih Kurumu, Uluğ Iğdemir, Director. Architects: Turgut Cansever,* chief architect; Ertur Yener, assistant architect. Consultants: Rasin Etiman, static engineer; Salim Berkman, lighting/electrical engineer; Hacik Eram, sanitary installation and climate control. Contractors: Ahmet Bakircioğlu, reinforced concrete; Adnan Golar, electrical installation; TOKAR, Yapi Ve Endüstri Tesisleri Sanayi Ve Ticaret A. Ş., sanitary installation and climate control; PROFILO, Sanayi Ticaret A. Ş., aluminum doors and windows. Site supervision: Nail Çambel.

*Turgut Cansever has practiced architecture in Turkey since 1946. Trained in Turkey, he developed a conceptual approach based on a search for regional expression in architecture. Among his best known projects are the Anatolian Club Hotel (1951–56) and the Demir Holiday Village in Bodrum (1971). As a planner, Cansever has headed projects in Istanbul on preservation and restoration, pedestrian zoning, and metropolitan development. Since 1974 he has been president of the Regional Union of Housing Cooperatives, and has been Planning Advisor to the Mayor of Istanbul.

b. *Project Timetable.* 1951–60: definition of project. 1960–61: brief and design. 1962–66: construction. 1966: occupancy.

c. *Project Geography.* Ankara, Turkey: 1) client, 2) labourers, 3) red Ankara stone, 4) brick, 5) concrete, 6) concrete block, 7) copper, 8) carpets, 9) window screen fabrication, 10) wood doors and bookshelf fabrication. Istanbul, Turkey: 1) architect, 2) assistant architect, 3) static engineer, 4) lighting/electrical engineer, 5) sanitary installation/heating consultant, 6) reinforced-concrete contractor, 7) HVAC installers, 8) window fabrication. Marmara Island, Turkey: 1) marble.

d. *Climate Data.* Ankara, Turkey: 39.57° N latitude, 32.53° E longitude, 894 m altitude.

Month	Temperature (C.°)	Relative Humidity (%)	Precipitation (mm)	Wind Direction	Wind Velocity (m/sec)	Solar Radiation (Langleys)
J	0.1	78	34.9	SW	22.7	144.04
F	0.9	75	38.2	S	28.3	202.46
M	5.0	66	35.9	SSW	25.4	303.53
A	11.1	57	36.6	SW	29.6	426.96
M	16.0	57	50.0	NE	22.6	499.64
J	20.0	50	50.6	WSW	21.8	529.32
J	23.2	42	12.7	SW	25.1	566.45
A	23.3	40	8.4	W	18.4	532.44
S	18.4	46	18.6	W	17.7	420.63
O	12.9	56	22.0	S	22.6	297.65
N	7.7	70	27.9	SSE	24.9	176.66
D	2.5	79	46.4	S	22.9	118.18

Source: temperature, relative humidity, precipitation, wind direction, and wind velocity—*Ankara:* Il Yilliği/1967. Ankara: City of Ankara, 1967; Solar radiation—courtesy of Dr. Sahap Aksoy, Director, Building Research Institute, The Scientific and Technical Research Council of Turkey, Ankara.

2. The client provided all funding for the project. The construction was accordingly delayed as the schedule had to accommodate the funding exigencies of the society. This also affected the overall costs, since inflation offset earlier savings. The total cost of the project including material, labour, and professional fees of 560,000 TL ($62,200 [U.S.]), considered a modest sum for a public building.

3. See Project Geography, note 1.

INTER-CONTINENTAL HOTEL AND CONFERENCE CENTRE
Mecca, Saudi Arabia

1. Project Documentation. (Credits, Project Timetable, and information on the origin of human and material resources listed in the Project Geography have been provided in the Award documentation by the client and the architects.)

a. *Project Personnel.* Client: Kingdom of Saudi Arabia, Ministry of Finance and National Economy. Architects: Rolf Gutbrod, Frei Otto; design team: Hermann Kendel (leader), E. Baur, A. Charif, A. Claar, H. J. Collmer, H. Dannen-

berg, I. Grimm, H. Kiess, V. Keckstein, D. Mailänder, P. Netzer, S. Schulze. Project Management: Olgierd Tarnowski. Islamic motif design: Munir Jundi. Consultants: Ove Arup and Partners, engineers; Widnell and Trollope, quantity surveyors; Dale and Ewbank, services. Contractors: Enterprise Thinet, Marcel Thinet, director; Voyer, for lightweight structures only. Hotel Management, Furnishings, and Equipment: Inter-Continental Hotels.

*Frei Otto was trained at the Technische Universitat (Berlin) where he received a Diploma of Engineering in 1952 and a Doctorate of Engineering in 1954. He has since established a specialised architectural practice that focuses on structural design. His best-known works are the German Pavilion for Expo in Montreal, Canada, designed with Rolf Gutbrod (1967) and the roof structure of the Olympic Sport Stadium in Munich, West Germany, with Behnisch and Leonhardt (1972). He has won numerous awards and honours in architecture.

b. *Project Timetable.* 1966: design competition. 1966–68: brief and design. 1968–73: construction. 1974: handover to client. 1975: occupancy.

c. *Project Geography.* Saudi Arabia: 1) client, 2) artisans, 3) concrete, 4) basaltic stone, 5) botanical material. West Germany: 1) architects. England: 1) engineers, 2) service consultants. France: 1) construction management/contractors, 2) steel. United States of America: 1) hotel management, 2) interior design. Turkey: 1) artisans. Lebanon: 1) construction finishes. Pakistan: 1) construction finishes. Yemen: 1) labourers. Italy: 1) marble. Scandinavia: 1) redwood.

d. *Climate Data.* Mecca, Saudi Arabia: 21.28° N latitude, 39.50° E longitude, 500 m altitude.

Month	Temperature (C.°)	Relative Humidity (%)	Precipitation (mm)	Wind Direction	Wind Velocity (Kts)	Solar Radiation* (MJm⁻²)
J	24.6	46	1.2	NNW	04	491.0
F	24.1	46	12.8	NW	05	507.9
M	27.6	44	3.0	SW	05	645.3
A	31.9	35	0.0	SSW	05	739.6
M	35.1	33	0.0	WNW	04	795.6
J	35.6	28	0.0	NNW	05	776.9
J	34.0	28	0.0	NW	05	796.3
A	33.6	32	0.0	S	05	742.8
S	34.8	31	0.0	SW	05	697.3
O	30.0	34	0.0	SW	04	639.7
N	28.4	40	0.8	SW	03	494.9
D	24.8	48	1.5	NW	03	507.7

*Data indicate astronomically possible global radiation; microclimatic effects not taken into account.

Source: temperature, relative humidity, precipitation, wind direction, and wind velocity—from the records of the Meteorology and Environmental Protection Agency, Ministry of Defence and Aviation, Kingdom of Saudi Arabia, courtesy of the Director General, Romaih M. Romaih; solar radiation—values adapted from radiation maps in World Meteorological Organisation, *Technical Note No. 172: Meteorological Aspects of the Utilization of Solar Radiation as an Energy Source;* Annex: World Maps of Relative Global Radiation. Geneva: WMO, 1981. (WMO—No. 557)

2. The project was funded entirely by the Saudi Arabian Ministry of Finance and National Economy. Inter-Continental Hotels acquired a contract to operate the facility year round when the project neared completion.

3. Since its completion, the centre has hosted a number of conferences. Among them: 1976: First International Conference on Islamic Economics (260 guests); 1977: First International Conference on Islamic Education (300 guests); 1977: Annual Hajj and Awqaf Ministers Conference (120 guests); 1977: First Meeting for the Governors of Islamic Bank for Development (100 guests); 1977: Arab Police Conference (150 guests); 1978: World Assembly of Muslim Youth (200 guests); 1978: Preparatory Conference for Celebrating the 15th Hijri Century (300 guests); 1978: Research Studies Conference on Capability for Hajj in Islamic Shariaa (90 guests); 1978: Monetary and Fiscal Economics of Islam (70 guests); 1979: Annual Hajj and Awqaf Conference (150 guests); 1979: First Meeting for the Mayors of Islamic Capitals (150 guests); 1979: International "Holy Quraan" Recital Competition (100 guests); 1979: Arab Health Ministers (80 guests); 1980: International "Holy Quraan" Recital Competition (100 guests); 1981: International "Holy Quraan" Recital Competition (100 guests).

4. For complete climate data, see note 1. Electrically powered air conditioning is provided for interior spaces. The hotel rooms have fan coil units behind the suspended ceilings of bathroom areas. In the large halls, air is supplied from peripheral walls.

5. For Project Geography, see note 1.

NATIONAL MUSEUM
Doha, Qatar

1. Project Documentation. (Credits, Project Timetable, and information on the origin of human and material resources listed in the Project Geography have been provided in the Award documentation by the client and the architects.)

a. *Project Personnel.* Client: H. H. Sheikh Khalifa bin Hamed Al-Thani; Ministry of Information, H.E. Isa Ghanim Al-Kawari; Department of Antiquities and Tourism. Planners: Michael Rice and Company, Ltd.* Architect for grounds and Museum of the State: Design Construction Group, Anthony Irving, principal architect. Consultants: Engineering Services Department, Qatar Department of Public Works, reconstruction engineers; K.L.P., structural engineers for the Museum of the State; Vahe Yacoubian, service engineers for the Museum of the State. Restoration: Qatar Department of Public Works, Ahmad Assad Al-Ansari, head of maintenance section, Engineer Services Department.

*Michael Rice and Company is a London-based information and public-relations consultant which, since 1969, has specialised in the planning and design of museums. To date the company has helped develop ten museums in the Arabian Peninsula: Qatar National Museum; Oman Museum; Museum of Archaeology and Ethnology, Riyadh, Saudi Arabia; Museum of the King Abd al-Aziz Military Academy, Riyadh, Saudi Arabia; six site museums in the Kingdom of Saudi Arabia.

b. *Project Timetable.* 1972: definition of the project, brief and design. 1973–75: construction. 1975: opening of Phase I: restoration and Museum of the State. 1977: opening of Phase II: Marine Museum and Aquarium.

c. Project Geography. Qatar: 1) client, 2) planners, 3) restorer, 4) carpenters, 5) labourers, 6) mortar *(juss)*. England: 1) planning supervision, 2) design and supervision of interiors and exhibitions, 3) academic research coordination, 4) structural engineering. Lebanon: 1) consulting architects, 2) service engineers.

d. Climate Data. Doha, Qatar: 25.16° N latitude, 51.33° E longitude, 11 m altitude.

Month	Temperature (C.°)	Relative Humidity (%)	Precipitation (mm)	Wind Direction	Wind Velocity (Kt)	Solar Radiation (Wh/cm²)
J	11.3	71	12.7	NW	9.4	11.42
F	13.4	73	30.8	NWN	9.5	11.31
M	14.3	62	6.6	ESE	9.8	15.15
A	15.0	49	0.0	NNW	9.6	17.42
M	16.0	44	0.7	NNW	8.9	20.45
J	17.7	41	0.0	NNW	10.1	18.49
J	23.8	56	0.0	NNW	8.5	17.08
A	20.6	48	0.0	NNW	8.7	18.33
S	22.4	61	0.0	NNE	6.6	16.48
O	19.1	60	0.0	NW	6.8	15.07
N	18.7	70	0.0	NNW	5.8	11.45
D	12.1	67	0.0	NW	7.8	8.69

Source: temperature, relative humidity, precipitation, wind direction, wind velocity, and solar radiation—*Annual Climatological Report, 1980.* State of Qatar, Ministry of Communication and Transport, Department of Meteorology, 1981.

2. For a complete description of the entire complex see: G. R. Wright, *The Old Amiri Palace, Doha, Qatar,* (Doha: Qatar National Museum), 1975 (unpaginated).

3. Wright, *The Old Amiri Palace,* page opposite fig. 9.

4. For an indepth look at these features, see Wright.

5. *The Qatar National Museum: Its Origins, Concepts, and Planning,* (Doha: Qatar National Museum), 1975 (unpaginated).

WATER TOWERS
Kuwait City, Kuwait

1. Project Documentation. (Credits, Project Timetable, and information on the origin of human and material resources listed in the Project Geography have been provided in the Award documentation by the client and the architects.)

a. Project Personnel. Client: His Highness Sheikh Jaber Al-Ahmed; Ministry of Electricity and Water. Planner: VBB, Consulting Engineers, Architects, and Economists. Architects: Sune Lindström, chief architect; Joe Lindström; Stig Egnell; Malene Björn, architect for the Kuwait Tower. Consultants: Ingmar Gullstrom, chief engineer and project manager; Erik Jonsson, chief engineer; Lenmart Gerde, chief construction engineer; Ake Lindstrom, construction engineer (all above, partners of VBB); Bergman & Co., electrical installations; Hugo Theorells Ingeniörsbyra, HAVC; B. Broms, general director of Swedish Geotechnical Institute, foundation engineer for the Kuwait Tower; Swedish Aerotechnical Institute, aerodynamic studies for the Kuwait Tower. Contractors: Strojexport and

Armabeton; Union Engineering, for the Kuwait Tower only; Raymond Piling Co., pilings for the Kuwait Tower; STEPRI, for pumping station and control buildings; SOCEA, for main pipelines with valves.

b. Project Timetable. 1967: project definition, 1967–68: brief and design. 1970–76: construction. 1977: system put into operation.

c. Project Geography. Kuwait: 1) client, 2) cement, 3) aggregate. Sweden: 1) planners, 2) architects, 3) structural engineers, 4) electrical engineers, 5) HAVC engineers, 6) construction supervision. Czechoslovakia: 1) contractor for the Kuwait Tower, 2) skilled labourers. Yugoslavia: 1) contractor, 2) skilled labourers. Italy: 1) marble, 2) glazed ceramics. England: 1) contractor for pilings of the Kuwait Tower. Belgium: 1) steel, 2) aluminum profiles, 3) glass. West Germany: 1) contractors. France: 1) contractors. India: 1) steel. Canada: 1) aluminum profiles. Iraq, Iran, and Lebanon: 1) skilled labourers, 2) unskilled labourers.

d. Climate Data. Kuwait City, Kuwait: * 29.2° N latitude, 48° E longitude, 4.9 m altitude.

Month	Temperature (C.°)	Relative Humidity (%)	Precipitation (mm)	Wind Velocity (miles/hr)	Solar Radiation (cal/cm²/day)
J	13.9	66	15	8.2	228
F	15.6	52	7	9.2	408
M	20.0	47	8	10.4	540
A	25.6	42	11	10.5	592
M	30.6	34	3	10.5	645
J	35.0	26	0	12.9	738
J	36.7	26	0	12.2	725
A	36.7	27	0	10.6	679
S	33.3	29	0	8.5	620
O	27.2	38	0	7.9	470
N	22.6	52	25	7.5	368
D	15.0	65	41	8.0	259

*Temperature, precipitation, and relative humidity for Shuwaikh, Kuwait; wind velocity and solar radiation from Kuwait International Airport.
Source: temperature, relative humidity, and precipitation—World Meteorological Organisation. *Climatological Normals (CLINO) for CLIMAT and CLIMAT Ship Stations for the Period 1931–1960.* Geneva: World Meteorological Organisation, 1971; (WMO–OMM—No. 117.T.P.52) Wind velocity and solar radiation—Directorate General of Civil Aviation, Meteorological Department, Climatological Division, Kuwait.

2. Kuwait's first commercial petroleum shipments began in 1946. Oil brought about immediate economic development as well as a significant increase in population. The population of Kuwait City rose from about 35,000 in 1914 to about 150,000 in 1950 (Ronald Lewcock, *Traditional Architecture in Kuwait,* London, 1978, p. 14). The population of Kuwait City (estimated at 1,100,000) and of the entire country (approximately 1,400,000) bears witness to the continuing boom.

3. Area served by project: 300 km². max. daily water consumption: fresh water—450,000 m³, brackish water—430,000 m³. Max. static water pressure: City of Kuwait—80 m, other areas: fresh water—50 m, other areas: brackish water—

30 m. Distribution pipe systems: total length of pipes—500 km; pipe diameters—400–1200 mm; pipe material—ductile cast iron, cem. lining. Pumping stations: six main stations with sixty-four pumps. Total pump capacity: 18 m³/sec. Pipework: ductile cast iron and stainless steel. Reservoirs: eight ground level res., tot. cap. 138,000 m³, thirty-one water towers in standard units of 3000 m³, five sites, tot. cap. 93,000 m³, two water towers in the Kuwait Tower, each 4500 m³, tot. cap. 9000 m³.

4. For complete climate data, see note 1.

5. VBB, *Water to Kuwait.* Cement types included ASTM I, II, and V. Type I is standard construction grade material; Type II is similar to Type I with a heat retardant added to reduce the amount of heat given off during the hydration process, reducing the possiblity of shrinkage cracks; Type V is a sulfate-resistant concrete used particularly for exposure to alkaline soils or sea water.

6. The siting of the Kuwait Tower group presented a number of unique structural problems. In order to counteract the low bearing pressure of the soil, the foundation had to consist of deep-bored Raymond concrete piles. Additionally, foundation slabs had to be prestressed in order to minimise the corrosive effect of saline ground water on the reinforcing. The reservoir design, based on the principles of shell structures, also employs prestressing to allow for the spherical shape. Calculations were carried out using FEM (Finite Element Method) computer programmes. The wind stresses could not be determined through computer analysis, requiring instead comprehensive wind-tunnel testing to ensure choice of the proper design.

7. Malene Björn has stated: "Of the Kuwait Tower, the head in the family of water towers in Kuwait, it has been said that it blends Islamic tradition with modern technology. It brings to mind the image of Muslim minarets as well as modern missiles. Still, when the Amir had expressed his wish for a specific attractive design for the Kuwait Tower, and I was asked to submit a design, I had no such idea.
"My fantasy went its own way. In that very moment I was not aware of the beautiful masterpieces of Islamic architecture which I so admire, and though my thoughts brushed by Brasilia and its construction, halfway buildings, halfway sculptures, the image did not at all persist in my mind. I asked myself: What's going on today, what's life, what's future? And so without really being conscious of it, there was 'the globe' the earthy human warmth, and there were 'the missiles' too, long sharp logic thoughts, fired against the heavens, and suddenly the globe was pierced and there were more globes, speared by the rockets. It was not my intention to make the towers look like minarets, but obviously they have something in common."

RESTORATION OF THE ALI QAPU, CHEHEL SUTUN, AND HASHT BEHESHT
Isfahan, Iran

1. Project Documentation. (Credits, Project Timetable, and information on the origin of human and material resources listed in the Project Geography have been provided in the Award documentation by the client, the architects, and the technical reviewer.)

a. Project Personnel. Client: National Organisation for Conservation of Historic Monuments of Iran (NOCHMI). Architects: Bagher Shirazi, chief architect (NOCHMI); Eugenio Galdieri, chief architect (IsMEO); H. Fehrenstenjad, A. Jabalameli, G. Tala'i, Habiti, Zamani, K. Karapetian, G. Zander, M. Ferrante, R. Orazi. Engineers: Tehrani, M. Kustermann, G. Kustermann, Kassaian. Painting restorers: Aghajani, Taheri, Qolami, Nadjarzadé, Tahebi, Nasri, Rahimian, Darab, Abadi, Mahoudian, Mansourian, Shajanian, R. Boenni, R. Cerbino, P. Mora. Structural technicians: Manchai, Razavi, Rapeima. Craftsmen: A. Maggiano, master craftsman and field assistant, Hasan, carpenter, Ochaqi, carpenter.

b. Project Timetable. For Maidan-i Shah and Ali Qapu: 1964: project definition; 1965–75: restoration; 1977: occupancy. For Chehel Sutun and Hasht Behesht: 1966: project definition; 1967–78: restoration; 1975–80: occupancy.

c. Project Geography. Iran: 1) client, 2) architects, 3) planner, 4) engineers, 5) restorers, 6) historians, 7) contractor, 8) craftsmen, 9) labourers, 10) construction material. Italy: 1) architects, 2) engineers, 3) restorers, 4) historians, 5) geologist, 6) craftsman.

d. Climate Data. Isfahan, Iran: 32.41° N latitude, 51.41° E longitude, 1597 m altitude.

Month	Temperature (C.°)	Relative Humidity (%)	Precipitation (mm)	Solar Radiation (cal/cm²*)
J	3.7	64	19	251
F	6.3	54	16	323
M	10.3	47	18	418
A	15.6	47	16	493
M	19.9	45	8	573
J	25.3	38	1	680
J	27.9	37	5	650
A	26.4	36	1	605
S	22.8	40	7	521
O	16.4	45	3	406
N	9.3	58	19	283
D	4.4	64	20	230

*Totals per day on a horizontal plate.
Source: temperature, relative humidity, and precipitation—World Meteorological Organisation; *Climatological Normals (CLINO) for CLIMAT and CLIMAT Ship Stations for the Period 1931–1960.* Geneva: World Meteorological Organisation, 1971; Solar radiation—M. Daneshvar, "Solar Radiation Statistics for Iran," *Solar Energy,* vol. 21, no. 4, 1978, p. 348.

2. The results of the investigations are presented in the following works: Galdieri, Eugenio and Roberto Orazi, *Progetto di Sistemazione del Maidan-i Shah di Isfahan,* Rome. 1969; Galdieri, Eugenio, *Apparenze e Realita nell'Architettura Safavide,* Venice 1978; Galdieri, Eugenio, "Two Building Phases of the Time of Shah Abbas I," *East and West,* XX, 1970; Galdieri, Eugenio, *Esfahan: Ali Qapu* Rome 1979; Orazi, Roberto, *Wooden Gratings in Safavid Architecture,* Rome, 1978; Zander, Guiseppe, ed., *Travaux de Restauration des Monuments Historiques en Iran,* Rome, 1969.

3. According to ISMEO, the total restoration budget for the years between 1966 and 1978 was in the order of 95 million rials ($1.3 million [U.S.]) and were provided by the Iranian (98%) and the Italian governments (2%).

MUGHAL SHERATON HOTEL
Agra, India

1. Project Documentation. (Credits, Project Timetable, and information on the origin of human and material resources listed in the Project Geography have been provided in the Award documentation by the client and the architects.)

a. Project Personnel. Client: Hotels Division of I.T.C., Ltd. (Indian Tobacco Company), A. N. Haksar, chairman. Architects: Arcop Design Group; Ramesh Khosla, partner-in-charge; Ranjit Sabikhi, partner; Ajoy Choudhury, partner; Ray Affleck, design advisor; Ravindra Bhan, partner-in-charge of landscape; Aguil Ali, Karl Fisher, D. Guha, Neela Kany, Jethy Chadha, Kamal Chadha, job captains. Consultants: Anil Verma of Anil Verma & Associates, interior design of guest rooms, speciality restaurant, and health club; Hotels Division of I.T.C., Ltd., kitchen planning; Gherzi Eastern, Ltd., structural, electrical, mechanical, and HVAC engineering. Contractor: G. S. Luthra & Sons Construction: G. S. Luthra & Sons, masonry construction; Nathu Ram, plaster of paris craftsman.

b. Project Timetable. 1974: project definition. 1974–75: brief and design. 1975–76: construction. 1977: occupancy.

c. Project Geography. Agra region, India: 1) labourers, 2) brick, 3) red sandstone, 4) sand, 5) aggregate, 6) carpet. New Delhi, India: 1) cement, 2) red brick tile, 3) furniture, 4) landscape architect, 5) interior designer (for guest rooms), 6) contractor, 7) plaster-of-paris craftsman. Calcutta, India: 1) client, 2) steel for reinforced concrete. Bombay, India: 1) engineers. Central India: 1) teak. India (general): 1) bathroom fixtures, 2) lighting fixtures, 3) kitchen equipment, 4) mechanical, plumbing, electrical, and HVAC equipment, 5) cement, 6) glass, 7) marble, 8) plaster of paris, 9) slate, 10) bitumen, 11) tar, 12) paint, 12) botanical material. Montreal, Canada: 1) architects.

d. Climate Data. Agra, India: 27.1° N latitude, 78.02° E longitude, 169 m altitude.

Month	Temperature (C.°)	Relative Humidity (%)	Precipitation (mm)	Wind Direction	Global Radiation* (tenths of cal/cm²)
J	14.8	61	16	WNW	334
F	18.0	48	9	WNW	425
M	23.8	36	11	WNW	516
A	29.7	26	5	WNW	584
M	34.5	27	10	WNW	610
J	35.0	41	60	W	550
J	30.9	71	210	E	455
A	29.3	79	263	WSW	426
S	28.9	69	154	WNW	468
O	26.2	52	23	WNW	447
N	20.6	45	2	WNW	383
D	16.1	55	4	WNW	324

*Data for global radiation are radiation observations for New Delhi, India.
Source: temperature, relative humidity, and precipitation—World Meteorological Organisation; *Climatological Normals (CLINO) for CLIMAT and CLIMAT Ship Stations for the Period 1931–1960.* Geneva: World Meteorological Or-

ganisation, 1971; Wind direction, wind velocity, and global radiation—courtesy of India Meteorological Department, Government of India, New Delhi.

2. Only three restaurants were originally planned. The fourth was a later addition, designed after the hotel had opened, and was constructed in what had been an outside amphitheatre.

3. The extensive gardens are irrigated by recycling water treated at an on-site sewage treatment plant.

4. The initial schedule aimed for construction to begin in October 1974. Design began in June 1974. By late August 1974, at the time the initial design was completed, a cement shortage developed in India and the government banned the use of the material. The architects then had to redesign the structure using lime concrete. This redesign process took an additional three months and was completed in early 1975. At that time cement was again available. For reasons of cost and flexibility, the architects returned to the original design. Note that the plans show the amphitheatre.

KAMPUNG IMPROVEMENT PROGRAMME
Jakarta, Indonesia

1. Project Documentation. (Credits, Project Timetable, and information on the origin of human and material resources listed in the Project Geography have been provided in the Award documentation by the client and the planners.)

a. Project Personnel. Client: Jakarta City Government, Ali Sadikin, former Governor. Architect/Planners: K.I.P. Technical Unit, Mr. Darrundono, Chief; Pik Mulyadi, Vice Governor of Jakarta, former Head of Regional Planning Office; People of the Kampungs. Contractors: PT. Yomas Jaya, K.I.P. Unit.

b. Project Timetable. 1969–74: First Five-Year Development Plan. 1974–79: Second Five-Year Development Plan. 1979–present: Third phase of development.

c. Project Geography. Indonesia: 1) planners, 2) administrators, 3) labourers, 4) construction materials. International: 1) planning and financial assistance through the World Bank (for second phase and third phase).

d. Climate Data. Jakarta, Indonesia: 6.11° S latitude, 106.5° E longitude, 8 m altitude.

Month	Temperature (C.°)	Relative Humidity (%)	Precipitation (mm)	Wind Direction	Wind Velocity (m/sec)	Solar Radiation (cal/cm²)
J	26.2	85	335	W	1.1	8438.2
F	26.3	85	241	NW	1.1	8156.4
M	27.1	83	201	W	1.0	9312.4
A	27.2	82	141	NE	0.9	9132.0
M	27.3	82	116	NE	0.9	9324.8
J	27.0	81	97	NE	0.8	8160.0
J	26.7	78	61	NE	0.9	10137.0
A	27.0	76	50	NE	0.9	9048.9
S	27.4	75	78	N	1.1	9450.0
O	27.4	77	91	N	0.9	12558.1
N	26.9	81	151	N	0.8	10122.0
D	26.6	82	193	W	1.0	10409.8

Source: temperature, relative humidity, and precipitation—World Meteorological Organisation; *Climatological Normals (CLINO) for CLIMAT and CLIMAT Ship Stations for the Period 1931–1960.* Geneva: World Meteorological Organisation, 1971; wind direction, wind velocity, and solar radiation—the Meteorological and Geophysical Institute, Department of Communication, Jakarta.

2. Political unrest, too, contributed to mass migration during the time period. Following the revolts in Sumatra and Sulawesi in 1958–59, Jakarta's population grew by one million people within a single year.

3. The first decade for which reliable census information is available.

4. Two thirds of this total, or 57,000 people per year, were in the prolific 15–59 age group. (Nathan Kufitzi, *Migrants into Jakarta, 1969–1971,* unpublished report, 1972).

5. Anticipating population growth, the World Bank (1976) estimated a need for 1.2 million houses in Jakarta in 1973–83, or about 120,000 units annually. Construction of permanent houses within the city was estimated then at about 25,000 units annually, available only to families with monthly incomes of Rp 35,000 or greater. Since the median household income for the city at the time was Rp 25,000 per month, this housing was beyond the means of most city residents.

6. A World Health Organisation study estimated that the city's uncollected garbage amounts to 30 percent of the daily load.

7. Nick Devas, *Indonesia's Kampung Improvement Programme, An Evaluative Study,* DAG Occasional Paper 10, August 1980, Joint Centre for Urban, Regional and Local Government Studies, p. 12.

8. Wells are contaminated either from septic tank seepage or from salinity due to depletion of freshwater aquifers and seawater encroachment (World Bank, Urban Projects Department, "Indonesia: Appraisal of the Second Urban Development Project," unpublished report, September 24, 1976, p. 5).

9. World Bank, Transportation and Urban Projects Department, "Appraisal of the Jakarta Urban Development Project in "Indonesia," unpublished report, August 30, 1974, p. 4.

10. *Jakarta's Kampung Improvement Program,* prepared by Directorate of Physical Development, Jakarta Capital City Government and K.I.P. Implementation Unit, 1976, p. 3.

11. Devas, p. 16.

12. Devas, p. 23.

13. *Jakarta's Kampung Improvement Program* p. 5.

14. In hardship cases where a significant portion of property is given over to such improvements, *camats* are permitted to collect funds from neighbourhood residents as a source of compensation.

PONDOK PESANTREN PABELAN
Central Java, Indonesia

1. Project Documentation. (Credits, Project Timetable, and information on the origin of human and material resources listed in the Project Geography have been provided in the Award documentation by the *pesantren.*)

   a. *Project Personnel.* Client: Hamam Dja'far, Kyai; Habib Chirzin, Deputy. Planners/Architects: Amin Arraihana, Fanani; LP3ES, Abdurrahman Wahid. Builders: People of the *Pesantren.*)

   b. *Project Timetable.* 1975: Ongoing since 1965.

   c. *Project Geography.* Indonesia (Central Java): 1) client, 2) planners, 3) architects, 4) craftsmen and labourers, 6) construction materials. Kuwait: 1) partial funding for the girls' dormitory built in 1976.

   d. *Climate Data.* Pabelan, Central Java, Indonesia.*

Month	Temperature (C.°)	Precipitation (mm)	Solar Radiation** (MJm⁻²)
J	25.7	319	601.1
F	25.9	343	523.8
M	25.8	308	587.9
A	26.0	217	530.4
M	25.7	214	501.6
J	24.8	153	468.0
J	23.8	79	464.2
A	23.4	26	548.0
S	24.4	36	574.2
O	25.5	111	592.3
N	25.8	235	608.0
D	25.8	255	596.6

*Temperature values are for Tasi Kmalaya, an inland town in Central Java, and the closet town to Pabelan for which data have been taken.
**Data indicate astronomically possible global radiation; microclimatic effects not taken into account.
Sources. Temperature: *World Weather Records: 1961–1970, Volume 6: Islands of the World.* Washington, U.S. Department of Commerce, National Oceanic and Atmospheric Administration, September 1981. Precipitation: courtesy of the Meteorological and Geophysical Institute, Department of Communication, Jakarta. Solar radiation: values adapted from global radiation maps in WMO, *Technical Note No. 172: Meteorological Aspects of the Utilization of Solar Radiation as an Energy Source;* Annex: World Maps of Relative Global Radiation. Geneva: WMO, 1981. (WMO—No. 557).

2. Many scholars suggest that *pesantrens* have pre-Islamic origins.

3. Estimates of numbers of *pesantrens* are highly unreliable. Government figures from *Annual Report, Directorate of Islamic Religious Education,* Ministry of Religious Affairs, Jakarta (1977), cite only 4752 schools with 830,850 students. Figures quoted are from Kyai Sahal Machfudz of Pesantren Naslakul Huda in Kajen, Central Java, as quoted by Sidney Jones in "Arabic Instruction and Literacy in Javanese Muslim schools," paper

presented at 1980 American Anthropological Association Meeting. The government figures include only those *pesantrens* which are registered with the Ministry of Religious Affairs. These amount to only a fraction of the total number.

4. *Pondok* is a place to stay, or a dormitory, derived from the Arabic *funduq* or hostel. *Pesantren* is a school; thus Pondok Pesantren is a boarding school.

5. As the *pesantren* expanded, requiring more space, several village houses were removed, relocated to the southern edge of the pesantren.

6. Refer to technical report by F. Afshar, Table 1 for breakdown of costs.

7. Although the amount of agricultural land actually owned by the pesantren is small, students work the neighboring fields on a shared basis with half the produce going to the landowner and half to the pesantren.

8. Vocational training includes the following skills: agriculture (farming, horticulture, animal husbandry, and fish breading); carpentry and construction; welding; handicrafts; radio and electronics; photography; family welfare education; administration and management; library skills; experience with the cooperative store.

HASSAN FATHY
Chairman's Award

Special thanks are due to Abdullah Kuwatli for photographic documentation and other detailed information on Hassan Fathy.

Curriculum Vitae. 23 March 1900: Born in Alexandria, Egypt; 1926: Graduated from the High School of Engineering, (Architectural Section), Giza, Cairo; 1926–30: Worked at the Department of Municipal Affairs, Cairo; 1930–46: Taught at the Faculty of Fine Arts, Cairo; 1940–41: Designed first mud brick structures, experimental housing in Bahtim, Egypt, commissioned by the Royal Society of Agriculture; 1946–53: Delegated to the Antiquities Department to design and supervise the project of New Gourna Village at Luxor, to displace the inhabitants of the Old Gourna from the Antiquities Zone; 1949–52: Appointed Director of the School Building Department, Ministry of Education; 1950: Delegated Consultant to U.N.-R.W.A.; 1953–57: Returned to teaching at the Faculty of Fine Arts, Cairo. Head of the Architectural Section in 1954; 1957–62: Joined Doxiadis Associates in Athens as consultant. Lecturer on Climate and Architecture at the Athens Technical Institute. Member of the Research Project for the City of the Future; 1963–65: Director of Pilot Projects for Housing. Ministry of Scientific Research, Cairo. Designed High Institute of Social Anthropology and Folk Art for the Ministry of Culture, Cairo. Designed and supervised Pilot Project of Bariz Village at Kharga Oasis for the Egyptian Desert Development Organisation. Worked as consultant to the Minister of Tourism, Cairo. Delegated by U.N.O. for Rural Development Project in Saudi Arabia; 1966: Lectured on philosophy and aesthetics in Town Planning and Architecture Department at al-Azhar University; 1970–80: Designed and constructed a series of private residences based on the construction techniques and aesthetics developed for the large, civic projects; 1975–77: Lectured on rural housing at the Faculty of Agriculture, Cairo University; 1977–present: Founder and Director, International Institute for Appropriate Technology;

1977–80: Member, Steering Committee, Aga Khan Award for Architecture; 1980: Designed and supervised the construction of a mosque in Abiquiun, New Mexico, U.S.A.

Affiliations. Honorary Fellow, American Institute of Architecture; Honorary Fellow, American Research Centre, Cairo; Member of the High Council of Arts and Letters, Egypt.

Publications. The Arab House in the Urban Setting: Past, Present and Future, Fourth Carreras Arab Lecture of the University of Essex, 3 November 1970, London: Longmans, 1972. *Architecture for the Poor: An Experiment in Rural Egypt*, Chicago: University of Chicago, 1973 (originally published in 1969 under the title *Gourna: A Tale of Two Villages*, by the Ministry of Culture, Arab Republic of Egypt). "Beyond the Human Scale—Hassan Fathy," interview by Yorick Blumenfeld, *Architectural Association Quarterly* 6, Nos. 3 & 4 (1974), pp. 53–57. "Constancy, Transposition and Change in the Arab City," *Madina to Metropolis*, edited by L. Carl Brown, Princeton, N.J.: Darwin Press, 1973, pp. 319–334. "An Ekistic Approach to the Problem of Roofing in Peasant House-Building," *Ekistics* 17 (June 1964), pp. 391–398. "Model Houses for El Dareeya, Saudi Arabia," *Ekistics* 21 (March 1966), pp. 214–219. "Le Pays d'Utopie," *La Revue du Caire* 24 (November 1949), pp. 8–35. "Planning and Building in the Arab Tradition: The Village Experiment at Gourna," *The New Metropolis in the Arab World*, edited by Morroe Berger, New Delhi: Allied Publishers, 1963, reprinted, New York: Octagon Books, 1974. "The Qa'a of the Cairene Arab House, Its Development and Some Usages for Its Design Concepts," *Colloque International sur l'Histoire du Caire*, 1969, Cairo: Ministry of Culture, Arab Republic of Egypt, 1972, pp. 135–152. "Rural Self-Help Housing," *International Labour Review* 85 (January 1962), pp. 1–17 (abstracted in *Ekistics* 13 [June 1962], pp. 398–401). *Urban Architecture in the Middle East*, Beirut: Beirut Arab University, 1971 (in Arabic). "La Voûte dans l'Architecture Egyptienne," *La Revue du Caire* 27 (May 1951), pp. 14–20.

Bibliography. Clark, Felicia, "Appropriate Invention," review of *Architecture for the Poor*, by Hassan Fathy, *Architectural Record* 168 (January 1980), p. 187. Cliff, Ursula, "Designers of Human Settlements. Hassan Fathy; The Logical Building Material Is What the Peasants Dig Out of the Ground: Mud Brick," *Design and Environment* 7 (Spring 1976), pp. 22–25. *Climate Study: Traditional Houses*, participants: Omar El Farouk, John Norton, Wendy Etchells, Joelyn Levaux, Allen Cain, Farroukh Afshar, London: Third World Studies Program, School of Architecture, Architecture Association, 1973 (includes air movement study of mud-brick test room built by Hassan Fathy at the Building Research Institute, Cairo). Cousin, Jean-Pierre, "Hassan Fathy," *L'Architecture d'Aujourd'hui* 195 (February 1978), pp. 42–78. Lobell, Mimi, review of *Architecture for the Poor*, by Hassan Fathy, *East/West Journal* (June 1976), pp. 52–53. Marquis, Robert B., "Egypt's Prophet of Appropriate Technology," *American Institute of Architects Journal* 69 (December 1980), pp. 38–39. "Nouveau Village de Gourna, Hassan Fathy, Architecte," *L'Architecture d'Aujourd'hui* 140 (October–November 1968), pp. 12–17. "Le Nouveau Village de Gournah, Egypte, Architecte: Hassan Fathy," *L'Architecture Française* 8, Nos. 73–74 (1947), pp. 78–82. Petruccioli, Attilio, "Tracking Down the Poet of Raw Bricks," *Spazio e Societa* 5 (1982), pp. 42–61. Prussin, Labelle, review of *Architecture for the Poor*, by Hassan Fathy, *Journal of the Society of Architectural Historians* 37 (March 1978), p. 55. Richards, J. M. "Gourna, a Lesson in Basic Architecture," *Architectural Review* 147 (February 1970), pp. 109–112. Schilling, Jakob, "Gourna, ein Architektonische Experiment in Aegypten," *Deutsche Bauzeitung* 99 (January 1965), pp. 46–50. "Self-Help/Mud Building, Egypt," *Architectural Design* 46 (October 1976), p. 596. Swan, Simone, "Hassan Fathy Demonstrates Ancient Construction Methods in New Mexico," *Architectural Record* 168 (December 1980), p. 39. U.S. Department of Housing and Urban Development, Office of International Affairs, *Mud Brick Roofs*, Ideas and Methods Exchange, No. 42, Washington, D.C., 1957. Ward, Colin, "For the Fellah with Nothing," review of *Architecture for the Poor*, by Hassan Fathy, *Royal Institute of British Architects Journal* 81 (February 1974), pp. 35–36.

SELECTED BIBLIOGRAPHY

Aga Khan Award for Architecture seminar proceedings:

Toward an Architecture in the Spirit of Islam, Renata Holod, ed. ("Architectural Transformation in the Islamic World," proceedings of Seminar 1, held at Aiglemont Gouvieux, France [April 1978]), Philadelphia, 1978.

Conservation as Cultural Survival, Renata Holod, ed. ("Architectural Transformations in the Islamic World," proceedings of Seminar 2, held in Istanbul, Turkey [September 26–28, 1978]), Philadelphia, 1980.

Housing: Process and Physical Form, Linda Safran, ed. ("Architectural Transformations in the Islamic World," proceedings of Seminar 3, held in Jakarta, Indonesia [March 26–29, 1979]), Philadelphia, 1980.

Architecture as Symbol and Self-Identity, Jonathan G. Katz, ed. ("Architectural Transformations in the Islamic World," proceedings of Seminar 4, held in Fez, Morocco [October 9–12, 1979]), Philadelphia, 1980.

Places of Public Gathering in Islam, Linda Safran, ed. ("Architectural Transformations in the Islamic World," proceedings of Seminar 5, held in Amman, Jordan [May 4–7, 1980]), Philadelphia, 1980.

Other Sources (listed chronologically):

Schmertz, Mildred F., "Design in the Spirit of Islam: The Aga Khan Award for Architecture," *Architectural Record* (New York) III (March 1979), pp. 117–124.

———, "Housing in Islam," *Architectural Record* (New York) VIII (August 1979), pp. 79–85.

———. "A Search for Meanings in the Architecture, of Islam," Architecture Record (New York) VIII (August 1980), pp. 86–89.

"The 1980 Winners in the First Aga Khan Award for Architecture," *Architectural Record* (New York) XI (November 1980), pp. 104–127.

Davey, Peter, "Islamic Identity," *The Architectural Review* (London) CLXVIII (November 1980), pp. 278–293.

"The Seven Lamps of Aladdin," *Domus* (Milano) DCXLL (December 1980), pp. 8–14.